UNWRITTEN RULE

A Volume in the Series
Cornell Series on Land: New Perspectives in Territory, Development, and Environment

Edited by Wendy Wolford, Nancy Lee Peluso, and Michael Goldman

A list of titles in this series is available at cornellpress.cornell.edu.

UNWRITTEN RULE

State-Making through Land Reform in Cambodia

Alice Beban

Copyright © 2021 by Cornell University

All rights reserved. Except for brief quotations in a review, this book, or parts thereof, must not be reproduced in any form without permission in writing from the publisher. For information, address Cornell University Press, Sage House, 512 East State Street, Ithaca, New York 14850. Visit our website at cornellpress.cornell.edu.

First published 2021 by Cornell University Press

Library of Congress Cataloging-in-Publication Data

Names: Beban, Alice, 1981– author.
Title: Unwritten rule : state-making through land reform in Cambodia / Alice Beban.
Description: Ithaca [New York] : Cornell University Press, 2021. | Series: Cornell series on land: new perspectives in territory, development, and environment | Includes bibliographical references and index.
Identifiers: LCCN 2020021631 (print) | LCCN 2020021632 (ebook) | ISBN 9781501753626 (hardcover) | ISBN 9781501754043 (paperback) | ISBN 9781501753633 (ebook) | ISBN 9781501753640 (pdf)
Subjects: LCSH: Land reform—Cambodia. | Land tenure—Political Aspects—Cambodia. | Power (Social sciences)—Cambodia. | Nation-building—Cambodia.
Classification: LCC HD1333.C17 B4 2921 (print) | LCC HD1333.C17 (ebook) | DDC 333.3/1596—dc23
LC record available at https://lccn.loc.gov/2020021631
LC ebook record available at https://lccn.loc.gov/2020021632

Contents

Preface	vii
Acknowledgments	xii
Abbreviations	xiii
Introduction	1
1. Donor-State Partnerships in the Cambodian Land Sector	32
2. Encountering the Leopard Skin Land Reform	58
3. Reconfiguring Local Authority through Land Reform	80
4. Youth Volunteers to the Frontier	104
5. Life in the Leopard Skin	136
6. Communal Land Struggles in the Wake of the Land Reform	166
7. An Ontology of Land Beyond State-Capital Formations	189
Conclusion	211
Notes	219
References	223
Index	237

Preface

When I set out to conduct research for this book in 2011, I did not think I would end up writing a book about land reform. I planned to research the violence with which state-facilitated economic land concessions (ELCs) for forestry and commodity crops were spreading across rural Cambodia and displacing smallholder farmers at a seemingly intractable pace. But while I was preparing for fieldwork in 2012, the Cambodian prime minister made a sudden announcement: a preelection land titling reform that promised to break up ELCs. The potential of this shift intrigued me, and I switched my empirical focus to look specifically at the rollout and implications of the land reform. I was able to observe the land survey during preliminary fieldwork in 2012. When I returned to Cambodia for eighteen months in 2013–2014, I undertook a multisited ethnography to understand how the land reform was reshaping people's relationships with land, with their communities, and with the Cambodian state. In this preface, I describe my research approach, rooted in a feminist ethics of research on violence that evolved during my fieldwork.

I based my ethnographic research in two Cambodian provinces: my primary field site in western Khang Cheung province and a comparative study in northeast Khang Leit province (note, all names of places and research participants are pseudonyms to protect people's safety). I lived primarily in Khang Cheung in 2013–2015, with regular trips to Khang Leit and Phnom Penh city, and spent much of my time hanging out talking with people at their homes and fields. I attended monthly village meetings, festivals, community network meetings, and community forest patrols, as well as land title displays and distribution ceremonies. In both provinces, I also interviewed smallholders and land claimants, unofficial community leaders, NGO officers, government officials, volunteer land surveyors, land brokers, plantation laborers, village elders, and youth. Although I speak Khmer (Cambodian language) and undertook interviews myself, I worked with local Khmer research assistants (one man and one woman) during my research in Khang Cheung and with an indigenous research assistant in Khang Leit province in order to build rapport with research participants. I complemented this ethnographic work with a household survey of 270 land claimant households in my study provinces with the help of two professors from Pannyasastra University in Phnom Penh and eight university students. In Khang Cheung, I randomly selected around twenty-five households to survey per village, across four randomly selected villages in each of my two study communes, for a total of 198 households. In Khang Leit, I similarly randomly selected four villages within each of my two study communes, although my team decided not to continue the survey in two villages due to concerns for participant safety after local officials intimidated team members and survey participants. Due to both the change in fieldwork schedule in Khang Leit and people's preference for group interviews, I completed only seventy-two surveys in Khang Leit.

Research in Violent Spaces

Research by privileged foreign researchers in the global south and in poorer communities is beset with ethical quandaries. Postconflict settings demand added questions about the researcher's responsibility and potential violence to those she or he works with. Fieldwork can be intrusive, demanding of people's time, and may expose people to unnecessary risk. In Cambodia, universities and research institutions complain that most international researchers leave the country without even leaving a copy of their theses or making a presentation (Sovachana Pou et al. 2016).

In this context, I came to my fieldwork committed to a postcolonial feminist scholarship that privileges awareness of positionality, self-reflexivity, and reciprocity and places importance on emancipatory epistemologies and methodologies in order to facilitate social transformation (see Smith 1999). In contrast to my previous experience working for an agricultural NGO in Cambodia as a single woman in 2006–2007, I arrived in 2012 with a husband and two children in tow (a six-month-old and a three-year-old when I began fieldwork). Motherhood can be a key marker of mutual identification between women researchers and participants, and I found that having children helped people to size me up as someone more familiar and therefore trustworthy (Warren 2001). This familiarity opened up new spaces for social interaction while it closed down others. Previously, my anomalous status as a childless single white woman made me strange enough to pass in situations where people gendered as women would not fit, such as at the village coffee shop in the evening when men gathered to drink local liquor or in the remote forest that was considered too dangerous for women. As a woman with children, though, I felt disapproval when I entered these male spaces and often stayed away from them (even if my children weren't with me), which meant being excluded from the spheres where much informal village politics took place. At the same time, my children helped ease me into new spaces and new relationships (Scheyvens, Scheyvens, and Nowak 2014). As my children played with kids at the playground, as I waited to pick them up from school, or as we sat in the shade while the pediatric nurse conducted wellness checks, I found myself in gendered sites of sociopolitical power that I had not appreciated before becoming a mother. These were feminine spaces of good-humored laughter, news about what was happening in the village, gossip about land sales, complaints about corrupt government officials, and ideas for how to solve village issues.

My desire for reciprocity in research practice was complicated. As a white middle-class woman from New Zealand, I was often assumed to be working with an NGO, but I did not have the political clout required to make a large intervention in land conflict, nor was I an NGO worker who could deliver resources to communities. Moreover, my first concern was for the safety of my research participants. At times, I felt tension between a desire people articulated for me to witness and help with their land struggles and a sense that I should abandon fieldwork in case I was putting people at risk (something I explore more deeply in my collaborative work with Laura Schoenberger [2018]). With an ethics of "do no harm" to guide the researcher, withdrawing from the field may seem the most ethical response to a violent field site, but if we are committed to an ethics of reciprocity and social justice, the measure of risk is much murkier. When does a responsibility to do no harm become a paternalistic position that denies any agency on behalf of research interlocutors to engage on their own terms?

I do not have a definitive solution to this quandary. But I settled on an ethical position guided by three principles: first, to place myself in a position where I could move in and out of my different fieldwork sites and methodologies if I sensed I was putting research participants in danger; second, to be honest with rural people that while I had provincial permission to conduct research, I was likely being watched by the local authorities and elite (I found, however, that people often considered me the vulnerable one in the interaction, as they were used to threat and intimidation); and third, to aim for an ethics of reciprocity and social justice. I stressed my academic affiliation and stayed away from political events when I felt that my presence might endanger me or my participants. Instead, I tried to find other ways to help. For example, I wrote grant applications for a local community activist group, and I worked with land rights NGOs to design a series of land rights workshops for women in my Khang Cheung and Khang Leit field sites, each of which brought together twenty women from different communities to share stories, learn, and network with each other.

Research Ghosts

This book is shaped by the people I was able to encounter in the field and by the ghosts of others. Because I based myself in rural villages, I interacted most with household members who live and work locally, including women (particularly those with young children), older people, and people who have retained their land. In particular, my data does not capture two significant groups of people: (1) people who consider themselves rural villagers but are not present in the village because they migrated for labor opportunities or left the village permanently and (2) the growing number of urban absentee landowners. I term these people the ghosts of my research because while their voices are missing from much of the analysis, they are certainly present in the discussions I had with their families, neighbors, and (in the case of absentee landowners) those impacted by their land acquisitions.

I tried to include migrant workers by interviewing people when they were home for New Year celebrations. I also talked with people on minivan taxi rides in and out of the villages, in provincial market towns, and in Phnom Penh. Absentee landowners were much more difficult to interview, however, and I believe the exclusion of this group from almost all research I have seen on land relations in rural Cambodia limits the ability of researchers to understand the changing composition of rural communities. I attempted to account for this through my qualitative research in two ways: first, I conducted interviews with land brokers who work with urban buyers, and I talked with local people employed to oversee land plots for absentee owners; second, I conducted interviews with an absentee landowner in Phnom Penh. A third group of voices largely absent from my study are concession company managers. I tried repeatedly to interview company management at the Pheapimex concession in Khang Cheung province, but my requests for interviews were turned down. Instead, I gained a sense of concession operations by talking with current and former laborers, looking over documents from the concession company and the government, and visiting the concession barracks to take food to friends who were working there.

Land and Emotions

Cambodia's land concessions are violent places. My research participants were regularly subjected to threats and intimidation from government officials and plantation security, and a pervasive fear permeated people's hushed conversations when they discussed politics and land tenure. As a foreign researcher with backing from my country embassy and provincial officials, I was not subject to the same level of threats as my research participants (although I was questioned by police and authorities in Khang Leit); at first, I found it difficult to understand why people reacted sharply to small things—repeated phone calls from an unknown number, a commune official strolling past the house, a motorbike accident in a nearby village. But I began to feel fear more deeply a few months into my fieldwork, when a friend from Phnom Penh who worked in the NGO sector was murdered. This changed the way I encountered the field. I became more attentive to potential threats and to my own, and other people's, fear. Soon after the murder, one of the village activists in Srai Saat disappeared. A mutual friend said he fled to another province because the village chief threatened him. Then an opposition party supporter had a motorbike accident and was taken to hospital. Rumors abounded. "He was run off the road...." "He was too outspoken...." "And did you hear about the activist who fled town?" None of these rumors were new, but now I experienced them in a bodily way. I started to record my senses, my jumpiness, the glances, turned backs, raised voices, and whispers out of range that I encountered during my daily life in the villages.

I realized that one of the biggest challenges I faced in this environment was making sense of the way fear shaped people's daily lives and relationships with land and communities. Attention to emotion—in both our interlocutors and ourselves—is an important pathway to knowledge in violent settings (Macek 2014, 2). Emotions matter in struggles over land; they influence resource access, use, and control, and they shape people's everyday lives and relations with each other and with the state. (I develop this theme further in coauthored work with Laura Schoenberger [Beban and Schoenberger 2019; Schoenberger and Beban 2018].) Throughout this book, I aim to bring an awareness of emotion, particularly the way that fear and uncertainty are generated through collective memory of violence and intimidation from the politico-business elite, and how fear shapes—but never fully determines—social struggle.

Acknowledgments

Knowledge is never created in isolation. This book was coproduced with the histories and stories of research participants and the research assistants who aided me in the field. To the hundreds of people in Cambodia who welcomed me into their homes, shared their stories with me, and allowed me to witness their extraordinary struggles, I am forever indebted. To my hosts in Khang Cheung and Khang Leit and the other activists in the community network whom I cannot name here, and to my three research assistants and their families, who became such good friends with my own family, thank you for your generosity. To my research colleagues at the Cambodian Institute for Cooperation and Peace (CICP), Pannyasastra University, and the Center for Khmer Studies, I am grateful for your support and for the chance to work with you and witness your committed scholarship.

Many of the ideas in this book have been developed in conversation and formal collaborations with fellow researchers who became such a support during my research: Laura Schoenberger, Courtney Work, Tim Gorman, Bunthoeun So, Kheang Un, and others. Aspects of our collaborative work are cited in the text where they appear. During my doctoral studies at Cornell University, I had the privilege of working with inspirational scholars and friends. My supervisor, Wendy Wolford, gave just the right balance of kick in the pants and hands-off mentoring that enabled me to grow into my topic and emerge feeling more confident, more curious, and more resolute in my desire to enact change through my teaching and research. My supervision team, Phil McMichael, Lindy Williams, and Andy Mertha, always pushed me theoretically and provided personal and professional support. I am also indebted to Nekkru Hannah, to the Southeast Asia Program community, to the Wolford Lab grad students, to all the Development Sociology administrative staff, grad students, and professors, and to my friends and students for your unwavering support.

To my family: my parents Helen and Russ, my siblings, and my France family, thank you for all your support along the way. My daughters, Siena and Rosa, cheered Mummy on through all the late nights and trips away, facilitated many of the closest relationships I developed during my fieldwork, and continue to embrace life wherever we go. And finally, to Justin, who took on the challenge of moving across the world for me, and who astounds me every single day with his depth of love for our kids: Thank you. Every word of this book has made it onto the page because of your support.

Abbreviations

BMZ	German Ministry of Economic Cooperation and Development
CF	community forest
CLT	communal land title
CNRP	Cambodia National Rescue Party
CPP	Cambodian People's Party
ELC	economic land concession
FA	Forestry Administration
GIZ	German aid agency (formerly GTZ)
LMAP	Land Management and Administration Program
LRP	Land Rights Program
MAFF	Ministry of Agriculture, Forestry, and Fisheries (Ministry of Agriculture)
MFI	microfinance institution
MLMUPC	Ministry of Land Management, Urban Planning and Construction (Ministry of Land, Land Ministry)
MWA	Ministry of Women's Affairs
NGO	non-governmental organization
NTFP	non-timber forest products
SLC	social land concession
SLR	Systematic Land Registration
UNHCR	United Nations Refugee Agency

Cambodian Vocabulary

aekadom	high-ranking government official
bunn	merit (Buddhist)
jaa tum	indigenous elder
kbal dae	headland (land around the rice field)
khsae	strings (used for political chains of power)
koit	broken
komlang	power/energy
nayk taa	land spirit

ABBREVIATIONS

nayk thom big man (powerful, rich person)
oknha politico-business strongman (awarded to people who donate US$10,000 or more to the CPP)
omnaich power
wat temple

UNWRITTEN RULE

Introduction

The Land Titling Ceremony

I drove my motorbike into the grounds of the Buddhist temple in Tmor Muoy village and stopped in front of a large marquee adorned with red and yellow streamers (see figure 1). Hundreds of people sat around the marquee, waiting for the village land titling ceremony to begin. My research assistant, a local university student named Sokun, left our motorbike under the trees and we hurried over to some friends. "Do you think we'll actually get the land titles today?" one woman asked nervously as I sat on the grass next to her. "I don't know; what do you think?" I replied cautiously. Everything about the government's policy was so unexpected; I wasn't sure what would happen. In 2012, the Cambodian prime minister had announced a national land reform before the election. This announcement came as a shock in a country where violent plantation-fueled land dispossession is rife. The Cambodian government recruited thousands of university student volunteers to survey plots of land that formally lay within agribusiness concessions in order to provide land title to smallholder farmers who claimed the land. The land reform captured widespread attention as a potential solution to the growing problems of land grabbing around the world. But the reform was chaotic and people in Tmor Muoy village had waited for over a year to get their land titles. Now, in March 2014, people gathered at the temple to receive the long-awaited titles. "She thinks we will get the titles," said another woman, nodding her head at the older woman next to her. "But I don't think so; they will just keep us waiting again."

INTRODUCTION

FIGURE 1. People wait for the provincial official to speak at a land titling ceremony in Khang Cheung province in Cambodia.

(Photo: Alice Beban.)

A senior provincial official took the stage at the front of the marquee, and people quieted in anticipation. "Look at everyone here," he began, waving his arms at the assembled crowd:

> Look at all these people coming together! The opposition party say that we can't rule the country, that the different ministries aren't cooperating. But look at this. We have taken land from the companies to donate to the people. Land title is important because you can take loans to grow your farm, you can sell your land for more money, and it means the land is yours.
>
> Now the country is developing. Look at all the factories around here. At 5 p.m. it's hard to drive on the road around Khang Cheung city with all the workers pouring out of the factories! I want to send a message to the villagers who have children working in the factories. Don't believe the bad gossip you hear about the election, about the protests. You don't get any benefits from protesting. All you get is danger.... Even if the [opposition party] doesn't support the country, the country keeps moving forward. We have the factories, soon the bridge will be built ... the airport will be developed.... Khang Cheung will be the center of this development. Nowadays, life in our country is very easy.... Some countries are at war, but we are not. Khang Cheung is a dragon of Cambodia.

Sokun leaned over to me and whispered angrily, "A dragon! He means a dragon that eats snails!" Sokun was referring to an interview we had just completed with a poor man in a nearby village whose only protein source was wild snails that he caught and ate raw. Sokun's remark was cutting; the dragon is the most powerful creature in Cambodian mythology, but a dragon forced to eat snails to survive was a poor symbol of power.

The ritual involved in land titling ceremonies performs a world in which the state is unified and beneficent, citizens affirm political loyalty, and land is legible, ordered, and secure (Mathews 2011). The state claims power via the language of postconflict stability and economic development, while the "material power of these actors ensures people remain silent" (Mathews 2011, 109). The provincial official's speech confirmed that the postconflict Cambodian state brings good jobs, mobility, and infrastructure to all; the state supports the people over the companies; and land title provides wealth and security. To question this conception of development is to fuel the bad gossip the official speaks of; to raise one's voice in protest leads to danger. The official doesn't specify what this ominous danger is, but the implicit message is clear: People who want to ride on the back of this dragon will perform their roles as good citizens—do not complain, use your land title to deepen your connections to markets, be grateful for your jobs at the factories, vote for the ruling party. If you do not, the country could be plunged back into chaos.

After an hour of speeches, people surged into the village temple to claim their land titles. I lost my friends in the throng as people pressed in expectantly around government officials seated on the floor surrounded by documents. We met up again later outside the temple. "What do you think?" one woman asked me, thrusting her land titles into my hand. "I can't read," she said. "Do you think it's okay?" I leafed through her five land titles, each for a small plot of land of around 0.1–0.2 hectares. As we looked over the papers together, another woman joined us. "I didn't get any!" she exclaimed. "Did you ask anyone about it?" I asked. "The officials or the commune chief over there?" She shrugged and looked away. "No, I can't be bothered; I'm just going home."

This conversation at the land titling ceremony reveals the uncertainty the land reform left in its wake; no one in Tmor Muoy knew why some people got land titles and some didn't, or even what having the titles meant. In this book, I show how this uncertainty over land relations is productive for state power by exploring the multiple understandings—of state, land, and power—that play out in men's and women's everyday lives in rural Cambodia. Land plays a key role in the enduring rule of Cambodia's prime minister, Hun Sen, the world's longest-serving prime minister. Over the last three decades, Cambodia's uplands have become a frontier for rapacious capital as the government allocates massive logging and economic land concessions to investors, resulting in the widespread displacement of rural people, the loss of ancestral lands, and a pillaging of the nation's forests. I argue that Cambodia's hierarchical and extractive political economic system is maintained through a politics of fear, violence, and uncertainty. Central to Hun Sen's power is his use of unwritten rules—ambiguous legal directives; secretive, informal politics; and unexpected oral pronouncements—that enable the prime minister and his inner circle flexibility to rapidly shift policy in order to main personal control. My empirical focus on the leopard skin land reform, a national land titling program that was organized hastily by the prime minister before the national election in 2012, sheds light on the central importance of land in postconflict state formation, and it gives insights into the durability of authoritarian rule at a moment when nationalist, authoritarian politics is gaining ascendency around the globe. This introduction presents my argument, sets out the context of postconflict Cambodia, and develops a conceptual framework that draws on a feminist political ecology of land and livelihood; critical agrarian studies; and theories of citizenship, property and everyday state formation.

Consolidation of Elite Control through Land Reform

As the provincial official declared in his speech, Cambodia has achieved peace—indeed, Cambodian Prime Minister Hun Sen announced in 2010 that "Cambodia is a successful postconflict society" (Hun Sen 2010, 1). In many ways, he is right. Cambodia was a testing ground in the 1990s for a new kind of peacebuilding intervention in which the United Nations and international financial institutions took an active role in attempting to shape a liberal peace through the promotion of rule of law, constitutional democracy, human rights, neoliberal economic development, and civil peace (Richmond 2005). Cambodia has fulfilled much of the international community's desires for a liberal peace: economic growth rates of 8 percent for a decade, rule of law promoted by a democratically elected government, and opening up to a market economy (Heder 2011; Hughes and Un 2011). Donors cite the land administration program and its distribution of property titles to smallholder farmers as a cornerstone of capitalist economic development, helping to forge new state society relationships based on recognition of citizens' rights by, and responsibilities to, the state (Hughes 2003; Sikor 2009). Cambodia's joint land titles issued in the names of both husband and wife promise to empower women (MWA 2015), and communal land titles promise to safeguard indigenous people's rights. The success of the land administration project is therefore intimately tied to the success of democratic liberal peace in Cambodia.

But the liberal peace is itself undergirded by violence. The rapid shift from violent totalitarian rule to the celebration of the democratic, most "investor friendly economy in Southeast Asia" (Hun Sen 2010) came about on the backs of the country's peasant farmers and poor urban dwellers. Hun Sen and other Khmer Rouge defectors took over a country in chaos when they were installed in power by the Vietnamese in 1979. People's relations with land had been torn apart during the 1970s, first by civil war and US bombing, and then by the catastrophic Khmer Rouge communist experiment of 1975–1979, which resulted in the deaths of between a fifth to a quarter of the population (Kiernan 2008) and placed all land under state control (Collins 2016). People scrambled to accumulate land after the Vietnamese occupation pulled out of Cambodia in the late 1980s, and the political elite manipulated land control as the main component of state building (Le Billon 2002; Springer 2011). Hun Sen (who had risen to the premiership in 1985) allocated forest concessions to politico-business people who financed his campaign (Le Billon 2002). Then, as valuable timber grew scarce in the 1990s and international pressure mounted for Cambodia's leaders to conserve remaining forest, Hun Sen's government switched from forest concessions to a policy of allocating economic land concessions (ELCs) for agribusiness ventures. The passing of a national land law in 2001 enabled the state to demarcate vast swathes of land for ELCs, as the Land Law assumed all land was state property unless farmers could demonstrate ownership or cultivation of the land for five years before the promulgation of the law (Springer 2013). The scope of land conversion is huge. ELCs are estimated to cover over one-third of arable land (Neef et al. 2013), and Cambodia has the dubious distinction of having the highest deforestation rate in the world (Davis, Yu, and Rulli 2015). This rapid forest loss is linked to low groundwater reserves around the Tonle Sap lake, prolonged drought, and flash floods that are wreaking havoc in rural areas.[1] The ELCs are controlled by a small group of powerful tycoons including high-ranking politicians connected with international capital (primarily from Vietnam and China) (Global Witness 2013), while nearly one million people have been adversely affected (ADHOC 2014, 2).

The expansion of ELCs in Cambodia is part of a global phenomenon of land grabbing that ramped up in the mid-2000s as the confluence of the 2007–2008 global food, financial, and fuel crises encouraged a rush of investment (Baird 2014; Schoenberger, Hall, and Vandergeest 2017). The food crisis marked a shift from what Philip McMichael (2012) terms a "food surplus" regime, in which wealthy countries dumped cheap food imports in the global south, to a "food deficit regime," which has accelerated land dispossession as food-insecure countries lease land in other countries to grow food for their own people. By 2011, reports of land deals in Sub-Saharan Africa and Asia estimated that between 20 million and 227 million hectares of land had changed hands since the mid-2000s (Franco et al. 2013; Wolford et al. 2013; Zagema 2011). The rush of investment in countries like Cambodia offered a vehicle for finance capital to restore profits, for states to future-proof the domestic food supply, and for development agencies to renew their legitimacy by constructing acceptable codes of conduct for large-scale land investment. But for countries in the global south, these land deals foment displacement among vulnerable people (Borras and Franco 2012). The term *land grab*, first used in a 2008 report by the nonprofit advocacy group GRAIN, became a rallying cry for activists and academics who sought to draw attention to the violent, often secretive processes underpinning the wave of international land investments.

Many authors explain global land grabbing as an expression of the crises of neoliberal capitalism, using the Marxist concept of primitive accumulation to analyze the violent processes that turn land into a commodity. Marx ([1867] 1976) saw primitive accumulation as a historic process in which extra-economic forces kickstarted capitalist relations in Britain through the enclosure of the commons, the expulsion of peasants from their land, and their transformation into wage laborers. Later scholars show how this process is inherent to ongoing capitalist development; capital continues to depend on a diversity of noncapitalist forms upon which it "parasitically feeds" for its expansion (Ince 2014, 117; Tsing 2005). This viewpoint recognizes the key roles state actors play in facilitating extra-economic land deals, and it makes visible diverse processes of accumulation and displacement that the term *global land grab* can obscure (Schoenberger et al. 2017). We can't always be sure who is grabbing land; smallholder farmers are incorporated in new social relations and patterns of accumulation both as victims and agents of land grabbing, as they migrate in search of land and adopt cash crops for production on global markets (Hall 2013; see chapter 5).

Viewing land grabs through the lens of primitive accumulation also enables us to recognize how land grabbing changes what land is. In rural Cambodia, where projects of colonial and state rule and the discourse of modernization have never fully achieved hegemony over the meaning of land, diverse practices and understandings of land use continue alongside land's role in commercial production. In agrarian households, people's labor processes occur on, with, and through the land: they grow food for eating and selling on private or communal plots, gather wild food and firewood from common forest areas, graze animals on surrounding shrubland, and fish from nearby streams. This assemblage of diverse labor practices necessary for the sustenance of life—or what scholars term *social reproduction*—produces a strong unity between what are often seen as separate productive and reproductive spheres (Chung 2017). Furthermore, humans occupy an uneasy control over land; many people believe that land spirits that lie beyond the human realm are the ultimate owners of land and water (Work 2011). Global capitalism commodifies nature, life, and labor by subordinating these diverse processes of caring and food provisioning to the market value of land (Harvey 2005). This turns land into an abstract, fungible factor of production, incorporating and devaluing people, activities, and lands that were previously controlled by noncapitalist modes of social and ecological life (McMichael 2011).

State actors play crucial roles in facilitating primitive accumulation through force (and the threat of force), regulation, and discourses of development. Many land grabs have occurred on state land that is leased to private developers for capitalist production, thus creating new frontiers for capital on these lands (Kelly and Peluso 2015). In Cambodia, Western donors have encouraged ELCs as a way to achieve economic growth through foreign investment, alongside national land registration schemes that promise to strengthen bureaucratic institutions and safeguard land tenure security for those whose land is threatened by agribusiness and speculative investment (Biddulph and Williams 2016; Üllenberg 2009). Essentially, land titles are supposed to protect against land grabbing (Dwyer 2015). For more than a decade, however, the Cambodian government directed land titling programs to the lowland rice-growing regions, while avoiding the upland areas where the political elite and international investors displaced people to make way for ELC expansion (Dwyer 2015; Grimsditch and Henderson 2009; Schoenberger 2017). The uplands became frontiers for capitalism—not frontiers in the sense of wild places that meet civilization, but frontiers produced through the state's recasting of these areas as unpopulated and in need of development, thus throwing open existing social orders and creating a scramble for land (Peluso and Lund 2011; Rasmussen and Lund 2018).

When the commodification of land and life goes too far, diverse sectors of society, including the state, can mobilize to defend social protections against "disembedded" market capitalism (Polanyi 1944). This "double movement" can be pronounced in rural areas where livelihoods and identity are tied to the land (Li 2014). In Cambodia, protests against land grabbing grew in magnitude during the mid-2000s. The country was thrust into the global spotlight as rural people protested their violent displacement from the land, and transnational campaigns such as "blood sugar" exposed desperate labor conditions in the country's plantations. By 2012, Prime Minister Hun Sen found himself under pressure from displaced rural people and the growing numbers of restless urban youth. This spurred him to a sudden announcement: the preelection land titling reform. The prime minister's land reform excised land from within ELCs and provided land title to rural people who could prove they were using the land. This land reform was officially termed "Order 01" (or, in full, "Order 01BB: Measures reinforcing and increasing the efficiency of Economic Land Concessions"), but the prime minister dubbed the land titling program the "leopard skin policy" because land inhabited by farmers was excised from ELCs and other state land areas, leaving the cultivated areas resembling a spotted leopard skin pattern of smallholders and agribusiness operations (Oldenburg and Neef 2014). The leopard skin policy theoretically allowed for a win-win scenario for smallholder farmers and ELC companies, as the companies would have a stable local labor force and farmers would gain tenure security, access to credit, and employment at ELCs to finance their small farm enterprises. The prime minister mobilized 2,500 university student volunteers, who donned military uniforms and fanned out around the country to demarcate more than half a million land plots across twenty provinces.[2] The land reform also downsized or canceled ELCs that had not developed their land holdings, thereby demonstrating the power of the state to discipline concessionaires. Remarkably, the government carried out the majority of actions within just one year, with no assistance provided—or even allowed—by the international donor community.

I was attracted to Cambodia's leopard skin land reform as a focus of study because it potentially marked a major shift in land relations. But no one knew what to expect. For rural Cambodians living in fear of losing their land, the land reform offered hope that the prime minister would protect them. For local authorities and ministries who enjoyed some discretion over land control, the land reform threatened to shift control to the direct purview of the prime minister. And for development agencies and multilateral institutions, the land reform promised to strengthen bureaucratic land administration and provided a potential model for other countries. I felt the reform could go in two directions. On the one hand, my theoretical basis in critical agrarian studies made me skeptical about the potential for this reform to help rural people. Land reforms can be a vehicle for commodification and state control, and I expected land concentration, inequality, and state control to increase, with the potential for exploitative taxation and state surveillance (Akram-Lodhi, Borras, and Kay 2007; Borras, Kay, and Lahiff 2008; de Janvry 1981; James Scott 1998). Furthermore, I expected that the policy implementation would be chaotic because inequalities in wealth, power, and information in isolated rural areas meant that people in the know could easily take advantage of whatever benefits the land reform might offer (Hirsch 2011). On the other hand, I expected that if nothing happened (that is, in the absence of land reform), people in the uplands would continue to lose their land to ELCs. Forests would continue to be destroyed. People's access to land, water, and trees needed for survival would continue to erode. Many people felt they had little response to the powerful legal claims made by companies and the political elite, and they hoped that the land title might provide some form of protection from land grabbing. This hope felt partial, fragile, something to be nurtured for its possibilities rather than knocked by academic critique.

But my field research during and after the land reform's implementation revealed that my initial hope for a reassertion of rural people's foothold in Cambodia was largely misplaced. I found that Cambodia's leopard skin land reform could be considered a failure from the perspective of economists promoting land reform. Rules were unclear, elite capture was rife, and implementation was secretive and uncertain. The prime minister's oral pronouncements often trumped written rules, leaving policymakers scrambling to issue new legal documents. In total, the central state wrote more than two hundred documents to facilitate Order 01, a number unparalleled in the government's thirty years of rule (Focus on the Global South 2013). The prime minister first announced that disputed land would be surveyed, but then he backtracked and issued surveyors with new instructions not to measure land when multiple parties claimed ownership. This meant that people could only claim title for land they currently cultivated, not land that ELC companies had already grabbed for plantations. On the ground, survey practices varied between and even within teams. People who already had political power and wealth used the land reform to clear and claim forestland, while those who did not have the power to stake their claims, or whose land relations did not conform to notions of productive agriculture, lost access to land. Land earmarked for communal land title was titled out to individuals, creating tensions within communities.

The constantly changing policies and negotiations on the ground meant that land reform outcomes were diverse. Approximately 75 percent of people in Grimsditch and Schoenberger's (2015) national survey gained title to only part of their land. In my survey of 270 land claimants, 40 percent did not have any land surveyed, and many people whose land was surveyed received a title to only some of the land (see chapter 5). Land title recipients tell me they still do not feel fully secure in their tenure, they are scared of the companies and state officials, and they cannot access the state institutions that administer titles and adjudicate disputes. When I asked people about current perceptions of land tenure two years after the land reform, I found no statistical difference in people's perceptions of tenure security between those whose land was surveyed and those whose land was not surveyed during the reform.

But this failure—the confusion and uncertainty the land reform produced in rural areas—shows precisely why the campaign was successful for the Cambodian state elite. Land title recipients were not sure whether the land title would help them, but they saw the title as a gift from Hun Sen that tied them more tightly to the prime minister's personal protection. This flies in the face of the idea—held by both economists promoting land titling reform and scholars critical of land reform—that formal property institutions will tie people more tightly to the bureaucratic state. In Cambodia, the extension of formal property rights did not strengthen rural people's relationships with bureaucratic institutions; instead, land titling strengthened the patronage-based politics that Western development agencies hoped to subvert. The land title became part of the economy of personal gifts from the government, within a broader political economy in which the ruling elite use the production of fear and uncertainty to strengthen their grip on power. The tension between the possibility of receiving state and development agency services such as the land title (as personal gifts from the prime minister) and the possibility of not receiving them (or receiving them on uncertain terms) is a powerful mechanism that encourages people to remain loyal to the regime and to produce themselves as good state subjects. Social categories of gender, race, and class are central markers of difference in this constitution of the state-citizen relationship; they contain the other who is the foil for the unitary, modern nation-state. The possibility of violent repression for those who do not conform always lurks close to the surface, and people's fear of speaking out against the state is maintained through constant surveillance and everyday threats. And while the land reform buttressed the personal power of the prime minister in the short term by giving people hope that he may protect them, it undermined rural communities in the long term by enclosing communal resources and facilitating predatory capitalist relations.

These encounters with land reform are power laden, but the outcomes are never fully predetermined. Policy is always made on the ground as surveyors, land claimants, state officials, land activists, and agribusiness concessionaires' claims for recognition and powerful actors' claims to bestow property rights produce state authority and shape people's relationships with land (Gupta 1995; Joseph and Nugent 1994; Sikor 2009; Wolford 2010). In this book, I draw on eighteen months of ethnographic fieldwork in two upland communes on the foothills of the Aural mountains of Khang Cheung province, where Khmer peasant farmers struggle to maintain a rural foothold inside the country's largest ELC.[3] I also include a smaller study of two communes in northeast Khang Leit province, where indigenous ethnic groups face land dispossession from Khmer migrants, government assimilation schemes, and ELCs. My research reveals stories of uncertainty and negotiation, stories that show the power of fear but also leave room for hope and for agency that reaches beyond established networks of power. I contend that this uncertainty is precisely what allows Cambodia's political regime to continue and what makes Cambodian state power, and the predatory patrimonial and capitalist logics on which it is built, inherently unstable.

I (and likely my readers) am also implicated in these predatory relations through my consumption. Cambodia's ELCs are financed by global capital from China and Vietnam as well as Europe and North America, and they produce rubber, sugar, and cassava that are shipped offshore to be transformed into value-added products: rubber for car tires and consumer products in China, sugar for ethanol and packaged food products in Europe and the United States, cassava for animal feed and biofuel in Thailand and China. Surplus value is captured outside of Cambodia, and consumers benefit from cheap goods that further fuel our societies' hyperconsumerism. The stories in this book, therefore, highlight the ways in which Cambodia (and other countries in the global south) are connected to all of us: Cambodia's land conflicts are situated within global capitalist relations, in which Cambodia occupies a place at the bottom of the global hierarchy.

Constructing the Postconflict State

For a piece of work dealing with state formation, my discussion throughout the book may be curious, for I spend little time discussing Cambodia's bureaucratic structure. My epistemological commitment to understanding national and global change from the view of rural women and men shapes my representation of the state. When I asked people to talk about the state, discussion centered on the manifestation of the state in people's daily lives and imaginations. The state was the village and commune authorities, the prime minister, the land reform volunteers. This is the state that rural people can access. The workings of the judiciary, in contrast, were almost never discussed because they held little meaning for people. I was repeatedly told, "People like us [that is, poor, rural, uneducated] cannot access the judicial system." How, then, does the law matter? "People like us are constantly rebuffed when we seek assistance from higher-level provincial authorities or the central authorities in Phnom Penh." The ministries, then, have little meaning from villagers' perspectives. The opposition Cambodia National Rescue Party (CNRP) was gaining support at the time of my research, but many people in my study areas did not openly support (or even talk about) the opposition for fear of state retaliation, and all of my study areas were controlled by ruling party officials. But the village chief matters. The commune council matters. The NGOs might matter. And, most importantly, Prime Minister Hun Sen matters. This is the state that people related to, and this is the state that features in my account. While I do discuss broader state structures, much can be gained from the silences in the text. It is imperative, however, that this discussion be situated within a broader view of state power, which I build in this section.

The Cambodian state that formed in the 1990s carried the West's expectation that development could be achieved through the simple importation of known solutions into postconflict, postsocialist states: a free market, parliamentary democracy, human rights. The 1991 Paris Peace Agreements that led to the United Nations' peacekeeping mission in Cambodia (UNTAC) was a historic moment—the first occasion in which the UN took over as the government of a state and the test ground for the implementation of a democratic capitalist state in postsocialist, postconflict regimes. But this assumed "end of history" (Fukuyama 2004) has not transpired in Cambodia nor in many other states subject to international reforms. Nazneen Barma (2016) argues that peace agreements too often fail to institute long-lasting democratic peace. Peacebuilding interventions go awry, she argues, when international institutions select particular elites to partner with, conferring legitimacy, resources, and power to these groups. In turn, domestic elites "use that power to enact subtle strategies of institutional conversion to their own ends" (4), by "restrict[ing] political competition and dominat[ing] the process of postconflict institutional design" (9). The resulting political system is a "neopatrimonial order" in which a patrimonial system of political relationships mediated through personal connections coexists with bureaucratic government's pretensions of impersonality and the rule of law (Pitcher, Moran, and Johnston 2009; James Scott 1976; Weber 1978).

This argument certainly has relevance to Cambodia, where peacebuilding efforts have paradoxically worked to strengthen patrimonial relations that form the basis of power on (and through) which state institutions are constructed, leading scholars to term the political system a "mirage" of democracy (Strangio 2014), a "neopatrimonial system" (Beban, So, and Un 2017) and a "shadow state" (Le Billon 2002). The discourse of the neopatrimonial state is useful to explain the shortcomings of liberal peacebuilding efforts, but it can be problematic when invoked to explain state abuses of power across vastly different countries (see Pitcher, Moran, and Johnston [2009] for a critique of the literature), and it smacks of cultural essentialism when used to describe patronage relations across hundreds of years of history as though these are static (Creak and Barney 2018). Too often, this approach focuses attention on what is not there, in terms of impersonal institutions such as an independent judiciary and functional markets, to the exclusion of what is there: "the myriad ways in which politicians, state makers and different sectors of society make claims and engage with each other" (Strauss and Cruise O'Brian 2007, 2).

Recent Cambodian scholarship moves beyond these traps by analyzing the shifting constructs of neopatrimonial governing networks (Milne 2015). The ruling Cambodian People's Party (CPP) gained power in the postwar period by combining legal, pseudolegal, and illegal mechanisms of financing to pacify opponents and consolidate networks of supporters, including the expropriation of large tracts of forest- and coastal land and funds from development agencies earmarked for formal budget lines (Jacobsen and Stuart-Fox 2013). Violence was central to the CPP's consolidation of support. A violent coup against the main opposition party in 1997 disposed Hun Sen's rival. The United Nations' intervention accepted the legitimacy of the CPP despite the violence that propelled it to power after the country's first elections. As Andrew Cock (2016) wryly suggests, donor countries promoting capitalist reforms seemed primarily interested in ensuring that Cambodia's integration into the regional and global economy advanced, no matter how the politics of reform played out. Over time, the CPP has turned the armed forces and government bureaucracy into "organs of the party" by strengthening the patron-client network within and among the state, party, and military apparatuses (Barma 2016, 155). The Cambodian state therefore defies any easy delineation; it includes not only the political elite who hold formal positions of state power but also the broader ruling elite who are intertwined with state structures in formal and informal positions (such as business or military capacities) and thus in a position to exercise influence over how the country is governed (Cock 2016).

This system of political power rests largely on the provision of land, timber, and natural resource licenses to the politico-business elite and international investors in exchange for party financing for state projects and loyalty. Political power (*omnaich*[4]) flows through social connections called *khsae* (strings) linking patrons (*knong*), who provide protection and assistance, with clients, who are expected to pass on a portion of any benefit they receive (Chandler 2008; Jacobsen and Stuart-Fox 2013; Un 2005). Financial flows from resource extraction are used to provide the gifts to rural voters (in the form of donations, food, infrastructure, and state services) that aim to secure their loyalty. Hun Sen's government has built up its base since the 1980s through such practices of gift giving in rural areas, allowing the party to marginalize opposition and build an elaborate system of mass patronage and mobilization (Hughes 2006, 2013; Norén-Nilsson 2016; Un and So 2009). The CPP manages this gift distribution through its *choh moulothan* (going down to the base) strategy, in which a network of CPP working groups (*krom kar ngear*) are in charge of distributing donations (Craig and Kimchoeun 2011). This top-down structure stretches from the prime minister at the apex, through the ministries to the subnational provincial level, down to the village level. Even when infrastructure is provided for under decentralized commune funding (established in 2001) rather than through CPP networks, voters are led to credit the CPP for the state's services (Craig and Kimchoeun 2011).

At the top of this system, the ruler's status is secured through the cultivation of political networks and through his claim to semi-divinity, a tradition of the divine king (*devaraja*) that emerges from Brahman and Theravada Buddhist influences (Stuart-Fox 2008). In this way, power is held in individuals, due to the merit (*bunn*) they possess, rather than in institutions. Prime Minister Hun Sen embodies much of the flexibility and charisma of earlier personalistic leaders (notably independence-era leader Prince Sihanouk [Chandler 2008]); he manipulates the symbols of kingship and spirituality to enhance his legitimacy, styling himself as both a kingly power and a reformist committed to building a modern nation (Strangio 2014). He is also an adept orator who weaves together collective memories of conflict to stoke an aggrieved sense of nationhood that is in stark contrast to the West's narrative of postconflict liberation. Many Cambodians feel that the land of the Khmer (or *Srok Khmer*), which was once a distinct cultural empire in Southeast Asia, has for centuries been besieged by powerful outsiders (Goshal, Ku, and Hawk 1995, 27). The United States is associated with a 1970 coup that pushed out the prince, a bombing campaign from 1969 to 1973 that helped bring the Khmer Rouge to power, and a prolonging of the conflict by supporting the Khmer Rouge at the UN in the 1980s (Chandler 2008). The 1991 Paris Peace Accords that ended the conflict, therefore, hold an ambivalence for Cambodians—they mark the transition to peace, but they can also be seen as the dawn of a new foreign project to re-create Cambodia in the West's own image and for its own ends (Virak 2017). It is not surprising, then, that as the Cambodian elite have maintained relations with Western donors in the years since the Paris Accords, they have also cultivated a growing relationship with China, with whom they have a long history of bilateral cooperation with few strings attached.

Development agencies continue to play important roles in the patronage system when they form partnerships with Cambodian state actors and their contributions are funneled through CPP networks. As Sophal Ear (2006) argues, this flow of revenue means the state has not had to install effective taxation systems, thus avoiding relations of responsibility that tax-paying citizens may be better placed to demand. But international actors can also pose a threat if they demand too much transparency and good governance, too much focus on human rights, or conversely too much overt land dispossession. These threats became increasingly visible as a connected civil society emerged through the mid-2000s, with translocal movements of NGOs, activist networks, and opposition party supporters calling out the complicity of financial firms and development agencies in the land sector (Beban, So, and Un 2017).

Hun Sen has built formidable power at the apex of this system, but his power is not absolute. Hun Sen's continued rule relies on ongoing negotiation of internal tensions within the CPP and the broader political elite, which includes competing factions of politico-business strongmen (*oknha*), who are integrated into the state but retain a degree of autonomy in their domains of extraction (Milne

2015; Verver and Dahles 2015). Fierce rivalries over which domains of the state will control land also play out within the leadership networks of ministries—the Ministry of Agriculture, Forestry and Fisheries (MAFF), responsible for land concessions; the Ministry of Environment (MoE), responsible for conservation estate; and the Ministry of Land Management (MLMUPC), responsible for governing land use through land titling. Some reformist politicians in these ministries have become popular for their public statements committing to stamping out corruption in their institutions.[5] In general, though, these factional disputes within the ruling party revolve around obtaining lucrative positions and securing revenues from extraction, rather than other ideological stances, and most do not seek to challenge the structure of power (Cock 2016). Rumors abound about factions within the CPP, but with the deaths of long-term CPP stalwarts Chea Sim and Sok An and the political risks that potential challengers would take if they were to openly oppose Hun Sen, a shift of power seems unlikely anytime soon. Hun Sen has sought to hedge his reliance on other state elites through the cultivation of personalized networks of clients, the elevation of his sons into senior military and administrative positions, and close ties of marriage and kinship with the military apparatus (Cock 2016). But he faces the regime's fundamental contradiction: it requires ever-greater resources to satisfy patrons and to maintain the flow of gifts down to local levels, even as it eats away at Cambodian territory.

Fear, Uncertainty, and the Durability of Authoritarian Rule

Given that the elite's control is unstable and depends on constant negotiation, why has Hun Sen's personal power been so strong for more than thirty years? While some scholars look to Hun Sen's spiritual bases of power to explain his continued legitimacy (Jacobsen and Stuart-Fox 2013), and while others look to the CPP's success in negotiating the end of violent civil conflict (Hughes and Un 2011; Sovachana Pou, Wade, and Hong 2012), these explanations assume a popular legitimacy for the CPP that I did not find in the rural uplands. Rural people living in spaces of land conflict and prolonged drought that has devastated rice yields frequently told me, "The government has abandoned us." "Hun Sen doesn't see us." Some people even said that life was better during the Khmer Rouge regime than it is now.

I found this reference to the Khmer Rouge shocking at first, as I perceived the Khmer Rouge regime only in terms of a horrific violence that seemed beyond comparison. But I believe the shock was intended. The people who said this were not former Khmer Rouge cadres who had life relatively easy during the regime, but villagers who had suffered and lost family members. People's comments centered on two connected aspects of life. First, "in the Khmer Rouge time, everyone got rice, however little." Second, "at least we were all equal then." When I pressed them, these people firmly said they did not want to return to that time of conflict. Rather, the comparisons were a form of postsocialist nostalgia that told me more about people's views of the current administration and their expectation that the paternalistic state should maintain people's capacity for social reproduction and community cohesion (a sentiment also observed in the former Soviet states [Verdery 2003]).

Although people's comments stressed the need for equality (at least everyone got rice), I don't think it is inequality per se that people are complaining about here. After all, social order in Cambodia is cleaved along lines of race, gender, generation, and other social markers, with peasants seen to be low status (Chandler 2008). But this hierarchy is only respected when those higher up in the social order protect those below in exchange for loyalty. Rulers are expected to (personally) protect state subjects (Hughes 2006). It is this basic relationship that people say has shifted: instead of a paternalism toward Khmer peasants, the elite look after some people now, and they abandon others.

These sentiments give pause to the suggestion made by some scholars that Hun Sen's right to rule is "freely given" due to his superior power (*omnaich*) rather than "grudgingly given" in response to the threat of his coercive power (Jacobsen and Stuart-Fox 2013, 18). I found that in the rural villages where I conducted research, Hun Sen's *omnaich* is always perceived to be backed by the threat of force. For rural people increasingly aware of rising inequality and connected with alternative networks of power through NGOs and translocal activism, support for the ruling regime is much more complicated than for a noncoercive, freely given right to rule. Hun Sen's cultivation of himself as a benevolent leader does not preclude the cultivation of himself as militarily powerful, with the ever-present possibility that he could turn to force to maintain his position if required. This potential for outright violence became abundantly clear before the 2018 national election, when the government moved to shut down growing support for the opposition party (the CNRP) by dissolving the party and cracking down on independent media and activists. Indeed, it is the cultivation of fear and uncertainty over the state's potential for both protection and for violence that encourages people's obedience in upland areas.

I want to dwell on this point to show how fear and uncertainty stabilize Hun Sen's regime. Fear is pervasive in rural Cambodia. Fear of the state is layered over collective memories of the civil war, the Khmer Rouge regime, and Buddhist traditions of nonconfrontation. The Khmer Rouge installed a legacy of "radical mistrust" (Zucker 2013); the Khmer Rouge leadership fomented distrust and fear through a discourse of traitors and enemies penetrating the party ranks (Path and Kanavou 2015) and sought to break apart the bonds of trust in families and communities (Zucker 2013). The move to a free market economy in the 1990s further built on these layers of fear, as agrarian solidarity groups were dismantled and the field of action for resistance was reduced (Hughes 2003). The state's socialist authoritarian building blocks established in the 1980s have persisted through post-1993 democratization, including central planning, tight surveillance, and social control mechanisms at the village level that aim to prevent the establishment of antigovernment resistance (Milne 2015). In rural areas, surveillance networks persist down to the level of neighborhood chiefs, who oversee groups of around ten households. Hun Sen frequently reminds people that the country could plunge back into chaos if his party loses support (Strangio 2014). The layers of fear and continued surveillance produce an "ontological insecurity" that contributes to social fragmentation and a deep fear of resumed violence (Ojendal and Sedara 2006).

Fear of state power is of course a normal part of rule in any nation state; it is what allows the state to work. As part of the social contract, we (citizens of a nation state) recognize that if we do something wrong, the police and judicial system can punish us. (It is not just a moral imperative that encourages us not to speed when driving, for example; it is the threat of state retaliation.) But in Cambodia (and in electoral authoritarian states more generally) the nature of the rules and the potential for state discipline is unclear (Schedler 2013). People rarely know when they have crossed the line from norms to deviance, from legality to illegality, from supporter to antigovernment organizer, because the prime minister's oral pronouncements and secretive unwritten rules guide state actions, and the state elite lean on both legal institutions and extralegal means to re-create the rules in each social encounter. This uncertainty over (il)legal norms allows the state to criminalize people's actions. Uncertainty also foments distrust in others, because people never know where others stand relative to this shifting line of government supporter/antigovernment activist. And it encourages self-discipline, as people fear possible retribution for any actions that may be deemed antigovernment and make sure to stand well inside the line of acceptable behavior that the state would require, were the line to be clearer (Banmer and Smithson 2008, 21).

Throughout this book, I use the idea of uncertainty in reference to political practice and its effects in Cambodia in three broad senses. First, I argue that Cambodian state actors produce uncertainty over the people and processes involved in governance. The state elite's patronage networks use practices including obfuscation, secrecy, confusion, and delay, as well as the selective application of law, to maintain control of resources. This aspect of state practice is examined in a burgeoning social science literature, which recognizes that the ability to "withhold information, deny observation and dictate the terms of knowledge" is an integral element of political power (Abrams 1988, 62). While a state's ability to know populations and territories through making them legible (measuring, systematizing, and simplifying them) is a central process of rule (James Scott 1998), the production of illegibility, ignorance, and murkiness is also productive for state power (Das 2004; Mathews 2011). In Southeast Asia, as Derek Hall and colleagues (2011) argue, informalization of state rule is not just about deficient state capacity; the confusion of fuzzy, overlapping land boundaries is actually productive, as it enables different constituencies to argue that right is on their side. Elsewhere, I have termed this form of state power state the "power of informality" (Beban, So, and Un 2017). I don't use that term here, preferring the broader (and therefore less precise) term *uncertainty*, as I am interested in the effects of state practice in people's everyday emotional lives—that is, uncertainty as lived experience. The production of uncertainty may allow smallholder farmers flexible accommodations, but it also allows officials at various levels to "disorient, undermine, confuse, or defer political challenges" from people in rural areas (Whitington 2019, 150).

Second, uncertainty is a temporal phenomenon: the uncertain potential for the state to deliver gifts of development and prosperity or, conversely, punishment and violence. People's anticipation of and desire for prosperity and the possibility that the state may be able to provide development encourages people to continue supporting the government. While people in rural areas complain of being abandoned by the state, the regime continues to carry support through the promise that abandonment is not total. Some people do receive state protection. Sometimes state officials arrive to distribute food rations, toilets, land plots, a health clinic, and infrastructure, often provided as personal gifts from the CPP to communities who demonstrate loyal support for the party. Similar to the Laos state characterized by Sarinda Singh (2012), the potential for state protection and prosperity is so important in encouraging self-discipline. The state and development agencies' rhetoric of economic development and poverty reduction deemphasizes inequality, allowing tensions between the rural poor and urban wealthy to be balanced by a shared aspiration for wealth and modern development that, as in Laos and other Southeast Asian states, "allows state authority to be conceived of as a mutual interest that links the state and the people" (122). Holly High (2014) similarly argues that desire and aspiration legitimize the developmental state. While people see the state as exploitative, they also see it as a possible source of nurture and expect the state to provide resources needed for wealth, education, and health care. The difficulty for the Cambodian state is that expectations are not static; the CPP's success in bringing about stability and rapid growth in the postwar era, alongside the explosion of information technology and urbanization, has created new expectations, particularly among the generation of young people who didn't live through war. People are keenly aware of what prosperity could look like, and of the state's failure to provide it.

Third, I recognize that uncertainty is not always deliberately produced; uncertainty can also be due to ineptitude, mistakes, chance, and inadequate information. The character of the Cambodian state leads to confusion and problems on the ground, in part because much of the state bureaucracy is staffed by people who gained their positions through family or *khsae* connections rather than those with the most relevant skills. Even competent civil servants must make decisions where political calculus is the overriding factor. The flexibility enabled by oral decision making also lends the regime a tendency toward reactive, rapidly changing policies in order to conceal immediate problems, which can lead to a confusing flurry of policy changes from central government (Maclean 2013). The point here is that uncertainty is both intentional and also likely unintentional; uncertainty can be "part tactics, part negotiation, part due to chance and part due to lack of resources" (Whitington 2019, 68), and these work together to reinforce the primacy of personalized nodes of power.

For the state, uncertainty is politically useful because it enables tensions to be privately negotiated between state actors rather than threatening state stability (Cock 2016, 133) and maintains the state elite's flexibility over resources so they can engage in both future-proofing (taking on selected reforms imposed by donor countries while regaining hold of financial flows for later projects of rule) and "past-proofing" (ensuring that past mistakes cannot be traced to any one institution or person) (Roy 2016). Donor agencies and capitalist firms in Cambodia also participate in the production of uncertainty, although through different means and for a different purpose than the Cambodian government. While the Cambodian elite produce uncertainty in order to retain personalized control over state revenues, the donors do so in order to maintain the performance of democratization and the stability necessary for international investment, and to paper over what appear to be irreconcilable differences in understandings of state authority and land (see chapter 1).

The Cambodian state's production of uncertainty is particularly evident in the land sector. Cambodian state officials go to great lengths to maintain secrecy over who is involved in land deals and what the details of the deals are. The shadowy network around ELCs includes state, capital, and military elements, often with the same people playing multiple roles, such as when Cambodian military personnel are employed as private security guards for concessions (Milne 2015). But rural (non-elite) people rarely know who is involved in these deals. Cambodian state actors regularly produce uncertainty over who and what are involved in land deals through bureaucratic delay, obfuscation, silencing, denial, secrecy, and ambiguous legal directives. This has a paralyzing effect on possibilities for resistance (Milne 2015). As Whitington (2019, 151) notes, the production of uncertainty is an "act of disempowerment" for those who lack access to information; ignorance is a central part of people's feelings of exclusion and comes to form a hierarchical structural condition that excludes the rural poor from both complex bureaucracies and informal power relations. And even if rural people know who is involved in land deals, it is not at all clear where people can go for help because those who are in positions of power are often involved in land grabbing. During the Order 01 land reform, the opaque, patchy implementation created uncertainty for people on the ground about whether they would receive a land title and, for those who did eventually receive one, uncertainty over what this gift from the prime minister signified.

The lexicon of uncertainty over the state's provision of gifts to reward or discipline citizens is important—these state services are gifts, not rights. Contrary to a state service provided through bureaucratic structures that implies some sense of accountability to tax-paying, voting citizens, a gift does not imply accountability (Carrier 1991; Mauss 1954). A gift implies a more personal relationship of obligation, protection or kindness, rather than something citizens have a right to demand. This aspect of gifts is discussed in a rich history of anthropological scholarship distinguishing impersonal commodity exchange from personalized gift exchange that creates qualitative relationships between givers and receivers, making them reciprocally dependent (Carrier 1991; Mauss 1954; Rus 2008). More recently, scholars have pointed to the coexistence of commodity exchange and gift exchange, disentangling the components of both in any exchange situation (Tsing 2015). Gifts not only continue to embody the identity of the giver but also impose this identity upon the receiver (Carrier 1991). As a result, the receiver, in bearing (a part of) the identity of the giver, becomes subordinated to the latter (Strathern 1992). State gifts in Cambodia bear this sense of obligation—preelection cash handouts are often distributed with an explicit reminder to vote for the ruling party; infrastructural development may be awarded to communities loyal to the ruling party and withheld from those deemed problematic (Craig and Kimchoeun 2011).

But land title as a gift may seem contradictory. After all, with a centralized property registry, the bureaucratic state ostensibly bestows the future promise of property protection backed by the power of the judiciary, which appears to reshape land control away from patronage relations (Boone 2007). However, the way that the prime minister designed and managed the land reform exemplifies the attributes of CPP gifts and merges this phenomenon of political gift giving with the promised neoliberal benefits of commodifying land. During the leopard skin reform, the state focused on implementing the reform quickly before the election, holding elaborate land titling ceremonies, maintaining secrecy and confusion over the details of the reform, and instituting rapid policy changes according to Hun Sen's oral pronouncements—all attributes of CPP gift giving (Hughes 2006; Norén-Nilsson 2016). From Order 01's inception in May 2012, Prime Minister Hun Sen made clear that he personally organized and funded the initiative. In public speeches he stated that volunteer students' bonuses came from "uncle, auntie and the party."[6] Supplementary funding came from the CPP as well as from private domestic and international firms associated with the party, and the campaign was coordinated by Hun Sen and his son, army colonel Hun Manit (Grimsditch and Schoenberger 2015). The volunteer surveyors were dubbed "Heroic Samdech Techo Volunteer Youth" in reference to the prime minister's full name, thereby reinforcing the land title's status as a personal gift from him (see chapter 4).

The land reform was thus a political campaign in the guise of land reform. While the land reform was motivated by multiple factors, the primary motive appears to have been the need to gain electoral support and to underline the legitimacy of the prime minister as rural people's patron in the lead-up to the national election. As one Cambodian woman working in a land rights NGO said to me, "Why didn't they do this a long time ago? Why wait until just before the election, when they knew that things were so tense then? It is obviously a political move." The commune elections in 2012 were a wake-up call for the government, with ruling party support lagging in areas with land disputes as well as in urban areas where growing populations of educated, networked young people are less afraid than older people and less loyal to the regime (Un 2015). According to one Khmer researcher I interviewed, panic set in within the CPP ranks. The challenge, in Cambodia's political context, was to ensure Hun Sen's survival (and the broader dominance of the CPP). This meant doing something about land evictions to win rural people's support, while also retaining the support of elite concession holders who finance informal payments and development projects. But herein lies the difficulty for the government: A complete implementation of this reform would have entailed erasing earning opportunities for many of the CPP's key business and military clients and the local authorities who mediate and profit from the flow of new settlers into these areas. But to do nothing risked losing support from people whose capacity for social reproduction is being eroded. The resulting political calculus was the partial land survey I analyze here, which provided government recognition for some people while also shoring up relationships with investors and loyal supporters. This analysis reveals that the key problematic for political power in rural Cambodia lies in the tension between the potential for state protection and the potential for state repression at the site of social reproduction. Land relations is a prime site of this tension, due to land's crucial role in financing state provisioning and elite wealth and providing capacities for rural people's social reproduction.

To simply recognize the incompleteness of the land survey, however, is to conceal the ways in which this process produces disciplined subjects, deepening social cleavages including gender, race, and class. To understand this production of subjectivities, we must understand how state power in Cambodia is fundamentally gendered. This analysis reveals the relations between the power of the state, the distribution of its resources, and the masculinity of its representatives, for gender and politics are not separate/separable categories: sexual difference is constituted by politics, and challenges to gender norms also pose challenges to political power (Joan Scott 1988).

Gendered State Power in Cambodia

Cambodia's neopatrimonial state is also a patriarchal state. Gender is a central marker of political power; men are generally perceived as having (and able to acquire) more *omnaich* than women (Jacobsen and Stuart-Fox 2013). While women can possess *omnaich* in their own right, women's power works largely through cultivating backdoor relationships with influential male kin and local officials (Resurreccion and Elmhirst 2008). These gender norms are in tension with contemporary designs for reducing gender inequality and for increasing economic opportunities (particularly jobs in the garment industry) that draw young women into new social spheres away from the direct control of parents and relatives (Brickell 2011; Derks 2008). However, government spokespeople and rural women and men I spoke with still make reference to the traditional texts describing appropriate codes of conduct: women are expected to maintain a harmonious household, including managing household finances, raising children, and performing domestic work, as well as engaging in trade and crop production; men are tasked with protection and governance (Brickell and Springer 2016; Ledgerwood 1996). Women's role as protectors of family harmony is tied up with protection of the Khmer nation (Frieson 2001). State promotional pamphlets from the 1950s independence era instruct women to fulfill their "duties as good housewives" in order to make the country prosperous (quoted in Frieson 2001, 4). Hun Sen has stated that he is "tired of listening" to women "always demanding rights," when "many men in Cambodia are oppressed by wives who do not let them go to wedding parties."[7] This joke belies the point that women are valued insofar as they produce themselves as good housewives (to be treated carefully by men). Those women who demand rights and do not maintain family harmony will not be listened to (and, by extension, will not be treated carefully by male household members or by the state [Kent 2014]).

The gendered norm that women oversee family harmony and manage household finances provides a higher status for women in Cambodia than in many societies with strictly patriarchal gender norms (Errington 1990); although in everyday life the power and prestige afforded to men exceed that afforded to women (Brickell 2011). Women's status is reproduced through land inheritance practices. Norms of bilateral land inheritance, in which land is shared equally among sons and daughters upon marriage, is a common practice among Khmer families in Khang Cheung; many parents also provide extra land to the daughter who cares for them in old age. Among the diverse inheritance practices of indigenous communities in Khang Leit, many have strong traditions of communal land management, as well as matrilocality and matrilineal land inheritance, in which the family name and landholding are passed down the female line, and newly married couples settle in the wife's home village. Cultural practices are always in flux, however, and the arrival of ELCs and lowland migrants in upland communities are reconfiguring inheritance norms. People can no longer rely on moving onto communal forestland, and the ability to inherit land has become central to the transfer of wealth for those families who manage to hold on to or accumulate land, while increasing numbers of land-poor families are reliant on off-farm labor. Furthermore, women's status as landowners does not always equal control over land and control over decisions to mortgage or sell the land or to plant risky cash crops (Jacobs 2009a; Park 2015).

The Cambodian Civil Code actually mandates equal bilateral inheritance for girls and boys, although I have never met anyone in rural Cambodia who was aware of this provision in the code or seemed to feel that the law was relevant at all. As one man in Khang Leit told me, "In other countries they follow the law; here we follow our parents." The law did, however, become relevant during the Order 01 land reform. The land reform was widely celebrated as gender inclusive for its focus on providing joint title in both husband's and wife's names. This avoided the worst effects of gendered dispossession seen in contexts such as Malawi and Ghana, where land was titled only in men's names in matrilineal communities, leading to upheaval in social norms and the loss of status for women (Agarwal 1994; Jacobs 2009b; Peters 2010). But the celebration over joint title in Cambodia ignores the ways that land formalization may disrupt social norms in communities with matrilineal or communal traditions of land inheritance, and it also ignores the broader political economy of rising land inequality that leaves some families who lack land and labor for off-farm work—such as widowed women—in a precarious position (Lee 2006; Park 2015).

This brief analysis of gender constructions shows how women are largely excluded from networks of political power (and incorporated problematically as protectors of family and national harmony), thereby connecting resource control, state formation, and patriarchal relations within and beyond farming households (Sikor 2009). However, work on the state in Cambodia, with its complex treatment of the articulation of neoliberal capitalism and patrimonial politics, has been largely separate from work on gender. The literature on gender produced by NGOs and development agencies often equates gender with women, and specifically with poor (and vulnerable) women (MWA 2008; STAR Kampuchea 2013). When the state is discussed in these texts, it is generally in terms of formal policy and representation. I do not mean to dismiss this approach. Rates of women's political representation are low.[8] Important work is being done to bring gender-sensitive institutions into key ministries and subnational commune councils, and some of the political gains made by the opposition party CNRP are from women standing for local body election. But it is useful to reflect on the differences between what we see as the state from the expansive literature on neopatrimonialism and what we see as the state in work on gender in Cambodia. The literature on neopatrimonialism recognizes the Cambodian state as a "hybrid of largely rhetorical and symbolic acquiescence to democratic norms built on the foundation of a patrimonial and highly predatory state structure" (Cock 2010, 10), while work on gender discusses political power largely in terms of gendered representation in formal institutions. This focus risks turning to the "largely rhetorical and symbolic" (10) bureaucratic institutions in order to empower women, despite political power being structurally embedded in patrimonial networks.

Of course, the problem of patriarchal state power is not limited to Cambodia, and the point here is one that has vexed feminist scholars for many years: How can we turn to the patriarchal state in order to find liberation from the patriarchy? (Brown 1995). And to relate this discussion to the question of land and property rights—what does it mean to prioritize joint land title (for husband-wife dyads) in the 2001 Land Law and through the leopard skin land reform? I argue that in the land reform, formal land title reproduced the authority of Hun Sen (and the domain of patrimonial power) and reproduced the authority of men over women. As state authority was negotiated through encounters on the ground, however, gender relations were also renegotiated, creating space for women and men to produce new subjectivities that challenge gender norms.

Theoretical Foundations: Agrarian Change, Property, and Formation of State Power

All modern states engage in processes of "territorialization," dividing their territories into complex political and economic zones, rearranging people and resources within these units, and creating rules delineating how these areas can be used (Vandergeest and Peluso 1995; Peluso and Lund 2011). Land that is privately owned still remains within state territory, and the recording of property through land titling—from measurement (land surveys and mapping) and recording in a cadastre (registry) to issuance of a title deed—empowers state authorities by establishing a state agency as the arbiter of rights and arbitrator of disputes (Peluso and Lund 2011; Rosset et al. 2006). States seek to change land ownership customs and regulations through land reform policies that establish property rights (in individual or communal ownership) and that may decentralize state ownership of land, tax landowners, and redistribute land to the landless (Murtazashvili and Murtazashvili 2017). Land reforms range from tenure formalization programs that commodify land to radical agrarian reforms that seek to break up large estates and redistribute this land to landless farmers. In Indonesia, for example, almost two-thirds of the land acquired by business interests to develop plantations during the Suharto era was not developed, leaving large amounts of "sleeping lands" (*tanah tidur*) that were then reclaimed and redistributed (Lucas and Warren 2013). Land reform programs have shifted away from the "golden age" of state-led redistributive reform popular from the 1950s to the 1970s to market-led approaches focused on land titling that became dominant in development discourse from the 1990s. Market-led reform programs are underpinned by the idea that land title provides tenure security and stimulates investment as farmers can enter land markets and use land title to collateralize land for productive loans, thereby raising land values and moving people out of poverty (de Soto 2000).

Critics argue that economists' presumed links between formal title, tenure security, productivity, credit access, and poverty reduction are not borne out by empirical research. In a review of studies on land titling reforms across ten developing countries, Akram-Lodhi et al. (2007) conclude that poverty reduction was mixed. States, such as Vietnam, that carried out large-scale land reform alongside support for input-output markets and pro-poor social policies were able to reduce poverty, while in other contexts, such as Bolivia, where land reform was not accompanied by broader agrarian reform, poverty was not reduced. In some contexts, such as Armenia and Zimbabwe, poverty worsened. Furthermore, inequality worsened in all studies. Even in successful reforms such as Vietnam, where poverty reduced, market-led agrarian reform facilitated dramatic land-price increases and led to the emergence of a small group of commercial farmers holding high quality land alongside large groups of landless and land-poor farmers. Where land titling reforms do bring benefits, these are often captured by those who have the access to information and resources necessary to use the reform to their advantage, such as by clearing forestland in order to claim it under private title and bribing or intimidating others into recognizing illicit claims to land

(Cleary and Eaton 1996; Hirsch 2011). There is also no guarantee that poverty reduction benefits are shared equally within households. Rosset et al. (2006) find that in Thailand, where land titling reform saw a push in the 1980s, results benefited landlords who engaged in land speculation and grabbed communal land and water and forest resources, marginalizing poor families, particularly women, whose livelihoods were closely tied to communal resources. Musembi (2007, 1469) points out that land titling reforms not only fail to benefit the poor but may also further impoverish those people who cannot access formal land title and are relegated to the extralegal customary realm. In this way, "Title spells both security and insecurity.... [The question is] security for whom?"

Beyond the notion of improving rural livelihoods, states often use land titling to create a fiscally legible landscape that is very different from the overlapping land management systems of peasant society (James Scott 1998). But this doesn't fit the Cambodian case. While Cambodian people tried to make their claims legible to the state, the leopard skin land reform did not make the population legible. Prime Minister Hun Sen repeatedly stated that he would not introduce taxation on agricultural land (Hun Sen 2012b). And even if taxation is the end goal, the national cadastre will be of little use because the property registries produced through Cambodia's land titling programs are hopelessly out of date and large swathes of land were left untitled during the land reform. Rather than blame this mess on incompetence (or the donor favorite, lack of state capacity), I suggest that maintaining illegibility is also a form of state power (Maclean 2013; Mathews 2011). That is, while state actors may seek to establish legibility in the form of monocrop concessions as an exercise of power (incentivized by foreign and domestic capital), this does not extend to the bureaucratic legibility of rural populations in the form of clear landownership papers and legal regulations; on the contrary, for the state elite it is imperative that rural land relations remain unclear in order for the state to exercise flexible control over land and rural people. Those in power produce uncertainty over land relations through the myriad practices of obfuscation, secrecy, and unwritten rules that I detail throughout this book.

I tried at first to theorize the land reform as an act that produces illegibility rather than legibility. But this formulation reproduces a false binary. The state is certainly not all-seeing in its encounters with rural people, but neither did the land reform produce complete chaos. Christian Lund's (2016) work provides a way through this theoretical block. Lund argues that rather than expect property reform to reproduce the power of the high modernist state (or argue that it fails to do so), focusing on property as productive of authority—and therefore constitutive of the state itself—refocuses analysis on thinking through the ways that policies are construed and constructed within a particular balance of forces. The formation of state power through property rights depends on both the recognition of rights by an institution and the recognition of an institution's authority by its subjects (1209). Rasmussen and Lund (2018) extend these ideas to show how state power is always under negotiation through a constant process of forming and eroding social orders of property rights, legal identities, and institutions. The production of new frontiers (understood as the discovery or invention of new resources that undo existing social orders at particular moments and places) is intimately linked to the subsequent creation of new systems of resource control—a cycle of "frontier–territorialization–frontier–territorialization" (Rasmussen and Lund 2018, 389). This cycle reconfigures socioecological relations: as governing institutions build or lose authority, people become or disappear as rights subjects, and nature is transformed into resources and commodities. This conceptualization is in some ways similar to the Polanyian (1944) double movement of protectionist logics that mediate capital's effects on society when commodification goes too far, but the frontier-territorialization dynamic does not necessitate that territorialization works to halt commodification (if we take land formalization as a way to control frontier land markets, for example, this can have a profoundly commodifying effect); rather, this relationship draws our attention to the constitution of political authority in frontier moments as "facts to settle" rather than "settled facts" (Rasmussen and Lund 2018, 389).

This competitive process of state formation resonates with the Cambodian prime minister's need to wrest authority over property from both local authorities and from the Western donors championing land titling. But the Cambodian case is curious because half of the people who claimed land did not have their land surveyed. An important dimension of land reform, then, is how power and authority are inscribed by authorizing some people's claims and by denying others', raising questions of who are able to become visible to have their claims recognized (and, conversely, who are able to produce themselves as invisible to state power).

This process of authorizing or denying people's claims is not just one of choosing some people or groups over others; this is also a process of producing political subjectivities (Ansoms and Cioffo 2016). Sarah Byrne and colleagues (2016) use feminist theory of subjectivities to build on Lund's (2016) work, arguing that the next step in a theory of the production of authority through property relations is to explain why certain forms of authority emerge as more durable than others. They locate the durability of authority in the production of subjectivities that are rooted in cultural codes embedded within domains of development, bureaucracy, and patronage politics (Byrne, Nightingale, and Korf 2016, 1272). I build on this work to consider how practices of state formation enacted through land reform produce state subjects, and I consider the various ways in which people struggle to appropriate and subvert these practices. States use variable practices of policing resource use (at times repressive, at times tolerant of illegality) to buttress state power and to reproduce the other that is both outside the state and constitutive of citizenship (Foucault 2004). The state does not always see, and this act of not seeing is constituent of state power (Maclean 2013; Mathews 2011). In Foucauldian terms, the uneven exercise of state power is advantageous; by alternating tolerance and repression, by choosing to see or unsee social acts, state authorities create a "usable asymmetry" that can deepen state power (Boelens 2009). I relate acts of not seeing to the importance of uncertainty. State officials and other elites produce uncertainty over the potential for state discipline through contingent, often unpredictable, acts of seeing/unseeing.

I contend, therefore, that the power of the land reform (which is reflective of the power of Hun Sen's rule more broadly) is precisely in the tension between legibility and illegibility. That is, the performances of the volunteers' GIS units, the lavish titling ceremonies, and the material maps and title documents produce a very real hope in the potential of the state to recognize people's claims, while the majority of people are left waiting for land titles or unsure of how the titles will help them. The land titles in this way powerfully reproduce the uncertain potential of the state to deliver prosperity or, conversely, punishment. Land governance understood in this way is a bodily act. Some people are disciplined through fear, uncertainty, surveillance, punishment, and the construction of infrastructure that spatially excludes certain people and makes certain land use practices difficult. Other people receive differential privileges and protections in relation to their participation in informal networks of power and globalized market activities (Ong 2000). In the choice of gift and the distribution among particular people within the village, the gift confirms and reshapes gender, race, and class divides. The Order 01 land reform worked in this way to include some and exclude others. For example, a male farmer in his forties from Tmor Muoy village in Khang Cheung described a meeting he attended before the land reform, at which local authorities promised to distribute one-hectare plots of forestland to villagers: "The district officials said if we voted for the opposition, they wouldn't give us land titles and wouldn't give presents and wouldn't solve the problems in the village. They said they were marking out a big area of forestland to clear and distribute to people when the student volunteers came to survey the land. But we could only get that land if we were loyal to the government."

In this man's recollection, the officials promised to give gifts in the form of land plots to loyal voters and also threatened to exclude other people from access to communal land that they depended on. Alongside this discourse of political loyalty, state officials deployed a discourse of neoliberal development to reward and create productive farms. The land reform provided land title only to privately farmed, productive cropland. And in public speeches, Hun Sen focused not only on the CPP's personal bestowal of the gift of land title but also on the links between land title, rice-based farming productivity, and poverty reduction. His discourse connected land title to his goals for increased rice exports as a key aspect of the national development strategy: "Titles will achieve stability on issues of land possession and occupation, social safety, effective land use, poverty reduction and economic growth. We will see new houses and new cultivations on our people's land. . . . We no longer have to give them rice but they will give us pounded rice [*ambok*] in return" (Hun Sen 2012a). In this speech, the land title allows for the creation of a productive, prosperous farmer who will help the nation by providing rice. This discourse also presumes the subject who can (and wants to) be molded into the prosperous farmer. Only some can fit this category. Cambodian hierarchy recasts peasant as below urban dweller, woman as below man, indigenous woman as below indigenous men and all Khmer. And this racialized gendered social order is constituted through the ways that people use and relate to land: the settled, commercial paddy rice farmer is the modern citizen who will provide for the nation. This marginalizes indigenous people as well as Khmer peasants who use private rice land in conjunction with communal forestland and grazing land as a core part of their farming/food system.

But the state's power to define the terms of the gift is not absolute. Some people interpreted this gift more cynically as a state ploy to win support, such as one woman farmer in her thirties who exclaimed, "The land titles are a trap! They just dangle them in front of us so that we will support them, but it's a poisonous gift. Because the people are so happy to take the title, and we don't see all the land being destroyed around us. But some people don't believe the CPP anymore; we are sick of it." I heard a similar distrust toward the ruling party from many rural people during my research, suggesting that the CPP's legitimacy is waning (Baaz and Lilja 2014). If (as some of my interviewees suggest) a central strategy of the titling campaign was to win votes, this begs the question of whether this was successful and why. It is difficult to know the extent to which the land titling campaign influenced people's votes, not least because there are no reliable pre-vote polls, and asking about people's voting behavior is politically sensitive. However, it appears to have been unsuccessful in many areas. In the ensuing 2013 national election, the opposition party (CNRP) picked up fifty-five seats in the national assembly while the CPP won sixty-eight seats. The increase in opposition vote was a shock to many people within and outside the ruling party. The opposition support was concentrated largely in urban areas where people have greater access to non-CPP support networks. In my rural study areas, the CPP won all local electorates, although the CNRP made substantial gains. Local activists suggested to me that the land titles did increase support in their communes; the vote would have tilted even further toward the opposition if the land reform had not taken place. One man who is an activist in a village that narrowly elected the CPP told me, "Oh definitely, th[e vote buying] was the point of it. I think that if they hadn't dangled the land titles in front of people it would have been 60 percent in favor of CNRP at least here." During interviews, three other people in this activist's village told me they had voted for the CPP so the village chief would distribute their land titles, but they were still waiting for them. The election outcome therefore suggests that, at least in my rural study areas, the land titles did encourage people to vote for the CPP. But the ruling party's gift-giving strategies are losing legitimacy.

Outline of Chapters

In this introduction, in order to provide an understanding of Cambodian state power, I presented the encounters through which the land title gains meaning and produces state subjects. In chapter 1, I examine the formation of Cambodia's postwar property rights regime by tracing the evolving relationship between the German donor agency GIZ and the Cambodian state. For years, donor agencies ignored the failures of Cambodia's Land Rights Program, and donor practices turned the political issue of land control into a technical problem (unclear property delineation) with a technical solution (land titling) (Ferguson 1994; Li 2007; Mitchell 2002). Ultimately, these practices justified the donors' continued presence, even as they created uncertainty over what was actually happening on the ground and shut down space for deeper questions about the relationships between land titling and tenure security—until the problems became so acute they could not be ignored.

In chapter 2, I turn from national and global actors to the rural people I encountered during two years of research during and after the land reform. To understand why the state's strategies are losing legitimacy among rural people, I connect rural people's sense that the state has abandoned them to expectations of state power molded by precolonial and socialist-era discourses of the paternalistic state and to the rapid increase in rural inequality in Cambodia's contemporary market economy.

In chapter 3, I show how the land titling reform worked to wrest power away from local-level officials into the hands of the central government and how this effort was resisted and subverted with sometimes surprising results. Some local officials managed to amass land by clearing forest in expectation of the land reform, while in other areas local people mobilized to prevent the elite's capture of the reform and to produce new relationships with local officials.

Chapter 4 turns to the volunteer university student land surveyors who formed the front line of the state in the land titling reform. The prime minister's ability to sidestep local officials and gain the trust of rural land claimants depended on the mobilization of the student volunteers. I draw on interviews with those students to argue that the volunteers were central to the way the land reform reproduced Hun Sen's personal power.

In the second part of the book, I turn from the implementation to the aftereffects of land reform. In chapter 5, by following the experiences of several hundred land title recipients one year after the leopard skin campaign, I consider the ways in which those recipients living in leopard skin landscapes within agribusiness concessions use and give meaning to land title. My analysis reveals how the production of subjectivities through land titling is explicitly racialized and gendered heteronormative and has deepened cleavages of class relations in rural areas.

In chapter 6, I turn attention to struggles for communal land recognition, examining the detrimental effects of the land titling reform on collective mobilization. I find that, ultimately, both private and communal land titles as tools for land rights advocacy in Cambodia are limited. The power to define these interventions is in the hands of state actors whose own interests often run counter to the demands of rural communities. The government has thwarted the process through the same production of uncertainty I observe in other areas of state practices.

In chapter 7, I examine successful cases in which people have reclaimed land under dispute. I then work through prospects for land and property relations that move beyond the primacy of state-capital formations and the idea of a singular social contract between citizens and an (unaccountable) state system. I outline an alternative feminist ontology of land that seeks to reestablish the agency of nature through building a human relationship with lands and resources beyond the imperatives of commodification.

1
DONOR-STATE PARTNERSHIPS IN THE CAMBODIAN LAND SECTOR

The Roundtable Dialogue

In mid-2016, the German government agency GIZ became the last Western donor to terminate its Land Rights Program with the Cambodian Ministry of Land, after what one GIZ employee described to me as the program's "abject failure."[1] The program—as with other efforts at land formalization in postconflict Cambodia—had failed to protect marginalized people's land rights and failed to institute a sustainable cadastral registry. The Cambodian government had supported the donor-funded land titling program in the settled lowlands, while ensuring that this policy did not place constraints on state discretionary power in the ELC economy of the uplands, which is marked by land deals shrouded in secrecy and enacted through brute violence. These problems were evident from the early 2000s, yet GIZ, the largest donor in the land sector, continued to work laboriously to build a systematic national land registration system. This raises a two-part question: Why did the donors consider that land titling would be effective at all in a country without an impartial rule of law, and why did they continue to focus so much funding on formalizing property rights amid growing evidence of problems and public concern with the project?

In this chapter, I chart the unfolding relationship between GIZ and the Cambodian Ministry of Land since 1995 to examine how donor interventions have actually worked to strengthen the state elite's grip on power. I argue that the donors continued to justify their interventions in the land sector by ignoring the failures of the program, in part due to their ideological certainty in the benefits of land title, and in part due to donors' intentional efforts to divert attention from problematic outcomes by marginalizing critical voices and producing reams of documents focused on technical outputs. These practices papered over what was actually happening on the ground, and in this way the donors contributed to the landscape of uncertainty that is central to Hun Sen's grip on power. This perspective recognizes the work that development actors do to hide the actual contingencies and messiness of practice, so as to "allow reason to rule, and allow history to be arranged as the unfolding of a location-less logic" to which expertise is attached (Mitchell 2002). Development actors with very different interests and whose everyday practice contradicts the policy prescriptions nonetheless work to sustain an official interpretation of events that articulates with donor policy, because this is how project success, and their own interests, are secured (Mosse 2005). Successful projects can thus be seen as those that conceal their own contradictions.

While the Land Rights Program failed to create a sustainable land registry, the promotion of neoliberal property reform in Cambodia has succeeded on a discursive level in establishing central state-authorized land title as the only legitimate source of land tenure security in Cambodian public discourse. For many Cambodian state agencies, donors, civil society organizations, and researchers, there is now an "unquestionable truth" that "land property does not exist without a formal title" (Latorre 2015, 1556), which renders precarious those not granted land title and now deemed illegal and those who have a land title but still don't feel secure. I begin this chapter with a story that illustrates how faith in the efficacy of land title is produced in public discourse through oversimplified technical data and veiled threats that silence deeper questions.

In late 2014, I worked with a Cambodian research institute to organize a roundtable that brought together fifteen people from government, NGOs, and communities dealing with land conflict to engage in dialogue and to help set the research agenda. I prepared four questions to guide discussion, including a question that asked people to consider what kind of institutions besides formal land title might provide land tenure security. We held the meeting in the stark boardroom of the research institute, with seats arranged around a large board table. I paced nervously as people took their time finding seats. Two Ministry of Land officials sat at one end; NGO and donor agency representatives, community land activists, and local officials spread around the table; and I sat at the other end. After a short presentation, I opened the floor to discuss people's experiences of land conflict. Two women wearing red headbands and T-shirts proclaiming *Boeung Kak 13* to signify their solidarity with a group of thirteen imprisoned land activists spoke passionately about their struggles against eviction. The NGO officers, local government officials, and a representative from GIZ spoke next, detailing their various initiatives to protect people's land rights. I struggled to spark conversation, but the "dialogue" was really a series of monologues with little interaction between speakers. I glanced at the time. An hour had passed and the Ministry of Land representatives had not uttered a word. I was not even sure if they were listening; they both had their phones out on the table and they seemed busy texting. Finally, after everyone had spoken, the senior ministry official put down his phone and sat forward in his chair. "Now we would like to speak," he began.

> The problem with this meeting is that the research is not good. What does this even mean, this question about sources of tenure security beyond land title? That completely overlooks the work of the ministry for many years. The ministry has provided 3.8 million land titles. When people have land titles, they are secure. With the prime minister's land titling program, we have issued more than 500,000 land titles this year, and we have cut out one million hectares from state land to give to people. We need to do seven million land titles. We will do that. And that will solve all land conflict. The NGOs and the researchers who say there are problems make it hard for us to protect people.

When the official finished speaking, everyone at the table sat looking at me, waiting to see what I would do. I asked if anyone had comments, but no one spoke. The GIZ representative eventually raised his hand. "You have to remember where the country has come from," he said. "Land title gives people a chance to stand up in land conflicts and to invest in their land." Then the GIZ representative gave his apologies; he had another meeting. Time was up. I thanked everyone. I felt miserable. I had failed to muster any response to the ministry representative. His narrative felt vaguely threatening—it suggested that researchers and NGOs investigating land rights were working against poor people because they were calling into question state actions. In a context where the government could shut down researchers and civil society organizations for speaking out against policy, questioning the official would have positioned myself as antigovernment and antidevelopment.

As people filed out, I approached the Ministry of Land official and asked him about his work at the ministry. He said he had been at the ministry since the 1990s, even before the donors became involved with land administration. "Look," he said to me. "The problem with the title is this." He dug a piece of paper from his pocket and started sketching a timeline from the 1990s to now. "This is when we introduced the land titling registry," he said, stabbing his pen at a point in the early 2000s. "But everything else, it hasn't kept up. Most people don't get marriage certificates, birth certificate, ID cards. And the courts aren't functioning, other things aren't functioning, so you have this idea of private property title, but nothing around to back it up, nothing to actually ensure that rural livelihoods are secure in other ways." I was struck by the difference in the official's narratives: in the meeting, he asserted that the land title would solve all conflict; in his conversation with me, he conceded that there was nothing to back the idea of land title up because other forms of bureaucracy had not kept up with the land titling program. This encounter showed me how performative state practices are crucial to reproducing authority, as they seek to produce the idea of the state and define the realm of the political (Lund 2016; Mathews 2011). The official himself doubted the government's achievements, but in the roundtable, he reproduced the "fact" that land title provides land tenure security through his impressive land titling statistics that oversimplified questions of tenure security. His proclamations of success were underpinned by implicit threats if others present questioned his claims.

In reality, holding a land title in Cambodia does not ensure that people will enjoy land tenure security. The politically aligned judiciary and sudden policy changes guided by the prime minister's unwritten rules and oral proclamations make the possibility of state protection inherently uncertain. I found that in cases where people with land titles take their complaints to officials, the state's discursive production of land title as equivalent with land tenure security can actually allow officials to deny claims of land encroachment and to avoid investigating complaints, because (according to their logic) if land title is equivalent with tenure security, the complaints simply cannot be true. During my fieldwork, I encountered people in both Khang Cheung and Khang Leit who told me that powerful people encroached on their land after they received a land title. In most cases, it was difficult for me to ascertain exactly what happened, not least because representatives from the companies involved would not talk with me about the issue. Nor was there any documentation, because most people did not press their cases through the court system. In two instances, however, the complainants did attempt to find justice by soliciting the assistance of powerful people and land rights NGOs. In both cases, officials silenced the complaints through the discursive production of land title as equivalent to tenure security.

In one case, the European Commission (EC) investigated a village in Khang Leit after eleven families signed statements reporting that a concession company took the villagers' land after they received Order 01 title. The EC confirmed the villagers' account and took a document outlining the case to the Ministry of Land. But one EC representative told me, "We haven't heard anything about a solution.... The authorities always work together; it's hard to get anything solved." When I finally secured a meeting with a senior official in the Ministry of Land near the conclusion of my fieldwork and presented the same document to him, he told me, "That can't be true. They must not have proper titles. Just notices from the commune. Land title is the only thing that provides security." When I showed him that the letter stated the documents to be full land titles, he repeated that it could not be true.

In a second case, ten families from Khang Cheung's neighboring province contacted the land rights NGO ADHOC (Cambodian Human Rights and Development Association) and complained that the Pheapimex concession company had cleared villagers' land after they received land titles. The complainants thumbprinted a petition detailing the amount of land each family lost and the dates and land titles they held. However, the NGO spokesman told me, "When I talked with the Land Ministry about the community whose land was taken after they had title under Order 01, the ministry told me they can't have been titles, just receipts. But I showed him the titles! It's frustrating. . . . The titles aren't working. They are still losing land. This needs to be talked about. But there is limited conversation. You can't say anything critical about titling. If you do, they say you must be wrong." This NGO officer's recollection of his meeting with the ministry, as well as my own experience being told that land title is the only thing that provides security, reveals how the steadfast belief—or at least the public performance of belief—in the land title's ability to protect landholders shuts the state off from any engagement with alternative narratives.

But facts take work to produce. In the remainder of this chapter, I reveal how the idea that land title equals land tenure security was constructed by donors and state actors despite radically different understandings of what land title could and should do. I draw on interviews with seven GIZ consultants (five foreign staff and two Cambodian nationals) and four Land Ministry officials, along with analysis of donor and ministry reports, to reveal that land title has no fixed meaning; the very idea of what land title is and what benefits it brings has shifted over time and space in response to political shifts in both Germany and Cambodia. I focus here on GIZ rather than the World Bank (which was the biggest donor to the land program in its early years) because the story of the World Bank's activities in the land sector are already well recounted (Biddulph 2014; Kent 2014) and because GIZ's priorities have shaped land relations both in and far beyond Cambodia. Some of the same staff members who were stationed in Cambodia moved on to Myanmar, transferring a very similar package of land administration to a new context.

Donor-State Partnerships in the Cambodian Land Sector 1995–2017
Uneven Geographies of Land Titling (1995–2006)

Cambodia's postconflict property regime needs to be understood in a longer history of upheavals in conceptions of property and state formation. In the precolonial period, the king owned all land in the kingdom, and lowland Khmer could claim land by clearing unclaimed forestland for uses as family homesteads and farms (known as "acquisition by the plow"); the people also had communal access to forests and grazing areas. This tradition emphasized possession of land rather than ownership of land as property (Springer 2013). In upland areas, indigenous groups developed sophisticated forms of common property management based on swidden cultivation (Padwe 2011a). The French colonial occupation made several attempts to institute land privatization, but this had little success because of incompatible conceptions of land tenure between colonial administrators and their Cambodian subjects and because of colonial bureaucratic weakness (Guillou 2006; Slocomb 2007). In the 1970s, the Khmer Rouge radically collectivized all land under state control. People were forcibly moved around the country and organized into collective work groups. The Vietnamese-supported People's Republic of Kampuchea (PRK) that occupied the country in 1979 continued the practice of communal solidarity groups, although most lowland Khmer drifted back to individualized tenure (Slocomb 2010, 263). Some people reclaimed the land they or their parents had farmed before the civil conflict, while in other areas, commune-level authorities distributed land plots, with the amount of land dependent on household size (Frings 1994). This process established a system of commune-allocated land certificates, or soft titles.

After the Vietnamese pulled out in 1989, the government embraced a market economy under the leadership of Hun Sen. Land was a central concern from the early years of the Hun Sen regime. Land disputes became the most high-profile threat to stability in the 1990s, as well-connected people grabbed land and rural people continued the customary practices of clearing and claiming land (Biddulph 2014). The Cambodian state moved toward a capitalist model of individual property reform in the lowlands in the 1980s, but it was not clear how customary and use rights would be enshrined in law (Biddulph 2011). When the UN intervened in Cambodia's conflict in the 1990s, donor agencies looked to make their mark on the land sector. Tensions between different donor agencies and the Cambodian Ministry of Land were evident from the start. The World Bank and GIZ sought a land law that championed a narrow approach to land security, focused on ownership rights, and acknowledged only limited customary rights (LMAP 2002).[2] Several donors put forward competing concepts, such as the Japanese, who touted an approach to more locally responsive land titles (Trzcinski and Upham 2012). The Cambodian government also had different ideas about what broad-ranging agrarian reform might look like.[3] However, the World Bank model prevailed, and Land Law 2001 introduced an Australian land registration system (the Torrens system), which emphasizes simplicity in land titling by recognizing ownership exclusively on the basis of formal registration with a centralized cadastral agency (RGC 2001). The Land Law did not replace other forms of customary land tenure, however; it created a new layer of legal control on top of ongoing social norms of acquisition by the plow and commune-authorized ownership. The Land Law ensured that the state retained land control by assuming that all land was state property, unless farmers could demonstrate ownership or cultivation of the land for five years before the promulgation of the law (Springer 2013). In tandem, the 2002 Forestry Law declared all natural forests to be state land, with only vague allowances for customary user rights (Milne 2015). Under the narrow notion of legality in the Land Law, poor people who move to the uplands to clear land are simply labeled "illegal settlers" on ELCs, and the state's law enforcement agencies and military forces can be used to violently exclude them (Beban, So, and Un 2017; Springer 2011).

The resurgence of neoliberal economic interest in property reform as a way to achieve economic development and institutional stability shaped donors' expectations for the national cadastral system (Deininger and Feder 1998; Fukuyama 2004; de Soto 2000). To achieve accurate and universal cadastral mapping, and thereby "reduce poverty, promote social stability, and stimulate economic development," the World Bank created the Land Management and Administration Project (LMAP) in 2002 with the support of GIZ. The Land Law also included Social Land Concessions (SLCs) to provide land for landless households, as well as Communal Land Title (CLT) for indigenous groups. These provisions provided the government with much-needed international legitimacy after a violent coup in 1997 that disposed Hun Sen's main rival. International movements for indigenous land rights were in ascendance, and the recognition of communal land rights in Cambodian law was a victory for indigenous communities as well as the NGOs and politicians that lobbied Hun Sen's government in the lead-up to the law (Ironside, Patterson, and Thomas 2017). GIZ helped fund both SLCs and CLTs, and this complemented their centerpiece program—the development of a sustainable, national cadastral database. GIZ planning experts worked with teams in the newly established Ministry of Land and subnational Department of Land units to implement the Land Law and develop provincial-level land use plans. GIZ also developed a bachelor's degree in land administration training program and supplied the technology to survey and register land in a process called Systematic Land Registration (SLR), wherein teams from the Ministry of Land surveyed all the eligible land in a village at one time.

The Cambodian state did not reject the donors' land administration project. However, the SLC and CLT programs were starved of funds, land, and the political power needed to push them forward. From the perspective of the Cambodian elite, the negotiation of the Land Law, as part of the opening up of Cambodia to electoral competition, seems to have largely been a pragmatic strategy to harness

Western aid after the Soviet Bloc withdrew economic assistance in the late 1980s and to prevent instability rather than any deeper turn to democratic ideals. Hun Sen's ambivalence toward liberal reform was evident in a letter he wrote to the Laotian Minister of Justice at the time: "We can conclude that reform is better than no reform. If there is no reform, there is greater danger than if there is reform" (quoted Gottesman 2003, 188). Through the early 2000s, the state elite took on selective reforms but ensured that upland areas remained untitled and therefore more easily claimed as state land that could be leased out to concessionaires. In figure 2, Mike Dwyer shows that before the Order 01 land reform, land titling areas (in the hatched polygons) were concentrated in the lowland rice paddy regions in which ownership is relatively uncontroversial, while ELCs (the unshaded polygons) were concentrated in the upland ecologies of forest, cropland, and shrubland where powerful politico-business-military networks exclude poor land claimants.

Despite the government's channeling of the program to areas where they arguably made little difference (Biddulph 2014), the LMAP project was spurred on by World Bank studies that predicted massive potential for economic development

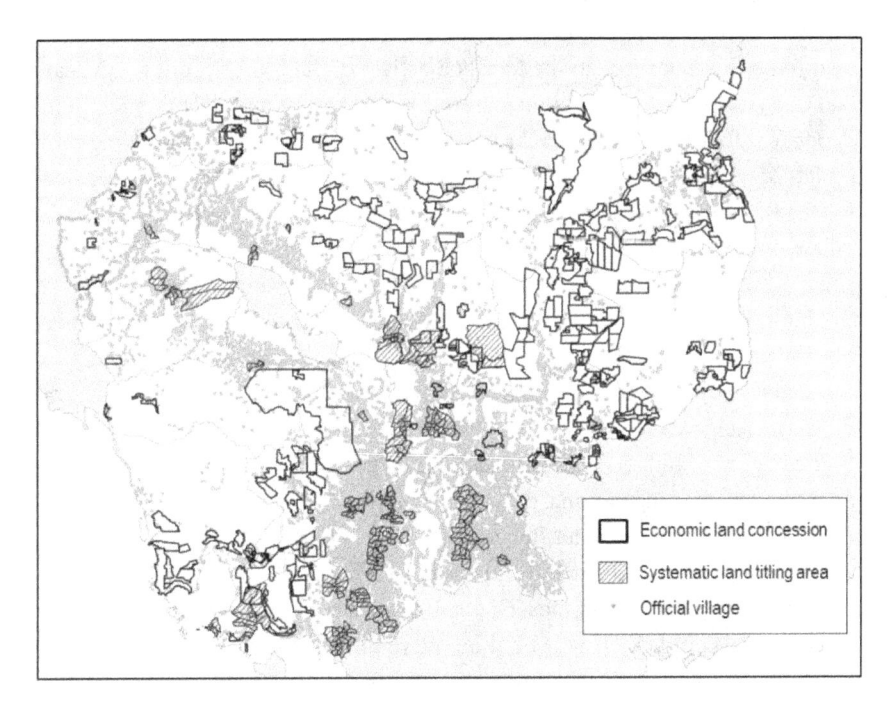

FIGURE 2. Titling areas versus ELCs. The diagonally hatched polygons are communes where LMAP operated (extracted from World Bank data).

(Source: Dwyer 2015. Reprinted by permission of the publisher, Taylor & Francis Ltd, http://www.tandfonline.com.)

through land titling and by project surveys that found people were satisfied with the titling process (Deutsch 2006; Deutsch and Makady 2009). However, several internal GIZ studies during the project's early years warned that the donor's optimistic vision may be overstated. The project's initial baseline study was somewhat schizophrenic; it went into great depth on the theoretical benefits expected from land titling, but it also warned that people may grab land, land markets may not change due to broader structural barriers (such as the high cost of health care), and broader governance and institutional reforms were needed (Ballard and So 2004). Despite plans to undertake a follow-up study, a researcher from Cambodia Development Resource Institute [CDRI], the research institute that did the original baseline research) told me this follow-up study was never carried out.

A string of critical reports in the mid-2000s consistently pointed to two problems with LMAP: first, that it excluded large areas from titling and in the process potentially made those who were passed over more insecure than before; second, that people's failure to register land transfers in the national registry calls into question how meaningful the registry is. An assessment of the SLR procedure in 2005 came to damning conclusions about the informal payments demanded by survey teams, the confusion and delays in the process, and the exclusions that meant "the poorest and most vulnerable households in a community would appear to be slipping through the social objectives of the LMAP project" (O'Leary 2005, 38). A GIZ adviser told me that this report was never made public. An independent follow-up report to the baseline study concluded that the titling project has "done little to realize economic growth for smallholders in the area studied" (ADI/LIC 2007, 14). The majority of land transfers were made extralegally at the village or commune level, coercive land sales were frequent, and land title did not correlate with improved access to credit (6). The report's authors noted that this finding raised a serious question: "Is LMAP's aim to promote the development of efficient land markets in conflict with its aim to reduce poverty?" (14).

Even if people made land transfers legally through the cadastral database, the database itself—the centerpiece of GIZ's program—overlapped with other contradictory state land records. The cadastral database was established without reference to two existing national databases, the Immovable Property Register Book (IPRB) and the Land Register Book (LRB) (World Bank et al. 2015). These other databases were not absorbed into the cadastral database but continued parallel to it, albeit unbeknownst to most GIZ staff I spoke with. This meant that the same piece of land could potentially be allocated to different people. More than half a million parcels—including controversial land allotments to ELCs—are registered in the IPRB alone, resulting in the government maintaining an "atmosphere of secrecy around IPRB data and [a] lack of willingness to put an end to it" (World Bank et al. 2015, 26). Yet, I heard no public discussion of this issue at GIZ or other donor fora. As one GIZ consultant said to me, "It seems like it was just easier for the Systematic Land Registration and its donors to forget about these two other cadastres. Obviously, there are big problems with the parallel existence of these three databases."

Despite noted problems with the accuracy of the cadastral database (both the parallel databases and the fact that most land title recipients do not record land transfers in the database), the database's statistics are frequently cited as unproblematic foundations for both donor and state reports. The World Bank et al. (2015) report, for example, draws on government data almost exclusively, even though the authors note their frustration with the "culture of not sharing data" (4) within the Cambodian government and the inaccuracy of the database (7). A GIZ report finds that more than 20 percent of records in the database are incomplete or inaccurate and lack critical information necessary for reporting (Deutsch and Makady 2009). Donors repeatedly blame this poor information on technological deficiencies associated with weak state capacity and urge greater spending on the cadastral database's technological capabilities. The World Bank consultant cited above, for example, recommends more funds to develop the technology underpinning the cadastral database, even as he recognizes that state officials regularly "play tricks" and produce false reports: "Because the stakes are high, everyone seems to have an incentive to misreport and hold on to information for their own benefit" (World Bank et al. 2015, 4).

This confusion over multiple databases is compounded within central state ministries, due to ministries' overlapping responsibility with land control (Un and So 2009). The Ministry of Defense (MoD), Ministry of Agriculture, Forestry and Fisheries (MAFF), and Ministry of Environment (MoE) have a great deal of power and manage a large amount of state land. The MAFF's power limits the reach of the Ministry of Land Management, Urban Planning and Construction (MLMUPC). Tensions between ministries over land control (and who will benefit materially from the expansion of ELCs) contribute to the secrecy over land maps, ELC records, and databases. This confusion enables government officials to deny responsibility and to push problems onto other institutions; one GIZ-commissioned report notes that "in the current system, it is hard to put anyone in the spotlight if something goes wrong" (Kelsall and Kimchoeun 2014, 7). A critical report of the land rights program from the German Institute for Human Rights goes even further to suggest that the "competing competencies" of different government ministries tasked with facilitating land management are a deliberate strategy that "enables a *divide et impera* style of rule and facilitates ignorance of the systematic implementation of human rights obligations" (Lüke 2013, 26). This statement is the clearest expression I have seen (at least, within the donor literature) that the confusion of overlapping responsibilities and rules is a strategic maneuver that not only reduces the power of any particular institution, therefore maintaining Hun Sen's position of power, but also enables officials to profess ignorance and deny any problems.

Increasing Pressure from Germany and Cambodia (2006–2012)

In 2006, the uneven geography of land titling broke into a scandal over LMAP's relocation of 4,250 families in the Boeung Kak Lake area of central Phnom Penh. Despite many households having strong evidence to prove their legal rights to the land, Boeung Kak residents were excluded from the titling system when land registration was carried out in their neighborhood. Shortly after, the Cambodian government granted the Boeung Kak lease to Shukaku, a large developer, and the families residing in the area were suddenly classified as illegal squatters on state-owned land (see Biddulph 2014). The political fallout led to the World Bank's withdrawal from LMAP in 2009 (World Bank 2009).

The Land Rights Program came under increasing criticism from within Germany after Boeung Kak Lake and particularly after 2010 as land grabs gained media and scholarly attention in the European Union. ELCs expanded rapidly in the mid-2000s, as investors took advantage of lax social and environmental safeguards and minimal formal fees to log valuable forests and grow commodity crops (Üllenberg 2009). Displaced rural people and NGOs began tapping into transnational networks, and a collaboration of NGOs and community groups launched a "blood sugar" campaign, pressuring European and American companies to discontinue sugar purchases from Cambodian plantations with poor labor and human rights records and calling on international consumers to denounce the global banks that fund these plantations. Critical reports from NGOs and academics claiming that the land rights program legitimized "blood sugar" and broader land grabbing in Cambodia were widely circulated in the German press (Neef, Touch, and Chiengthong 2013; Scheidel 2016).[4]

This negative attention dovetailed with political pressure to lower Germany's overseas aid spending in the wake of the economic recession and the EU sovereign debt crisis (Karbaum 2012). In 2011, GIZ came under the control of the German Ministry of Economic Cooperation and Development (BMZ), curtailing the agency's autonomy in Cambodia.[5] GIZ signed on for another funding round with the Cambodian government, and the LMAP became the Land Rights Program (LRP), which adopted an explicit human rights orientation for the first time, with the goal to secure socially balanced access to land (Trzcinski and Upham 2014). BMZ became increasingly touchy about criticism of its programs, as protests in Germany resulted in it scaling back its international food partnership,[6] and it sent a representative to oversee the GIZ Land Rights Program in Cambodia.[7] Internal tensions built within GIZ as the BMZ representative criticized GIZ's approach. This tension revealed deeper divisions within GIZ between a technical approach and a social approach to the land sector. As one GIZ officer explained to me, "There are all these tensions. Now the new German government BMZ representative here wants to come at this from a human rights perspective. And that rubs the land director up the wrong way; he has always been about the formalization, the technical side. Overall, they are very focused on the technical side.... It permeates the whole organization, I think. And then they can't look beyond that."

This shift from the technical side to a more politicized stance signaled a change in GIZ's relationship with the Cambodian government. When BMZ commissioned the German Institute for Human Rights to analyze the land situation in 2013, their report was so damning that, according to a GIZ foreign adviser, the Cambodian government apparently threatened "all Germans would be kicked out of the country if the report was made public before the election." The report criticized GIZ's "silent complicity" in human rights violations and argued that the Land Rights Program may unintentionally have a stabilizing effect on the political economy of land grabbing and forced evictions (see Lüke 2013). Neither this report nor broader policy discourse at GIZ at the time questioned the link between land title and land tenure security in Cambodia (the report repeatedly states that title will provide "legal certainty" and recommends the program continue, albeit with a qualitative rather than simply quantitative approach) (Lüke 2013, 14). But the report did signal a broader frustration with the narrow approach to land rights at GIZ.

Meanwhile, the Cambodian government was also shifting its attitude toward the land titling program and its partnerships with donor agencies. Government officials say that the process for writing policy on land has changed over the past fifteen years: initially foreign advisers completed the first policy draft and only later shared it with the ministry; today the process has been reversed (Trzcinski and Upham 2014). This reflects the CPP's increasing strength through the mid-2000s, as the party elite amassed power and wealth from their widening network of *oknha* and foreign investors. As the ruling party's grip on power tightened, keeping donors happy was less important than maintaining power, as one GIZ adviser described: "In 1998, Hun Sen didn't have such a hold on power. There was Funcinpec [the royalist political party], and there were two factions within CPP. Also, he didn't have the money from the elite that he does now; now he is bankrolled by them.... He doesn't need the donor money so much anymore, although it's still nice to have. So before, I could work with some sympathetic provincial leaders to secure land for people; now, they don't want to do anything that will upset Hun Sen."

This adviser is describing a paradox that I heard in many interviews: while decentralization reforms through the mid-2000s aimed to institute subnational decision making and accountability between local officials and rural people, the CPP's grip on power at the national level meant that local action became increasingly risky. The Cambodian state's decreased dependence on Western donor funds is also surely related to the reestablishment of China as Cambodia's main donor. As European donors have moved explicitly toward a more human rights–oriented position, with conditions for ongoing development aid tied to rights obligations, China's infrastructural-focused support provides large-scale development projects with few strings attached.[8] China's aid spending now dwarfs the Western partners; in 2017, China accounted for nearly 36 percent of US$732 million listed in bilateral aid—almost four times as much as from the United States—and 30 percent of foreign investment, again far more than any other country.[9] The Cambodian government has become more outspoken against the Western donor agenda as they are emboldened by China's support. The government's Cambodian Human Rights Committee produced a short video, widely viewed on Facebook, showing clips of the Libyan skyline at night (or at least what they claimed to be Libya) before and after the civil conflict, with the slogan, "Human rights are dangerous."[10] This is a vivid departure from the liberal peacebuilding discourse and is in direct contradiction to the German discourse of human rights in the Land Rights Program.

The shifts in the landscape in Cambodia, as in Germany, are also due in large part to the efforts of civil society groups who have developed local mobilization and transnational advocacy networks (Ojendal 2013). The Prey Lang Community Network in eastern Cambodia, for example, brought together community activists and domestic and international advocates to resist deforestation using local action, petitions, public demonstrations, and an international web presence (Parnell 2015). While some researchers are pessimistic about civil society's potential to challenge powerful state and corporate actors in Cambodia (Touch and Neef 2015), civil society groups have seen partial success, such as delaying ELC operations, targeting foreign finance and commodity companies with transnational campaigns, supporting communities to win land back through collective action, and creating (for a time) a united opposition party (Schoenberger 2017; Swift 2015). The announcement of Order 01 signaled a shift in the government's attitude toward land title that needs to be seen in this context of increased civil society and opposition party pressure.

Order 01: The Victory of the Land Rights Program?

Order 01 marked the victory of the Land Rights Program—finally answering the critics by moving titling into previously excluded spaces—and it also marked the total exclusion of the donors. GIZ was not allowed to watch or contribute to the policy (Müller and Zülsdorf 2013). One GIZ adviser who worked in the Ministry of Land building on the same floor as ministry staff recalled the day he arrived at work to find an empty building: "At first it was just silence. It was strange; we work in the office together and no one from the ministry was there. But of course people talk in elevators and coffee rooms. After a while, I would meet a friend from the ministry in the elevator and ask how they were, and they would say, 'Oh, I haven't been home in three nights. . . . I've been so busy I've been sleeping at work, doing Order 01 stuff.'" Another senior employee at GIZ said that the development agency staff were left "completely in the dark. . . . We can't touch Order 01. At the time it was put into place we weren't told anything. In the ministry, the GIZ partners had no idea what was happening. And at the university, all the students were seconded. We basically shut down for one year."

It wasn't just the donors left in the dark; land claimants, surveyors, and local authorities also found it very difficult to know what was happening because the land reform guidelines were based as much on Hun Sen's oral utterances as on paper policy, and the rules changed frequently. It is striking how difficult it is to discern what exactly the criteria were for a household or community to be eligible for survey. Indeed, Order 01 was a one-page notice that contained four bullet points outlining its goals. The original Order 01 did not contain reference to a land titling campaign. Instead, the prime minister announced the campaign to title land during a closed-door meeting with ministers and provincial governors on the implementation of the national development strategy. After the announcement, a TV station offered to distribute videos to anyone who requested a copy, and within days, hundreds of villagers sent in requests, saying they "would use it as insurance to solidify claims to their land if local authorities prove reluctant to implement the prime minister's orders."[11] Subnational officials also raced to procure a copy of the speech, because as one provincial governor remarked, "It's important to get the [videos] of the prime minister's order because some people heard and some people haven't heard what the prime minister ordered."[12]

This example of the power of Hun Sen's speech to override written land policy and shut out the donors is striking yet typical of Hun Sen's rule. Hun Sen's swift policy changes can mobilize networks of elites at short notice, and while the prime minister's constant shifts and maneuvers are, on the one hand, responses to resistance and perhaps mistakes, on the other hand, they strengthen Hun Sen's power over the legal realm as he makes, uses, and overturns law at short notice. The speed and confusion of these unwritten rules builds Hun Sen's power. As one NGO official said glumly, "They measured the land fast so that villagers didn't have the time or the information to know the advantages and disadvantages." This confusion provided space for people with access to knowledge, financial resources, and political networks to assert their own land claims.

Justifying the Land Rights Program after Order 01 (2013–2015)

The confluence of the donors' exclusion from Order 01 and pressure from Germany increased tensions between GIZ and the Cambodian government. The BMZ-commissioned German Institute for Human Rights report went so far as to suggest that "the limited transparency with which the Order 01 has been implemented also raises a suspicion that, possibly, one of the objectives of the campaign was to formalize and cover up the illegal land grabbing that has already taken place" (Lüke 2013, 26). Despite this criticism, the Land Rights Program continued, and reams of GIZ and Ministry of Land reports continued to laud the program's successes. Central to this construction of the Land Rights Program as a success was the use of expert knowledge and statistics to frame issues as technical problems and obscure alternative discourses. This is common in development and public policy (McGoey 2014) and has been employed by donors and state institutions since the early days of the Land Rights Program. Statistics are frequently trotted out in reports and meetings—titles distributed, plots surveyed, maps made, maps displayed, teams trained, and so on—and they take on a life of their own, endlessly repeated in state reports and also in the literature critiquing the program. This production of statistics seemed to gain energy after the land reform, and even the authors of a critical evaluation of Order 01 "put political calculations aside" and note that "Order 01 has achieved its intended outputs; despite some minor problems of corruption and informal fees . . . by January 2013 information sheets were filled for 434,014 parcels relating to 316,153 families. A total of 389,578 parcels were surveyed, comprising 505,347 hectares. A four week public display was undertaken for 183,295 parcels of 103,073 families comprising 293,348 hectares. So far, 117,548 ownership titles were distributed" (Kelsall and Kimchoeun 2014). This exhausting list of statistics echoes almost every donor and government land report I have ever read on Cambodia's land sector. The effect of this, as one former GIZ consultant told me, is to "muddy the waters" by focusing only on statistical outputs and diverting attention away from more challenging questions. Vast amounts of data presented as an impenetrable wall of numbers serve to frame the problem as the lack of titles and the solution as more titles and, in doing so, to obscure any alternative narratives on the outcomes of the land reform. This creates the state as a powerful bureaucratic machine and suggests the power of numbers to portray expert knowledge and precision that makes it difficult to ask other questions, so that actual outcomes of development programs remain uncertain (Allen 2014; McGoey 2014).

GIZ interviewees complained to me that it is difficult to talk about outcomes because there is no research available. The government has not released any detailed information from the cadastral database after Order 01, and there are limited studies on the outcomes of the reform (in terms of the relationships between land titles and perceived tenure security, conflicts, or other factors). But this is surely part of the production of uncertainty that is typical of the land sector in Cambodia generally. Recall, for example, that a follow-up study to the baseline survey under LMAP was never conducted, despite original plans to do so, and GIZ program evaluations rarely go beyond simple questions of outputs and people's satisfactions with titles (Deutsch 2006, 2014; Deutsch and Makady 2009). Critical NGO reports argue that the entire Land Rights Program rests on "an untested assumption," and if the outcomes were actually measured, "the results would in fact show an increase in land grabbing and conflicts" (Grimsditch and Henderson 2009, 28).

Even when one GIZ study did ask questions about outcomes and the land title appeared to have little long-term effect at the household level, the study reverted back to discussion of outputs. The *Survey of Food Security and Land Conflicts in LASSP Areas* compared households that had land title with those that did not, and it stated emphatically that "more than 3.7 million titles have been distributed. . . . There is broad agreement that this has resulted in improved security of land tenure and a reduction of land related conflicts" (Deutsch 2014, 4). However, while the report finds people are happy with the land titles, it also found that the titles had little to no effect on productivity or investment. One GIZ adviser told me he was surprised at the findings: "It didn't show what GIZ wanted, didn't show that the titles had positive effects. For most people there was no real effect on productivity, on investment. Even I was a bit surprised. This is the first report really that's gone into what the long-term effects are. Not just the superficial stuff about whether people are satisfied, because of course they say that to NGOs coming to interview them."

Furthermore, this evaluation found that only 12 percent of land transactions are registered, which means that the cadastre is out of date and also raises questions about whether land titling may actually make people more tenure-insecure if they purchase land without registering the transfer. My survey data does suggest this possibility. I found that only 9 percent of people who bought or sold land after the land reform in my Khang Cheung and Khang Leit field sites registered the transfer. This was primarily because they deemed it more prudent to ask the commune office to witness the transfer in order to cultivate their relationships with local authorities rather than register the transfer in the national database. In fact, several people showed me land titles that still had the previous owners' names on the title. These people who hold titles in other people's names are vulnerable to displacement if the previous owner wishes to legally claim the land in the future and has the political clout to push their claims. Despite these problematic findings, rather than raising deeper questions, the authors of the GIZ evaluation concluded by noting again the scope of the land titling outputs, repeating that people were happy with the land titles, and listing a set of recommendations entirely focused on improving training and technical changes to survey procedures.

Alongside this focus on statistical outputs rather than outcomes, GIZ and ministry reports also continued to justify the Land Rights Program after Order 01 by focusing on the successful achievement of gender empowerment in the program. I applaud the focus on gender in Cambodia's land sector (something that has often been forgotten in past land titling initiatives globally, with devastating results for women [Agarwal 2003]). But while reading the reports, I started to feel that there was something disingenuous about framing gender empowerment as an uncontroversial benefit of the program in ways that both twist the statistics and displace focus from program outcomes. For example, donor and state reports refer to the gender dimension of the land reform as evidence of a "trend in favor of women's rights" (World Bank et al. 2015, 34). The second Land Rights Program evaluation argues that the "statistics on land titles speak for themselves" when it comes to women's empowerment (34):

- 63 percent registered as shared property (husband and wife)
- 18 percent wife
- 8 percent husband
- 8 percent single
- 3 percent unknown

A senior Ministry of Land official similarly told me, "They have the PACP [gender equality] group. They do five days training. And they do land titles. We see the numbers are 63 percent joint, 18 percent women, 8 percent men. So gender is not a problem here."

These numbers do seem to suggest a strong bias toward promoting women's rights. And gender is frequently touted as the most successful aspect of the land rights program due to the focus on joint title. My research suggests, though, that this was relatively easy to achieve because most Khmer already recognize land as belonging to both husband and wife. (In fact, 79 percent of people in my survey who held commune-issued land certificates before the land reform had both husband's and wife's names on the certificate, suggesting that many Khmer communities regarded joint land possession as the social norm.) Furthermore, considering that over a quarter of households in Cambodia are female headed

(MWA 2015), the proportion of women's property titles (at 18 percent) actually seems too low and shows a bias against women (at least, it certainly does not suggest that "gender is not a problem here"). The primary reason I found for this discrepancy is that female-headed households have a higher than average rate of landlessness and land poverty. My survey results also showed that over and above the effects of landlessness and land poverty, women were less likely to have their land surveyed during the land reform (see chapter 5). That is, women faced systematic discrimination that is denied by the celebratory discourse of gender empowerment.

Furthermore, I found that some women were registered together with a dead or absent husband, an issue also observed in other research (Grimsditch 2013; STAR Kampuchea 2013). The World Bank report, however, "did not uncover a single case of a woman being forced to register land jointly with a missing spouse" (World Bank et al. 2015, 35). And the Land Rights Program evaluation found that "while twenty-five percent of female headed households' land parcels were actually registered as joint property with a dead or absent spouse, in all of these cases, the women were with their spouses at the time of the SLR process" (Deutsch and Makady 2009, vii). This means that married couples gained joint land title and then one spouse later died or left without a formal divorce or property transfer, so the absent spouse's name is still on the property title. But it makes little difference for the women in question whether their husband left them a month before or a month after registration; they still find themselves registered with a missing husband, which may inhibit their ability to formally sell or mortgage their land if authorities insist that the husband also sign the documents.

In the program evaluation, as in other donor and state reports on the Land Rights Program, the use of gender-disaggregated statistics to assert gender empowerment reinforces moral claims of a liberal capitalist project and silences deeper discussion of whether and how formal titles actually relate to gender equality (O'Laughlin 2007). In chapter 5, I take this argument further to investigate the (assumed) relationship between joint land title and women's ability to gain economic independence and escape abusive relationships.

GIZ Pulls Out (2016)

Donor agencies and international NGOs grew increasingly vocal in their criticism of Prime Minister Hun Sen as land conflict rose again after Order 01. The GIZ director found himself to be one of the last donor voices still supporting the Cambodian state's actions. Several former GIZ consultants and employees of other donors and NGOs told me they were embarrassed when the GIZ director supported Hun Sen's claim that he was donating land to people in Order 01. In a public speech, the GIZ director had argued that "this [land titling reform] can be considered a tremendous step towards the progressive realization of human rights of Cambodia's vulnerable and poor population in the rural areas. . . . Unauthorized settlers and other long term users of these lands, including those inside ELC, had been considered illegal before. Those of them who are poor now receive full property title by way of donation." This thorny issue of donated land illustrates how the Cambodian state and GIZ's use of this term confuses issues of land ownership, with potentially harmful implications for rural people. Prime Minister Hun Sen stated repeatedly that Order 01 land titles were a donation from him and the CPP.[13] This discourse was at the center of the prime minister's claims that the Order 01 land title was a personal gift, thereby legitimizing the land reform as part of Hun Sen's political gift giving in rural areas. And donating land does have a legal basis in Land Law 2001 (articles 15 and 18): "State public land cannot legally be the object of private acquisition unless donated by the State" (World Bank et al. 2015, 14).

The concept of donation is much more complex than this narrative suggests, however, for several reasons. Under the Land Law, people who have held land for five years before the promulgation of the law (i.e., before 2001) have legal right to land title. The incorporation of the Civil Code in 2010 (pushed by the Japanese government) relaxes these conditions to allow anyone who has possessed land for any five years to claim title. In my research and in a large survey conducted in several other provinces, many people who claimed land title during Order 01 had settled on the land before the promulgation of the Land Law, meaning they were legally eligible for land title and were certainly not "illegal settlers" (Grimsditch and Schoenberger 2017). I also found considerable confusion among GIZ and ministry officials over whether the designations of legal or illegal settlers even applied to land that had formally been granted as ELCs (an opaque process that requires the reclassification of state public land into state private land). The secrecy and confusion surrounding the state's conversion of land categories and the oversimplistic discourse of land donation that conflates rights to land with donated land titles have implications for the way people understand what land titles mean (see chapter 5) and may lead to the politicization of titling after the fact, as one NGO adviser pointed out: "I think that 01 titles are less secure than SLR. Some have a note at the bottom, 'gift from government . . . can be taken back at any time if needed for development.'" Furthermore, the presumption that Order 01 donated titles to otherwise illegal settlers produces uncertainty over who is actually committing illicit acts. The oversimplistic notion of donation ignores the state's secretive processes of land classification and leads to the conclusion that land claimants who did not receive a title must therefore (still) be illegal settlers.

This has dangerous implications for the state's ability to (legally) dispossess these people of their land.

Finally, in June 2016, under increasing criticism from home and in Cambodia, GIZ announced the termination of the Land Rights Program. They cited a lack of political will from the Cambodian government to create a transparent property system or a credible institution for settling disputes.[14] It is likely that the sudden death of the Land Rights Program director also contributed to GIZ's decision; the director was the staunchest supporter of the program and its relationship with the Cambodian government.

This brief overview of the Land Rights Program's history shows that problems with the program appeared many years before GIZ's decision to pull funding. Donors worked to maintain the program's legitimacy in the face of these challenges by discursively constructing the program as a success while ignoring deeper issues and generating uncertainty over program outcomes. State actors also worked to maintain their control over land distribution in resource-rich upland areas by first limiting the Land Rights Program to settled lowlands and then responding to political pressure by implementing land reform in the uplands in a rushed, secretive reform that strengthened Hun Sen's personalized control over land resources. A two-part question arises from this analysis: Why was partnership maintained for so long in the face of seemingly insurmountable problems, and why did the donors consider that land titling would be effective at all in a country without an impartial rule of law? I turn to this puzzle next.

Donor-State Partnerships in the Land Sector: The Terms of Engagement

It is likely that several factors played into Germany's central role in Cambodia's land sector and their tenacity to remain even as other donors pulled out. Germany saw itself as having a special relationship in the land sector, given how important private property was to building the unified Germany. The assumption that instituting private property rights would produce land tenure security and legibility was so taken for granted that perhaps the donors simply couldn't see when this assumption unraveled. Sarinda Singh's writing on Laos puts forward a similar suggestion that the categories of knowledge and power that the state elite function with in Southeast Asia are unrecognizable to donor agencies, except as seen in negative terms as low capacity, corruption, and falsified statistics. She argues that international observers are left blinded by their own categories, incapable of understanding the processes in which they participate. Certainly, in Cambodia, the magic of the land title to produce land tenure security and legibility of the population is a fundamental assumption of its land rights programs. Even those who recognized that the land title wasn't protecting marginalized people felt that it had the power to usher in a different political culture, that it was literally the ground on which a new form of capitalist democracy would be built. The German ambassador to Cambodia, for example, reiterated the need for strong land rights as the basis of democratic institutions "because we have seen ourselves in Germany after the wall came down—there was public land that East Germany had expropriated from private owners that had been reprivatized—how important it is to have clarity on land rights, because you will not get investors if this clarity is wanting."[15] The sense here is that if you just get the institutions right, then the political culture will follow.

For many long-term donor staffers I interviewed in Cambodia, however, this sense of blindness to incompatible cultural categories can't explain the whole story, as people were well aware of the fundamental problems with the program. What may have begun as naive blindness was now bitter cynicism. Long-term GIZ staff (along with others I have encountered at the World Bank and other donor agencies) spoke of the development community's lack of reflexivity and the institutional rigidity that made it near impossible to shift direction and to adapt programs on the ground, even as they sensed the program spiraling out of their control. Andrew Cock (2016) argues similarly that the irreconcilable differences between the approaches of the Cambodian government and its donors are not only recognized but also accounted for in aid programs: "Patterns of stonewalling, partial deflection and partial adoption that were manifestations of this external-internal interaction were broadly recognized by external actors. Indeed they seemed to be accounted for in the structuring of aid programs. At base, reform promoting external actors seemed to be primarily interested in ensuring that Cambodia's integration into the regional and global economy was advanced, no matter how the politics of policy reform played out at any particular moment" (Cock 2016, xi).

This damning assessment suggests that donors are complicit in the production of uncertainty over what is actually happening on the ground, because they are not keen to highlight their participation in a system that is working to enable the elite's land grabs. Even if they know they are "navigating in troubled waters" in Cambodia, as Cock (2016, 11) posits, they "seem to behave as if they have no choice but to turn a blind eye (as diplomacy obliges?) towards the negative repercussions of the actions of the national authorities." The donors have an imperative to provide aid as a central plank of their foreign relations with Cambodia, and geopolitically it has been important to donor countries that they do not sever relations with Hun Sen, particularly in the context of China's ballooning aid program. Germany, in particular, has a keen financial interest in maintaining positive relations with Cambodia, as one of the largest donors to Cambodia and one of Cambodia's five largest trading partners.[16]

I met many aid workers in the land sector who had genuinely good intentions of social justice. Many justified the continuance of the Land Rights Program because they felt it gave them influence, however small, on central state policy and practice. In the context of a system where many foreign donors and NGOs are considered outside this sphere of influence (and therefore combative to the state agenda), GIZ staff shared a common feeling that GIZ "walks a very thin line" as they try to partner with the Ministry of Land. Some said that GIZ's model of engagement with the government was untenable, as, according to a former GIZ adviser, "you should only work with [the government] on your own terms, never on their terms, which in practice probably means working with them is not possible." Other GIZ staff felt that critics were not generous enough to GIZ's delicate position, as one senior field officer noted: "Nothing can be done from this position unless we are friends with the government; it is a different form of engagement; it means we have to make concessions; we have to say some things that maintain the government's trust. But, also, it is about being in a position to do something."

The GIZ director echoed this field officer's stance after a critical article by Andreas Lorenz in the German newspaper *Spiegel* on 27 November 2013 pushed back against the German model of engagement. The article quoted a Khmer NGO director accusing Germans of being "part of the problem" of land grabbing because they glossed over the "fact that Prime Minister Hun Sen is merely using the [land titling] project to create the impression that the underhanded land grabs are legal, and that he has no intention of fairly distributing land." The GIZ director retorted in the article, "If you want to make anything happen, you have to work together with government agencies. This makes you vulnerable. It's a balancing act we have to put up with." The German ambassador to Cambodia was then quoted backing him up, arguing that "constructive engagement" is better than terminating the cooperative arrangement with Hun Sen, because "we can't achieve everything everywhere at the same time. . . . We will create legal certainty for six million people."

I want to highlight two points from this defense of engagement. First, the ambassador's narrative naturalizes the connection between land title and tenure security in a way that is reminiscent of the Land Ministry official who attended my roundtable discussion (quoted at the beginning of this chapter). The land title will provide legal certainty; therefore, criticism of the program is unwarranted (the benefits outweigh the drawbacks; we just can't achieve it all at once). Second, German officials recognize the vulnerability of their position; what is not said (though implied) is that the Cambodian prime minister could terminate the partnership if the donors do not give concessions and perform a balancing act.

What exactly constitutes a concession on the part of GIZ is not at all clear here. It may not even be clear to the donor agencies. The Cambodian government regularly excludes outspoken development agencies by claiming that the agencies have transgressed obscure legal codes (one NGO director, for example, told me her organization was shut down for misfiling a tax return, although she found nothing wrong) or passing laws that limit NGO activity, such as the restrictive NGO and Associations Law (2015). In this way, the government produces uncertainty over what constitutes permissible behavior, leading to the self-disciplining of NGOs as they seek to maintain engagement. One NGO adviser complained to me that fear of upsetting the government has led to a "NATO" culture of development agencies in Cambodia: "We say it's NATO for No Action Talk Only. There are always endless trainings and roundtable discussions, but limited change. The focus from the donors is so much on engagement, they won't raise anything critical." This culture of self-discipline is also evident from my interviews with GIZ staff. One Khmer female employee at GIZ said she couldn't do meaningful work on land issues because the ministry and senior GIZ officials suppressed what staff could say: "We can't talk. At GIZ we can't say anything.... It is shut down.... The bosses here told me not to talk."

I spoke with several NGO staff who hoped to shift tack away from state partnerships to more connections with transnational advocacy organizations, including one international NGO officer who told me, "We're giving up on the government here to make change. That can be a negative track when you just end up in limbo, waiting. Instead, we want to put pressure on the outside actors, really get to the consumers, or at least the finance companies investing in these companies." GIZ staff also discussed the ways in which they tried to make small changes from within government institutions. For example, a representative from the faculty of land management (founded by the World Bank and GIZ) said that he tries to "get people broad experience, like they do internships with critical land rights NGOs.... I want to give them both sides, not just the government's side. Many of them will go into working in government but not all of them." This adviser likened the GIZ approach to a "salami slice" strategy wherein the agency tries to change the ministry by influencing one person at a time; "they have to just push for a little now and then, but slowly, slowly, they turn towards our views." Another adviser said that he is always alert to small opportunities to make change beyond his formal job description: "I spend a lot of my time strategizing; what can I say to which person ... to make small changes, to have little effects.... Because often [the program] does nothing. If I was in the office now I couldn't be having this conversation with you; that's why I like meeting outside. You know, at times there's something admirable about sticking to the rules. But really, you can't do that over here; the rules don't work."

Despite this adviser's position that the rules don't work, he remains embedded within an agency whose mission is to stick to the rules (and make those rules stickier), and it seems he justifies this as it places him close to the powerful people that he hopes to influence. The real work of engagement for him is outside the rules, symbolized here through moving outside the physical space of the office where we "couldn't be having this conversation." My impression of this adviser was that he was adept at strategizing in the way he describes. For example, he worked closely with sympathetic Khmer staff at GIZ and the Ministry of Land to bring attention to indigenous communities who were still losing land after receiving government recognition. The irony of this adviser's stance is that donor institutions remain committed to installing a narrow program of private property rights as a basis for good governance in Cambodia with norms of transparent rules making, yet it is only through working in the murky corridors of informal political relations that he considers it possible for donors to make any change toward a rules-based order.

Conclusion: Moves toward Transparency?

Transparency is a term frequently thrown around among donor agencies in the land sector. As one of the pillars of good governance, transparency in decision making and financial flows is seen to be a core achievement of a centralized land cadastre, while opaque governance is the domain of patrimonial politics. In this chapter, however, I have sought to show that while donors frequently place blame for lack of transparency at the feet of the Cambodian government, nontransparency is reproduced through the discursive strategies of the Land Rights Program itself. The Cambodian government and GIZ are both implicated in the production of uncertainty over land relations, as the 2013 German Institute for Human Rights report suggests: "There is a lack of transparency: Nobody interviewed in the Ministry of Land has been able to provide information about the criteria for the selection of provinces, districts and communes for systematic registration. . . . In its moves towards more transparency, the Land Rights Program should reflect that it is itself bound by human rights. . . . Communication about what German development cooperation/the LRP is doing seems largely reactive and defensive" (Lüke 2013, 25). This report chides GIZ for lack of self-reflection and for reactive communication, but the suggestion of moves toward more transparency misunderstand what is at stake in maintaining opacity in the Cambodian land sector. For Hun Sen, the Order 01 land reform aimed to produce loyal subjects:

political supporters who would produce more rice and create a more prosperous nation. Hun Sen's government has built its power on the personalized control of land and is not likely to relinquish that power. For donors, the history of the Land Rights Program (as I have traced here) can be thought of as a series of decisions to not see the intransigent politics they were entwined with, thereby contributing to the production of uncertainty.

Moreover, the donors' focus on technical outputs discursively separates the violent political economy of the Cambodian uplands from the legal good governance sphere of land titling in the lowlands, thus precluding questions about how land grabbing is itself legitimated through the use of law and liberal economic doctrine. That is, land titling can only be posed as a solution to land grabbing if these are seen as completely separate (and separable) processes. In German government discourse, land grabbing emerges from poor governance and can be solved by "getting the governance right" so that public funds will "mobilize large amounts of private capital to permanently eradicate poverty, hunger and underdevelopment" (BMZ 2012, 3). In this private sector–led development model, development will be achieved through "free, prior and informed consent of the people affected" and the integration of local farmers into value chains (5). This discourse denies any possibility that the private capital being mobilized benefits from the lack of transparency and that state and corporate actors draw on both the legal framework of property rights and informal mechanisms of expropriation to procure land. But this is precisely the case. Global firms profit from Cambodia's lack of regulation, low labor costs, and legal flexibility, which means land titling benefits those who have the capital and clout to use the law to their own advantage (Global Witness 2013).

This researcher, too, is implicated in the production of uncertainty in the land sector. The roundtable discussions for the most part reproduced the same problems I saw in other Cambodian meetings—social hierarchies limiting whose ideas are heard, fear of state repercussion, and fundamentally different ideas about what land is and what ownership means that make any conversation difficult. Perhaps it is naive to think it could be any other way, for we researchers with a desire to work for social justice find ourselves trapped in the same predicament as the organizations I critique here—seeking to enact a different kind of politics while fully aware of the precarious political position we occupy, and thus directing our activities to those deemed acceptable to the state. In early iterations of my discussion prompts for the roundtables, I included a question that encouraged people to think beyond land titling. But I had such pushback that I took it out of later meetings with officials. This kind of self-censoring (the questions that we do not ask, the information that we do not gather) becomes a large part of what we are able to see—the limits that we build around our projects, our questions, and the answers we seek.

In the following chapter, I turn from the encounters between the central state and international donors to introduce the viewpoint of rural people living in areas of land conflict. This view helps us understand how "uncertainty is not only part of the give and take of political practice but comes to form a hierarchical structural condition" (Whitington 2019, 151) in which the rural poor are at the bottom of the hierarchy.

2

ENCOUNTERING THE LEOPARD SKIN LAND REFORM

Traveling to Khang Cheung

In the fifteen years I have been going back and forth to Cambodia, the country has changed almost beyond recognition: the urban centers are a hum of construction equipment and glossy shopping malls, and new roads slice their way through the countryside, ushering in investors and cash crops. In this chapter, I turn from the encounters between the central state and international donors to the viewpoint of rural people who must negotiate these rapid changes. Tracing my encounters with rural communities in western and northeastern Cambodia sets the scene for my analysis of the land titling reform in the following chapters by showing how fear and uncertainty become a "hierarchical structural condition" (Whitington 2019, 151) shaping everyday life in areas of land conflict. I first introduce the socioecology of rural Cambodia through the people I came to know best in these areas, the families with whom I lived, who all have diverse life stories but share a feeling that the government has abandoned them.

When I began fieldwork in rural Khang Cheung in 2012, the journey from Phnom Penh took five hours. I traveled alone by bus for my first visit so I could arrange a place for my family to live. The bus crawled through Phnom Penh's sprawling urban edge, past streets crowded with garment factories, markets, slums, and riverside apartments where construction workers perched on scaffolding high above. Phnom Penh is a city bursting at the seams. Cambodia's population rose from 6.7 million people in 1980 to currently over 16 million people. Almost a quarter of these people now live in Phnom Penh; the majority of these are recent migrants from rural areas, pulled by the lure of garment factory, construction, and service-sector jobs (NIS 2013). As the bus wound around the Tonle Sap lake, we passed glistening new wooden houses on stilts and small tin shacks mingled with rice fields, cattle, and fish farms. Despite rapid urbanization, Cambodia is still overwhelmingly rural (Ministry of Information 2019). Cambodia's booming economy has had uneven effects; over 90 percent of the poor reside in rural areas while the urban economy has grown, creating a deep social divide between rural and urban areas. Now, inequality within rural areas is also increasing, and 1 percent of Cambodia's population is said to own as much as 30 percent of arable land (Neef, Touch, and Chiengthong 2013, 1085).

The bus reached the edge of Khang Cheung town just as the provincial garment factories closed for the day. Women in colorful headscarves poured out of factory gates and into lines of waiting trucks that take them home to villages in every direction (figure 3). For these women and their families, rural life is not confined to farming or to the village. Land-based livelihoods remain crucial to rural people, but one in five rural households is landless, and rural people's lives are increasingly connected to urban garment factories, high-rise construction projects, and wage work across the border in Thailand.

The bus let me off near Khang Cheung's busy market, where I met up with Sokun, the university student who accompanied me for the first phase of my research. I bundled my bags on the back of Sokun's motorbike, and we started off

FIGURE 3. Garment workers travel home to rural villages after a day's work.

(Photo: Alice Beban.)

60   CHAPTER 2

on the two-hour motorbike ride to my field sites, flashing past wet-season fields dotted with sugar palms on the bunds. This land close to Khang Cheung town rose in price in the mid-2000s, precipitating a wave of land sales and land concentration. As we drove closer to the foot of the Aural mountains, the flat fields gave way to shrubs and rice, corn, mango, and yellowed grass. This more remote landscape has only recently grown in value, as infrastructure improves and speculative investors snap up roadside land. Most land here is legally state land (as is all land that has not been titled to individuals in the post–Khmer Rouge period), and forest use is subject to state rules including limits on logging. In reality, though, the state elite and the Pheapimex concession company control access to the logging industry and the in-migration of lowland Khmer. For this area lies within the massive Pheapimex concession, the largest ELC in the country at more than 300,000 hectares in size (shown by the large polygon in Khang Cheung in figure 4).

Within the concession area, I based my fieldwork in two communes in the neighboring districts of Tonle Leung (Phnom Mie commune) and Prey Jah (Srai Saat commune). I chose these areas because both communes were earmarked for land titling in the land reform, both are near the plantation zone, and people from both communes have actively resisted plantation development. I wanted to un-

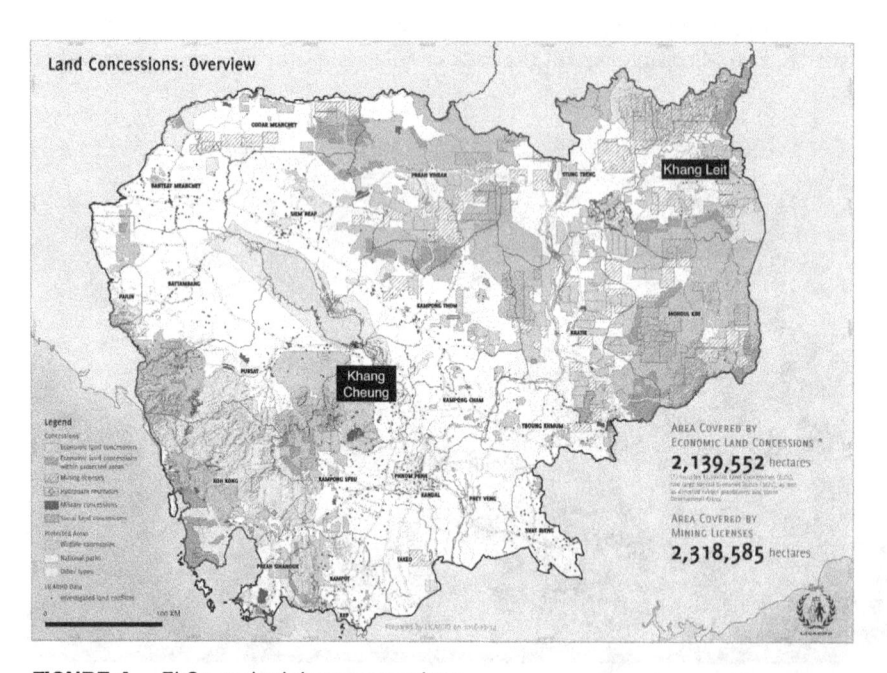

FIGURE 4.   ELCs and mining concessions.

(Source: Map licensed under a Creative Commons Attribution Generic License; LICADHO's original version is available at http://www.licadho-cambodia.org/land_concessions/.)

derstand what it meant to carry out land reform in an area that had a contentious history with ELCs, as these are the kinds of places where the leopard skin vision of improved relationships between ELCs and smallholders might be most meaningful. The two communes also had differences. While Phnom Mie is a longer-settled area with less forest cover and fewer land conflicts, Srai Saat is a commune still in formation with a history of military-led governance and land conflicts. And while the community network that connected people in their fight against the ELCs remains strong in Phnom Mie, it has fractured in Srai Saat, which allowed me to trace the importance of collective action in shaping relationships with ELCs and with the land reform. These communes are not separate spheres, however; they are mutually constituted through histories of conflict and cooperation. The district border has shifted over time; apparently the two district chiefs struck a deal in the 1980s to place the border further into Prey Jah territory, but the Prey Jah chief later produced a map that claimed more of Tonle Leung's territory. These local skirmishes are important because the forestland at stake is a key field of local power relations. Local government officials and business elite sell land to new migrants, give land to political supporters and family members, and profit from logging operations.

By the time I arrived in Srai Saat that first day, I was covered in orange film from the dusty road. Sokun and I sat at the front of a tin-roof shop sipping strong coffee from plastic bags. This area had a different feel from the villages we passed on the way. Seven villages (and several small settlements not yet recognized as villages[1]) cluster around the foothills with the Aural mountains looming in the distance. On either side of the coffee shop, several two-story solid timber houses stood in a commanding position along the main village road. These houses were owned by current and former military commanders, who first settled Srai Saat when conflict subsided here in the mid-1990s and still control large amounts of land around the village. Their houses were interspersed with more modest, one-room, tin-roof houses owned by people who moved here from the late 1990s and cleared the forest in search of farmland and small-scale logging opportunities. This first wave of settlers told me glorious stories about encounters with elephants and tigers as they struggled to clear thick shrubland by hand. These families sold land to a second wave of people in the early 2000s, who moved to the area from the crowded lowlands and refugee camps. A third wave of people has moved into Srai Saat commune since 2008, living at the back of the village in tiny thatched roof huts linked by networks of sandy walking tracks.

After a few days getting to know my way around Srai Saat, I drove my motorbike along the edge of the cassava plantation to neighboring Phnom Mie Commune. This commune is a collection of six villages that lies east of Srai Saat on the way back to Khang Cheung town, and people have been living and cultivating paddy rice here for generations. I didn't see so many two-story large homes along the main village road, nor did I see as many thatched roof shacks as in Srai Saat; people's homes here are mainly one story with tin or brick roofs, and rice fields, pigpens, and home gardens are dotted around the houses. The area has a more settled feel than Srai Saat. As with people in Srai Saat, though, this is a mobile population. The area was emptied during the civil conflict, and families drifted back to their preconflict villages in the 1980s–1990s. In some villages, state authorities allocated people the same land they had held in the prewar era; in other villages, land was doled out strictly according to household size.

In Srai Saat and Phnom Mie, the biggest structures are the school building and the Buddhist temple. Each village has one school with one teacher, and children who live along the sandy tracks walk more than an hour to school. Some children don't go to school; one eight-year-old boy in Srai Saat told me school is a waste of time because the teacher is rarely there. The teacher, Lok Kru Cheang, complained that it isn't his fault; he comes when he can, but his family lives in Khang Cheung town and he holds a second job in town in order to make ends meet. The nearest health center is ten kilometers away in the market town of Bakeal. For anything serious, though, people travel to Khang Cheung town hospital for treatment or, if they can afford it, all the way to Phnom Penh or Bangkok. The relative isolation of the area is revealed in a household survey I undertook in August–November 2014 (this included 270 households randomly selected from my study communes; see the preface). Only a quarter of the people in my survey said they lived near a large road, two-thirds lived near a small dirt road, and 10 percent did not live near a road at all; they accessed their house on sandy motorbike and bicycle trails. Out here, people must find their own ways to learn and to heal. I came across one grandmother in front of her house singing the ABCs in English with her preschool granddaughter; she showed me the English learner books she procured from visiting missionaries. Other women teach their grandchildren how to find medicinal plants in the forest.

Two things stood out for me as I settled into the area. Most notably, the quiet. I saw very few people. During the day, as I went from home to home introducing myself, I talked mainly with older women and men who tended the farm and cared for grandchildren. Only one garment factory truck pulled in here in the evenings to drop off tired workers. It was too far for most people to commute to town, and many women and men of working age migrated to Thailand or lived in Phnom Penh. The remittances that these workers sent home to their families became a central source of people's livelihoods, although the well-being of family members who went to Thailand informally (without proper documentation) and risked ending up in poor labor conditions or deported was a source of worry for those left behind. The second thing that stood out to me was the lack of presence of the ELC. Although the plantation zone had not yet reached my study area when I conducted research, both communes lay inside the ELC, and the expanding cassava plantation zone was only 2 kilometers from Srai Saat and 500 meters from Phnom Mie. But I may not have realized the ELC was there if I hadn't seen the maps. Most people did not talk to me about the ELC—at least, not at first. People were fearful of the day when the company would take their land, and this fear—of the company and of possible reprisal if people spoke badly about the company—likely kept people quiet about the ELC until they trusted me. It was only after living in the area for a few weeks that I realized how much the concession—the "Chinese company" as people called it—pervaded everyday life.

The "Chinese Company"

The ELC that borders Srai Saat and Phnom Mie is leased to Pheapimex, a Cambodian company run by powerful Chinese Cambodian tycoon Lao Meng Khin and his wife, Choeung Sopheap. This couple are part of the Chinese Cambodian ethnic minority, who number less than one percent of Cambodia's population, yet hold a great deal of economic and political power in Cambodia (Verver 2019). Chinese Cambodians are lauded as successful entrepreneurs, but their politico-business power and close ties with Chinese companies also invokes anti-Chinese sentiments in rural areas where ELCs have rapidly spread. The Pheapimex ELC and local villagers have a contentious history. When the government's MAFF granted Pheapimex a seventy-year ELC lease in the late 1990s, members of the Khmer Rouge still occupied part of the concession area, and the ELC contract was signed without notifying the thousands of people who live in eighty-five villages within the concession (Barney 2005). Chinese investments in agroindustry have come to be a central part of the Cambodia-China bilateral relationship, and the Pheapimex development was influenced by China's method of disbursing its official aid entirely through contracts to Chinese firms and the predominance of state-owned enterprises in financing and implementing large projects. The contract, which included no payment of rent for the land, enabled Pheapimex to use the land for agroindustrial development, and also included an agreement with a Chinese government entity—the China Corporation of State Farms Group—entailing investment of US$70 million from the Import-Export Bank of China for the cultivation of eucalyptus and the construction of a pulp and paper factory.

Pheapimex and the China Cooperative State Farm Group began clearing land in 2001 to develop acacia tree plantations. However, local landholders came together with the support of a local land rights NGO called Green Cambodia, which is led by a formidable Khmer woman in her fifties named Ming Tam. The landholders formed the Daoum Chuur Community Network (hereafter, the community network) and organized petitions, meetings, and a protest that mobilized more than two thousand people to block the main road to Phnom Penh. This community network marked a new kind of civil society mobilization in Cambodia, and it arose at the same time as several other networks across the country. Previous protests to land grabbing were largely local affairs, but the Daoum Chuur community network covered nine districts around the plantation zone across provincial lines, and it encouraged many local people (particularly women) to become active in community affairs. Although most of the people involved in the community network described themselves as farmers or rural people rather than activists, I use the term *community activists* throughout the book to describe people who play active roles in the community network, such as attending meetings and protests, taking on governance roles, and communicating with government and other villagers.

Pheapimex halted plantation development in 2004 following the community network's protests. But in 2010, with cassava markets on the rise, Pheapimex subcontractor Wuzushan began clearing forestland on the border of Khang Cheung province for a cassava plantation. Again, the community network resisted, but they could not stop the clearance. By the time I arrived in 2012, the plantation zone had grown to 50,000 hectares.[2] The former forest- and shrubland were cleared, ploughed, and formed into ridges. A plantation worker explained to me that cassava is planted throughout the year here; first, a preemergent herbicide and fertilizer are applied; then cassava cuttings are dipped in fungicide-insecticide solution and sown, reaching maturity in about six months. After harvest, the cassava is dried, processed into chips, and exported to China for ethanol and animal feed as part of Cambodia and China's "cassava diplomacy."[3]

Most people I talked with deeply resent the "Chinese company" for cutting down the forest and displacing rice land for chemical-intensive plantation agriculture. People often told me how clean the water was before the "Chinese company" came—children could swim in the rivers and drink from the village stream, cattle grazed freely in the woods, and people picked mushrooms and fruit to eat and sell at the market. But now the streams run a milky color, people (and livestock) complain of stomach illnesses if they drink the stream water, and wild food has been replaced by the "Chinese company's" cassava fields, fences, and guards. In fact, when I asked local people about deforestation (including forest clearance far from the plantation area), people almost always blamed the "Chinese company" rather than any specific perpetrators. Certainly, Pheapimex are responsible for a great deal of forest clearance in the area, but this use of the term "Chinese company" racializes blame and serves to obscure land grabbing and deforestation that is also linked to domestic landowners and the political elite.

I believe people's fear of the "Chinese company" emerges from a racialized fear of foreign land grabbing with deep roots in premodern Cambodia's history of land tussles with Vietnam and China, in its more recent history of China's role in the Khmer Rouge regime (Mertha 2014), and in the influx of Chinese companies and tourists into Cambodia (Verver 2019). Fear is always formed in layers of past and present threat (Pain 2009), and when people talked with me about the "Chinese company," their narratives frequently slipped between the plantation and the country's violent past. This past is present in stories, collective memories, and in the traces of land mines, Khmer Rouge–era canals, and spiritually potent mass graves embedded in the landscape. In this way, contemporary projects of state-making (and space-making) articulate with what Donald Moore (2005) terms "sedimented" histories, politics, and spatialities to remake contingent forms of sovereignty on top of existing territories.

An encounter I had with a community forest leader named Men Somning illustrates the ways that memories of fear are sedimented in the landscape to inform the present. I was on the back of Men Somning's motorbike one day heading to a community meeting, when he suddenly stopped the motorbike in the middle of a bridge near his house. He eased his foot off the pedal and pointed to the river below. "I dug that," he said. The channel was two cars wide, and deep, etched into the earth running through the village. "You know, hundreds of people died digging that," he said. "Maybe thousands." I wondered why he picked that moment to tell me; we drove past this spot often. But something in that moment had made him stop. And it made me see the landscape differently. The canals from Pol Pot's time snake their way through the area. Many of them are abandoned, considered unusable or irreparable. But they are always visible; they are symbols of the promise and the destruction of that time, and they shape people's reactions to current development projects. As we stood on the bridge, Men Somning's narrative moved easily between the Khmer Rouge canals and his fear of the "Chinese company": "Now is no different from Pol Pot. Now they suppress us just as before. If the government wants land for development, they take it. We can't do anything. And if we look at the Chinese company, this is a continuation of the project in Pol Pot's time. In Pol Pot's time, the Chinese were in control of building the big irrigation projects; they built this canal from here to the airport. There are many bodies in here, in this dirt. And now this continues. . . . Eventually we will be a minority. Khmer will be a minority."

For people like Men Somning, whose forestland is slowly being transformed into plantations around him, a palpable fear shadowed our conversations. This fear had a strange spatiotemporality; it was not just about the plantation itself but the area around it, the potential for land to be grabbed in the future. This was not a fear of acute eviction but of the "in situ dispossession" (Feldman and Geisler

2012) by the company's slow encroachment, a fear fed by the memories of past violence, the material loss of forests, and the appearance of bulldozers, cassava roots, engineers, and security guards. This fear is perpetuated by local state officials, company representatives, and military personnel, leading to widespread distrust. One elderly woman in Khang Cheung told me that she had spoken to several NGOs in the past, but "I never tell them anything. I just say everything is fine. Because they might record what we say and take it to the authorities. How do we know? If they do that, the [authorities] will kill us. So we can't speak." Fear shapes people's responses to land grabbing; not speaking or acting doesn't mean that people passively accept their subjugation. However, resistance often takes forms that I did not recognize until I became attuned to the way fear and threat pervades people's everyday lives.

Changing Political Ecologies of Rural Cambodia

The Political Ecology of Khang Cheung

My extended periods of fieldwork in Khang Cheung gave me a strong sense of how livelihoods and land tenure relations are in flux in rural Cambodia. After an initial three-month scoping study in 2012, I conducted my main period of field research from December 2013 to April 2015. The land reform was carried out between June 2012 and June 2013, during my scoping study, and I was able to accompany a volunteer land surveyor for a week in Khang Cheung and observe the land measurement. By the time I returned in late 2013, most people had completed one rice-growing season since the land reform. The changes were therefore both new enough that people still had strong memories of the allocation and old enough that I could assess the outcomes of the policy thus far.

It is difficult to separate the effects of the land reform from those caused by the other drivers of change in rural areas, as multiple factors have been pushing people out of agriculture over the past decade. Farmers have struggled through several years of drought, unstable markets for cash crops, a government clampdown on small-scale logging, and the plantation's expansion onto forest- and grazing land. The soil is acidic here, and modern high-yielding rice varieties do not grow well, so most people plant a mix of traditional heavy rice varietals that require six or more months to mature. Heavy rice is a gamble, though, because the rains that used to signal the start of the rice season in May are now arriving in June or July. With this shorter growing season, long-duration varieties risk becoming parched with drought and susceptible to disease. Severe drought in 2011 and 2013 forced several families to leave this area, and farmers tell me that every year the weather is more erratic, with scorching drought interrupted by torrential rainfall. Climate change is likely to further alter weather patterns here in the near future, with the traditional rainy season (May–November) expected to shorten into two periods of heavy rain (June–July and September–October) with a month of drought in August.[4] These changing weather patterns are a disaster for farmers in my study areas, almost all of whom rely on rain-fed rice systems.

While the changing climate and expanding plantation have forced some people to sell and leave the area, I did not meet any smallholder farmers who wanted to sell land. Even people who pushed their kids to get good jobs in the city still hoped to retain their rural landholding. Land is central to people's lives here. Land is a source of food and livelihood, a kind of insurance that people can sell in a crisis, and it is the main asset passed on to children when they marry. Land tenure is highly unequal, though. Average plot sizes are just over 1 hectare, and I estimated that around one in five households in Tmor Muoy village were landless by the time I arrived in 2012. In Phnom Mie commune, farther down the valley, an even greater number of households did not own any agricultural land. Land tenure is also highly gendered; women I surveyed in Khang Cheung reported owning around 1 hectare of agricultural land on average, compared to men's 2.1 hectares, primarily because women who are separated or widowed tend to have very small landholdings. Although land inheritance practices were generally gender neutral in Khang Cheung, with men and women receiving equal land upon marriage, families with male labor amassed more land by gradually clearing forest for agriculture, as land clearing was seen to be a masculine activity, while families that lacked male labor tended to have small landholdings.

The rice season still sets the rhythm of life. Notions of property ownership are fluid, and rice fields under private cultivation during the wet season (May–November) are used communally for grazing cattle in the dry season. This practice provides fodder for the cattle and manure for the rice fields. Forestland is used for livestock grazing, collection of timber and non-timber forest products (NTFPs), and upland rice nurseries. Families routinely claim forestland, which they mark out with sticks or simply have an understanding with neighbors that this is their land that they will gradually clear for rice when they have the labor available and need the extra food or money. Although all land here was formally state land under lease to the Pheapimex company before the land reform, families saw the forest- and shrubland as communal areas. I term this conception of forest tenure *communal* rather than *open access* because the people described the forest as a communal resource, owned by the spirit owner of the water and the land and, with proper negotiation (including using only enough resources to sustain one's family), available for all to use (Work and Beban 2016). Both rich and poor families in the village used the forestland before the land reform, but the poorest households had relatively less farmland and depended more on the forest for their food and livelihoods.

The village fills up with people for the rice transplant (June–July), as migrant workers come back to help their families, and there is a buzz of joy in the village as families are reunited. In the past, people shared labor at transplant time, doing a day's work on each family's field and slowly rotating around the village until all fields were planted. Now, though, most people don't have time for this. Migrant workers only stay a few days, and families who can afford it hire other villagers to help them transplant. I observed reciprocal labor arrangements in only one village in Phnom Mie commune. In June 2014, I squeezed onto a wooden cart with my friend Srey Sophorn and about fifteen other women and men from the village and spent four days traveling from field to field, wading out in the calf-deep sludge to transplant seedlings into muddy rice paddies. We worked together to transplant one full field belonging to one of the people participating, then moved to the next person's land and transplanted one of their fields, and so on, circulating around each of the participants' fields before we started back at the first farm and transplanted a second field. Participants left the group once all their fields were transplanted. In this way, the process was equitable, as people transplanted others' fields proportionate to the amount they owned themselves.

Just two farmers in the area (both with larger landholdings) broadcast seed rather than transplant their rice seedlings. One of these farmers, Puu Sothi, told me he learned about broadcasting rice seed when he worked in Thailand, and now he broadcasts his entire 10 hectares to save on labor costs. Other farmers complained that broadcasting only worked on Puu Sothi's fields because his land was less acidic, and broadcasting on other fields used too much seed and required more chemical fertilizer than people could afford. Most farmers choose their best fields as rice nurseries and use buffalo to plow manure and chemical fertilizer into the fields before transplanting. These practices, too, are changing, however, as two-wheeled tractors (known as "hand tractors") become more prevalent than cattle and buffalo. Tractors plow much faster than cattle. They also don't require grazing land, which is becoming increasingly scarce as the ELC and private owners enclose common forest- and shrubland around the village. But hand tractors cost around US$2,500 to $3,000, a price out of reach for many families in the area. Tractors also require ongoing costs in fuel and extra chemical fertilizer to maintain soil nutrients in the absence of manure.

After the rice transplant, the village is quiet until harvest time (November–December), when families gather to pick and dry their rice crop and celebrate the season with dances and feasts. Traders from Vietnam travel around the village weighing sacks of rice and giving farmers cash payment, minus any agrichemicals farmers bought on credit at the start of the season. All farmers I met in this area also keep some rice for their own consumption and save seed for the following season. Families with small plots often keep all their rice harvest for eating or sharing with relatives.

In the dry season, the fields become communal grazing areas, and people depend on other livelihoods, such as fishing (40 percent of Khang Cheung households I surveyed), gathering food and logs from the forest (31 percent), maintaining a home garden (28 percent), running a small business (25 percent), raising livestock (23 percent), and piecemeal laboring work (11 percent). Most families also send family members to work in Thailand, Phnom Penh, or other areas (68 percent). Women and men participate fairly evenly in most paid occupations, the exception being forest product collection (34 percent of men; 23 percent of women). This gendered difference reflects the importance of small-scale logging in the area, which is seen as men's work. But to make money in the logging business, you need money to purchase buffalo and a cart, or a hand tractor. By the mid-2000s, the nearby forest had already been logged of the most valuable timber, and large-scale loggers had taken control of forestland farther away inside a conservation zone. Poor families who cannot afford the equipment to access remote timber eke out a living from farming, piecemeal work, and migration remittances, and some have left the area completely.

While some people's fortunes fall, others manage to hang on to the threads of economic growth through their political connections, economic nous, wealthy relatives, or luck. My survey statistics reveal this inequality. Most people had very little formal education (60 percent of people in Khang Cheung had four years or less of schooling, and two-thirds of women in Khang Leit had no formal schooling at all). Levels of food insecurity also varied; more than a quarter of respondents in Khang Cheung and Khang Leit reported no problems with food insecurity, but 20 percent faced food shortages for more than half the year. Women reported a higher level of food insecurity than men, and deserted women (that is, women whose husbands had left them without a formal divorce) reported lacking food for almost eight months of the year.[5] People who are food-insecure are also most likely to be landless or have small landholdings and to depend on common land for food and livelihoods. But people's access to forests, water, and grazing land has decreased as common land is enclosed and urban investors snap up roadside land plots and clear forests. To illustrate the contours of everyday life amid this rising inequality, I turn now to the stories of two people I came to know best in Khang Cheung.

PUU TANAK

I met Puu Tanak on the first day I arrived in Srai Saat Commune.[6] Puu Tanak was a stocky man in his fifties with a huge smile, a shrewd economic sensibility, and a cutting political critique. Puu Tanak and his family—his wife, his wife's sister (who has lived with the family since her husband was killed in the civil war), his three sons and two daughters—lived on a side road in Tmor Muoy village. Puu Tanak's house was noticeable as one of the nicer houses on the road; it was raised off the ground and had red wooden sides and a tiled roof. The land activist with whom I had planned to live suggested that the Tanaks' house would be more comfortable for my family because the Tanak family had a toilet. Underlying this was his concern that if I lived with an activist, I would be seen as an activist myself, and local authorities might curtail my research or step up their surveillance of activists I associated with. Ming Tanak (Puu Tanak's wife) was not sure about taking me in at first, but she softened once my husband and kids arrived, and after a few days I became part of the landscape, rising at 5:00 a.m. to help boil sweet rice cakes in oil, tutoring the kids in English, and spending my days wandering around the village talking to people.

In the evenings, I sat in the shade under the house drinking homemade rice wine with Puu Tanak while he talked scathingly about local politics and the Cambodian government. This was always done at his house, in private. He supported the ruling party (CPP) at local political events when there was occasion to do so publicly, but he had deep misgivings over what he saw as the ineptitude of both the ruling party and the opposition party, and he took no part in local CPP networks. He was, therefore, a threat to the CPP village chief; he had no obvious connections to land activism or the opposition party, so it was difficult to pin any wrongdoing on him, and he did not ask for any gifts, so it was difficult to bribe him into silence. When the village chief distributed some forestland to selected villagers during the land reform, the Tanaks were left out of the land distribution (a fact Ming Tanak was bitter about). Puu Tanak did have a certain status with other villagers, though; he was known as a skilled buffalo healer, and there were rumors that this skill came from his deep connections to the land spirits in the area, whom he propitiously plied with daily supplies of food and drink at a small altar outside his house.

The Tanak family's five children (who ranged in age from seven to twenty-one) were still living at home. This was a point of pride for the parents, as Ming Tanak told me: "Most people here have to go away to Thailand or to work in the Chinese company. But we make sure the children can stay here and have work to do." The Tanaks explained their success at avoiding migration through their hard work and shrewd saving. The Tanaks sold their small landholding in the neighboring province and arrived in the village in 2005, just before the rise of land prices. They bought land from a family who left the village after a bad harvest and began to breed buffalo and chickens. They accumulated 8 hectares of rice fields as other people left the area. The Tanaks showed me letters issued by the commune office that confirmed their landholdings, but they had no formal land titles. The student volunteer surveyors had surveyed some of their land during the land reform, but the Tanaks, like many of their neighbors, were still waiting for the land titles more than a year later.

Beside farming, different livelihood opportunities came and went during the year. Ming Tanak and her sister managed a large home garden and sold produce at the market when they had extra. Ming Tanak and her daughter also negotiated a deal with the local chief and schoolteacher to set up a stall outside the school, selling pencils, notebooks, candy, and donuts. Ming Tanak grumbled that this was not always worth it; the schoolteacher didn't turn up to teach half the time, the village chief wanted a cut of the profits, and some children asked shyly if they could pay her back later, which she always agreed to. The Tanaks also had two wealthier relatives, who helped them out in various ways. One uncle in the neighboring province arranged for the Tanaks' elder daughter to train as a dessert maker in a nearby market town. An aunt in Phnom Penh visited once a month, and she always quietly left money on the table while the Tanaks' sons filled her car with rice and vegetables. When the Tanaks' younger daughter fell sick with a heart condition and required treatment in the city, this aunt took her in for several months. The Tanaks were careful not to overtax these relationships, though, and they took pride in doing things themselves.

Puu Tanak's position was better than most in the village, yet it was precarious. The Tanaks inhabited a social position on the edge of the local elite; Puu Tanak was a successful farmer and a self-educated man who had amassed a large amount of land, but the family lacked the ties to the military and local administration enjoyed by other elite landowners in the village. Puu Tanak planted mango and bananas to diversify his farm after the severe drought, but he worried about being so dependent on the land. "I'm always going up and down," he said to me one day. Indeed, just as I was finishing my fieldwork in mid-2015, the family suffered a setback when Ming Tanak's sister fell ill. She was treated in Khang Cheung and then Phnom Penh, and the family scrambled to pay the bills. Around the same time, the Tanaks' youngest son failed his high school graduation exam. This was a huge disappointment for the whole family, as they had worked hard to pay for his schooling and he had studied diligently. But he failed by one point. "One point!" Ming Tanak kept repeating when she found out. A passing grade would have been his ticket into a career as a civil servant. Puu Tanak exploded to me one evening, "The system is rigged. If you have connections, money, you can cheat on the exams, you can get jobs. If not, you don't get anywhere."

Two of the Tanaks' sons went to work at the "Chinese company" after that. I was shocked when he told me; he had persistently talked about how his family would never be "slaves of the company" like others. But, he said, "my sons aren't like normal laborers." The family had taken out a US$5,000 loan to purchase two hand tractors, which their sons used to transport laborers around the plantation. Each son earned US$250 per month, and Puu Tanak calculated this was enough to pay the hand tractors off in five years. "That way," he told me, "if the company takes all the grazing land in five years and we can't keep cattle anymore, then we'll be ready to plow the land with the hand tractors."

If Puu Tanak is an example of success, at least in terms of the family's relative landholding and farming operations compared to others in the area, then my host in my second study commune, Srey Sophorn, is an example of a household that struggles to get by with more limited land and labor assets. But she has built up a livelihood and considerable social networks through her connections with NGOs and land activism.

SREY SOPHORN

I first met Srey Sophorn in Khang Cheung town at a community network meeting. She spoke eloquently during the meeting, holding the floor as others listened quietly. I went back to stay at her house in Phnom Mie that evening, and I stayed there with my family often over the next two years. Srey Sophorn was in her mid-forties and lived with her older sister, Chimrouen. Chimrouen had stepped on a land mine in 1987, when she was just a girl and the family was venturing back into the area after the conflict. Now she had an ill-fitting prosthetic leg that on good days allowed her to go out to the fields, maintain a vegetable garden, and tend to two pigs. On bad days she could do little but sit under the house with her leg up. She did most of the cooking, though, even on bad days. With little money and no other household members available to fish or get food from the forest, Chimrouen's meals were simple: a heap of rice with vegetables from the garden and some marinated eggs or a little fish from the market. Srey Sophorn's husband had left the family years ago; there was no formal divorce and she had no idea where he was. "I'm better without him," she told me. "Things are hard, but now I can do what I want." Srey Sophorn had one daughter named Sayheang, in her twenties and living in Phnom Penh. Sayheang wanted to learn English and work in a hotel, but she was then employed as a cleaner and did not make enough money to send any remittances home.

Srey Sophorn and her sister squeaked by with their two hectares of rice fields they inherited from their parents. Before the land reform, the sisters had a letter from local officials stating that each of them held one hectare in her own name. During Order 01, the student volunteers surveyed their fields as two separate plots in the same manner as the local officials, and both women received land titles. Srey Sophorn told me she also had some forestland that she and her husband claimed years ago and used sporadically to grow mountain potatoes, but the "Chinese company" planted cassava on this land two years before the land reform, and she had no hope of getting it back.

The sisters produced enough rice to last them nine months of the year. After that, they ate sparingly with rice purchased from the market and small quantities of fish and meat. The rice land in this area was more fertile than Srai Saat, and most households did well with their rice harvest, although Srey Sophorn said that recent droughts had devastated rice yields. Also in contrast to Srai Saat, this area had been frequented by agricultural and livelihood NGOs in recent years, and Srey Sophorn experimented with organic rice cultivation methods she learned at NGO training sessions. These methods were more resistant to drought, and Srey Sophorn tried to persuade other people to try them, but the rice takes longer to transplant and maintain, so most people weren't interested. Srey Sophorn also got piecemeal work transplanting, weeding, and harvesting rice fields for larger landowners. She had a motorbike (a perk from an NGO to help her with her community work), and she sometimes collected other women's vegetables and took them 10 kilometers to the market to sell. She said she struggled sometimes but refused to work at the "Chinese company" because "they don't treat people well."

Most of Srey Sophorn's time was taken up with her role as an activist leader in the community network. "I help the people here," she told me. Srey Sophorn did not receive a salary for any of her NGO work, but she received per diem payments for attending meetings with NGOs or leading training sessions. She certainly wasn't getting rich from these activities, though; she did this work, she said, because someone had to do it: "There used to be more people who would participate, but now everyone is too busy. People go to Thailand for work, or Phnom Penh, or they are too scared to do anything against the company. The biggest problem here is with the Pheapimex company. The land issue. You know, I've been doing this for more than ten years, since the company started."

Srey Sophorn's lament at the lack of community involvement was something I heard frequently from activists in the area. Fear of company and state retribution dissuaded people from protesting; the pull of urban jobs and the precarity of life on the land also meant that many people did not have the time or resources to resist land appropriation.

CONNECTING SREY SOPHORN AND PUU TANAK

Neither Srey Sophorn nor Puu Tanak were typical villagers. They were each in different ways more food-secure and wealthier than the average household in my research, although their hold on success was shaky. This is a common situation in rural Cambodia, where poverty has more than halved in ten years; according to the World Bank, the loss of only about "thirty US cents per day in income would throw an estimated three million Cambodians back into poverty, doubling the poverty rate to 40 percent" (World Bank 2014, 1). For some people in Phnom Mie and Srai Saat, contingencies such as family illness, crop failure, or fines for informal labor migration to Thailand threw them into desperate poverty. Others had simply come too late. Newer arrivals to the area found the best land taken, property prices too high, and small-scale logging increasingly difficult due to the plantation's expansion and state crackdown on illegal logging. The land left for farming was sandy and drought-prone, and the erratic weather wreaked havoc on crops, leaving some households mired in debt as they struggled to cover food shortages.

Srey Sophorn and Puu Tanak's connection to the urban world of Phnom Penh expanded in 2014, when a large new road was constructed along the old colonial railway. Three vehicles could squeeze past each other on the expansive dirt road, and the drive out to Srai Saat became faster and more terrifying. The new road brought with it new vehicles. Large logging trucks that previously had to meet carts loaded with logs on the main road to Khang Cheung now roared right to the edge of the forest, trailing dust behind them. Black SUVs with dark windows careened up the road on the weekends. Whenever people noticed these vehicles coming through town, they watched keenly to see where they went—perhaps they were heading to the village chief's house, or maybe to Toung, the land broker. Sometimes the SUVs stopped by the side of the road, and men in shirts and smart pants emerged from the car, pointing up to plots of land. Speculation ensued from the people watching: "Oh, that's Ming Suon's plot of land; that's what they're looking at"; "No, no, the village chief got that land"; and so on.

The road is both a material transformation of social and ecological life in rural areas and a symbol of the ways that the state-society relationship is changing in rural Cambodia. Edwards (2006) argues that roads, like other infrastructural development gifts presented by Cambodia's ruling party in the postconflict era, have a regimenting effect: they allow mobility for some and trap others. For those who could afford motorbikes, cars, or a taxi fare, the new road promised to bring the urban world closer; others could only watch as the new road ushered in new vehicles and people from the urban world who bought up land and left with logs. I turn now to the other end of Cambodia: the upland province of Khang Leit, in which I conducted a smaller comparative study to gain a sense of state-society relations in a predominantly indigenous area.

The Political Ecology of Upland Khang Leit

Khang Leit province is an eleven-hour bus ride from Khang Cheung, up the Tonle Sap lake and across to the northeast of the country bordering Laos and Vietnam. I rode this bus up and down the lake four times during the course of my fieldwork to conduct interviews and a survey and to attend community meetings after the Order 01 land reform. I focused on two districts in which the land reform was carried out, with two study communes: Sai Tong (an ethnic Tampouan area), and Kam Chaa (an ethnic Kreung and Brao area). I chose these communes because villages within them had diverse responses to Order 01. In Sai Tong, people in one village welcomed the land surveyors because people hoped the land titles would protect their land from a Vietnamese rubber company; in another village, local people stood on the road to block the student volunteer surveyors entering the village. And in other villages, tensions rose as some people claimed individual title and others opted to wait for communal title.

Khang Leit is considered an upland province with a different history of relations to the state and a different population from Khang Cheung. The topography is mountainous, with plentiful mineral deposits and rich red soils. The province has been occupied by highland peoples for over a millennium. These groups are collectively termed *indigenous* (*Khmer Leur* or *Khmer Daom*), but they have diverse languages, cultures, and livelihood traditions.[7] Land tenure governance before the influx of lowlanders in the 1990s was based primarily on oral recognition of farming use rights for rotational cropping systems,[8] with governance of communal land areas headed by village elders (usually men) (Bourdier 2018; Fox et al. 2008). The forest makes up an integral component of people's livelihoods, with the collection of NTFPs, hunting, fishing, and firewood collection complementing resources from cultivation (Maffi 2009). Testimonies from around Khang Leit indicated that land scarcity was not an issue before the 1990s and families had equal access to land and forest resources (Fox et al. 2008; Gironde and Peeters 2015).

Violence is central to the history of Khmer/indigenous relations. During northeast Cambodia's early history, upland peoples were exploited as slaves by neighboring empires. With the independence fervor to build a Khmer nation in the 1950s, Prince Norodom Sihanouk attempted to bring upland peoples into the Khmer nation by classifying them as *Khmer Leur* (upland Khmer) and establishing a "Khmerization" campaign, which forced people to move to lower areas of the mountains and establish villages with people of different ethnic backgrounds (Padwe 2011b). The Khmer Rouge built its headquarters in the province in the 1960s, and uplanders joined the Khmer Rouge in large numbers. But once the Khmer Rouge took control of the country, upland villages were depopulated and people were forced into rice-farming collectives. Following the civil conflict, the government attempted to modernize the highlanders, sending state officials and public servants to live in the province and establishing new villages closer to roads and services. Cash crop booms during the 1990s saw the influx of cashew and soya into the uplands, which placed pressure on shifting cultivation systems (Padwe

2011b). This expansion of cash crops also transformed gender roles, as men became the money earners and gained more control within systems that were often based on matrilineal inheritance (Maffi 2009; Park 2015). At the same time, lowland Khmer started moving in large numbers to the uplands as migrant networks expanded (Gironde and Senties Portilla 2015). In the mid-2000s, a sharp increase in rubber prices triggered an unprecedented change in land use to rubber, driven by Khmer entrepreneurs, officials, in-migrants, and large ELCs (Fox et al. 2008). By 2012, sixteen ELCs covered 114,000 hectares in Khang Leit (Gironde and Peeters 2015). In the two communes in which I conducted research, some people have shifted completely to monocrop cash cropping, others have adapted their rotational systems to incorporate cash cropping, and many people still cultivate a diverse mix of upland rice, vegetables, and root crops.[9]

I found that people in Khang Leit resent the actions of the government and tie state actions to the loss of land in their communities. But they don't necessarily reject the state; many people told me they need more health and education services and more protection from land grabbers. The story of Siranii, a woman I met during fieldwork in Kam Chaa, illustrates the contradictions of indigenous people's relationships with the Cambodian state.

SIRANII

I met Siranii as I was leaving her neighbor's house. I had just arrived in the village the night before with my survey team, and I had completed my first interview with Siranii's neighbor, a relative of the village chief, who had talked about how good life was in the village. Siranii motioned me and my research assistant (an indigenous woman from a neighboring district) over to her house. When I got there, she blurted out, "My neighbor told you lies. It's bad here. The forest is gone. The company has taken it all; there is nothing left. And there is corruption in the village with the village chief and the commune chief. They make us pay for everything we need. And they got land from the student volunteers in the land survey and now I'm worried about our land."

Siranii, who is ethnic Kreung, has three young children and struggles to provide enough food for them. She uses two hectares of land within her village's communal land area for shifting agriculture, producing vegetables, rice, and cassava. Her use of the communal land is governed by village elders. Sometimes she doesn't have enough rice and borrows from her neighbors or her brother and sister in the next village, but she has to pay them back later, so she prefers not to do this. Siranii's husband, Tun, finds occasional work at a gold mine a couple of hours' motorbike ride away. When I first met her, Tun was away at the mine. She never knows how many days or weeks he will be away. She manages the household, caring for the kids, preparing meals, and tending the crops. Some days she leaves the kids with a friend in the early morning and walks into the market (a ninety-minute walk each way) to sell her produce. Most of the produce sold in the market comes straight over the border from Vietnam, she tells me, and the Vietnamese traders undercut the indigenous sellers. She laughs bitterly, "The trucks from Vietnam come in with vegetables and leave with black gold" (i.e., hardwood timber). Still, Siranii can make enough money to buy a little meat for dinner. She tells me that the women in her village don't go away for work like the men. "What would I do?" she says. "We don't know the [Khmer] language properly, I don't know how to do anything, I don't have schooling. . . . I would be cheated or couldn't find any work." I was struck by how different Siranii's narrative was from the situation of Khmer women in Khang Cheung, where the garment industry's rise had propelled women into breadwinning roles as labor migrants.

In 2014, Siranii's son became ill with high fevers and died within a week. "I used to believe in the spirits," she said, "but they didn't help us. I took him to the traditional healer and it didn't help. I took him to the hospital but they couldn't do anything." Siranii thinks every day about health care. But she says her biggest worry is that the community will lose its forestland and the land they use for growing crops, because the nearby Vietnamese-owned rubber ELC is edging closer to her village: "I see that the Vietnamese company comes. Maybe next year, if they get my land, I'm not sure what we will do. I will try to ask the village chief and commune chief. I don't know anyone else to ask. I can't write; I don't have any connections. The government has the power. And the government and the company work together. . . . If the communal land is gone, maybe we will have to go to a different place."

The following day I met Siranii again at her home, a small hut near the village meetinghouse. She said that she does not have any title for her land, neither an individual nor a communal land title. When the student land surveyors came to her village, some people got individual land titles, but the surveyors left before she had a turn. "I think we need to wait for communal title anyway," she tells me. "That's what the village elders say. We are waiting for the government to recognize our communal land." Siranii's young children played outside as we talked. Siranii pointed at them and said:

> I don't know what to do if they get sick. I want a health center, a school, a good road, a land title. If I have an individual land title, then the company can't take the land, and I can leave it for my children, and then if they need money they can sell it. But I don't want individual land title, because I want land for my children and their children, and I want to keep our culture. If we have communal land, we can still have wood to build houses and land for agriculture. But we are still waiting for the communal land title. The government doesn't see us.

Siranii's ambivalence over the value of communal and individual land title was something I heard from others in her village, and in other areas of Khang Leit, as people implored the government to see them and recognize their communal land claims. People told me the government didn't care about them and their cultural claims to communal land. Even if they felt that individual land title disrupted cultural practices and identities, some indigenous people felt they had little choice but to accept individual title or lose their land.

Conclusion: Abandonment

What Puu Tanak, Srey Sophorn, and Siranii share with many others I interviewed is a sense of injustice because state promises of prosperity and protection are unfulfilled; they feel that the government has abandoned them. In this chapter, I have developed a view of Cambodia's postconflict capitalist development from the ground to show how contemporary state-making projects articulate with sedimented histories and political ecologies. People's sense of fear and uncertainty emerges from histories of colonial rule, genocide, and civil conflict layered with contemporary state repression and violent extractive development. The stories in this chapter reveal an ambivalent desire for the potentiality of state-led development and gratitude to the government for delivering the country from war, while also lamenting what is being lost in the contemporary political economy, at times revealing deep anger toward the state. The new economy of garment factories, high-rise construction, and international mobility has blurred the boundaries of rural and urban communities as the sons and daughters of farmers become low-wage urban workers, and this has contributed to a shifting politics in the countryside. Rural people's desire—and expectations—for development grows as they see others in their community benefiting from the new economy and hear stories about luxurious urban lifestyles. But for those struggling to survive on low urban wages and a depleting land base, they see a government that has abandoned them and a community that is ever-more unequal and unsupportive. As fences and fines take the place of cattle and trees, this incurs a violent ontological shift in people's understanding of land as one's home and community.

When I asked people what made them most insecure, people across Khang Cheung and Khang Leit talked about poverty, land grabbing, floods, and droughts; people in Khang Leit spoke about food insecurity and the lack of access to health care and education. These myriad insecurities feed into each other and multiply over time. One woman in Khang Cheung explained her livelihood problems: "My family used to do logging but we have stopped now. The authorities fine us if we get logs. The people from outside have taken the land; there are fences everywhere now.

There is no space for the cattle. They suppress us. Everything we try to do, they stop us. People here just want to die. The rich people (*nayk thom*) can go into the forest but we can't go anywhere." The anger and desperation this woman expresses ("people just want to die") emerge from the threat of having one's land and access to forest livelihoods taken away, as well as from the visible inequalities in wealth within the village. For this woman, as for many people I encountered in land-conflict areas, everyday life is imbued with a sense of being gradually displaced.

My experiences conducting fieldwork in Khang Leit forced me to reflect on the fear I sensed in the field. I abandoned two field sites in Khang Leit after police and state officials intimidated my team and our research participants. In one case, a high-ranking police officer stopped me and escorted me back to his office, where he waved away the various letters and permission documents I had secured. "You can conduct your research," he shrugged, "but I can't guarantee your safety." He then marked areas on a map where he could provide protection. All of these were villages far from land concessions and seemed irrelevant for my study. I vividly remember the police chief standing up from his desk and stabbing his pen at the village we had hoped to visit. "That area," he said, standing over me and speaking in a low, slow voice, "that area is very dangerous. I don't know what could happen to you if you go there." I felt suddenly nauseous and retreated outside the police station, where my colleagues and I debated what to do. Exactly what line we were transgressing (or could transgress) was not clear to any of us. Perhaps we could have proceeded to our field site anyway. After all, he hadn't banned us from conducting research. But his warning had a sinister tone; none of us wanted to find out what "very dangerous" might mean. We decided to abandon the field site.

One striking aspect of this experience is the role local state officials play in enacting the state's potentiality. I had many encounters with officials, like this police chief, who subtly threatened me or put roadblocks in my way without fully banning me from conducting research. While other postsocialist states in the region have formalized procedures for research permission (Turner 2013), Cambodia has no clearly outlined procedure for noncitizens to conduct research. On the ground, this flexibility means that field access must be continually negotiated, with the implication that power is personalized in the hands of local chiefs and police. In rural areas, local officials also play a pivotal role in securing people's access to, or exclusion from, state services and land. In the following chapter, I examine the relationships between local state officials and their constituencies as they played out during the Order 01 land reform. I show how the land titling reform worked to wrest power away from local-level officials and into the hands of the central government and how this effort was resisted and subverted, with sometimes surprising results.

3
RECONFIGURING LOCAL AUTHORITY THROUGH LAND REFORM

The Community Forest Patrol

In rural Cambodia, the state is personified in the form of the village chief and the commune chief. If people have a problem, they turn to their local authorities. But these same figures are often part of the state-business-military nexus that controls land in upland areas. This presents a fundamental bind for local land claimants: village-level officials are often people's only connection to government, and it is in people's interests to have good relations with their village chiefs, even if they suspect that the officials are involved in land grabbing. The poorly paid local officials are also in a bind: even if they idealistically seek to curb land grabbing and corruption, they are expected to supplement their salaries with informal revenue gathering (particularly through land deals) and to pass benefits up to higher-level officials to secure promotions and accrue personal wealth. This results in an uneasy relationship in which rural people can never be sure whether their local authorities are on their side or not. I felt this uneasiness myself when I accompanied a community forest committee on a forestry patrol.

When I volunteered to join the weekly forest patrol, I expected to see forest. But the community forest in Phnom Mie is mostly shrubland, marked with an unassuming sign (figure 5). Our small group—three members of the community forest committee, the village chief, and I—hiked for an hour to the observation tower. I climbed the rickety wooden ladder, notebook and camera in hand, trying not to look down at the ground below, and we all sat cross-legged on the floor of the observation tower. The head of the forest committee, Men Somning, pointed

FIGURE 5. Poorly marked community forest.

(Photo: Alice Beban.)

to several patches of scorched, illegally cleared forest around us. "What we need is money from an NGO to get lighting," he said. "We need lighting and a car battery to power the lights, and then people won't be able to sneak in here and cut down the trees." The man on the other side of me nodded and said, "Yes, and we need a better tower. This one wobbles. We need better foundations for the tower; then we can sleep up here and see everything." Another man chimed in, "And we need a camera to have evidence of who is coming in. Like your one," he added, pointing at my digital camera. The others nodded in agreement. Then they all looked expectantly at the village chief. "Well," said the village chief, "we need to find out who cleared the land and who gave them permission to do it." He stood up as he spoke and I could feel the tower shake. "I will find out which village or commune chief gave permission. I will explain to them they can't just let people clear the community forest. I will think of ways to change their mind."

We continued on with our forest patrol, carefully walking the perimeter of each cleared area and using my phone to take GPS points and photos of the burned land. I headed back to Men Somning's house after assuring the group that I would have the photos processed. The village chief reiterated his promise to find the culprits. On the way back to Men Somning's house on his motorbike, Men Somning turned to me and said into the wind, so that I barely heard, "He won't do it, you know." He was referring to the village chief who had spoken valiantly about finding the person responsible for clearing the community forest. "He's with them.... He's all part of it," Men Somning continued. "He and the district chief and others. I think they're all in it together." I was confused. I knew the village chief well; I had interviewed him several times and my family even had a meal with his family. I remember him talking passionately about his commitment to his community. Indeed, he had been instrumental in helping to establish a community forest in the area. But Men Somning was adamant. We have to find another way, he told me.

Two months later, I returned to the observation tower. Men Somning had called me to let me know he was planning something. I saw new, sturdy wooden boards on the side of the tower and a bright red flag emblazoned with the logo of an environmental NGO (figure 6). A crowd of around eighty people waited below the tower.

A cart pulled up and five monks in bright orange robes emerged from the back. Men Somning handed around scarves made from the same orange material as the monks' robes, and we took turns tying the scarves around trees, while the monks lit incense and chanted (figure 7). Nothing more was said about the previous plan to find the people who were clearing the trees; the village chief had done nothing. The new strategy was to put a curse on the culprits, as Men Somning explained to me. "Even if we don't see them do it, they will be scared because they could have a car accident; something bad could happen to them."

These two performances—the community forest patrol and the tree ordination ceremony—both attempted to bring to light the shadowy work of those who are clearing forestland and those who granted them authority to do so in a pro-

FIGURE 6. Renovated observation tower in the community forest.

(Photo: Alice Beban.)

FIGURE 7. Monks chant at the tree ordination ceremony.

(Photo: Alice Beban.)

tected area. The first strategy was to literally illuminate the people cutting down the trees with lights, a camera, and an observation tower and to call on the village chief to intervene. When this failed, the second strategy used another form of intervention parallel to political power—spiritual power—suggesting that the spirits have an ability to see, and punish, immoral acts in ways that human observers cannot. These strategies were both employed to protect an area of shrubland and small trees for which *forest* is a very generous descriptor, particularly in comparison to the broad expanse of state-owned forest on the hills in the distance. Yet, donor agencies have poured money into this community forest and others like it.

I recount this story of the community forest patrol to draw attention to the complex relationships between local state officials and rural Cambodians. My confusion when Men Somning whispered that the village chief was implicated in the logging network was a feeling I had frequently during my fieldwork. The problem, as I quickly discovered, was that powerful people maintained secrecy over their actions in order to produce uncertainty over who was involved in land grab networks. Were the local authorities in this area involved in land grabbing? Were they helping villagers to fight against it? Were they impotent to do either? Sometimes subjects' positions seemed to change from day to day.

I found myself sized up by others in this way too. Rumor, secrecy, fearful glances, whispered declarations on the back of a motorbike—these are constitutive of everyday life for communities in and around areas of land conflict. Even those who were pretty sure they knew what was happening were often too fearful to report land grabbing, or they were faced with the problem that the very person to whom they might report such a crime—the village or commune chief—was likely involved. In this way, as I described in the research dialogue meeting where people's silences produced the state official's authority (chapter 2), certain things cannot be fully known or acknowledged, even if they are suspected and transmitted through gossip and rumor (Mathews 2011). The story of Men Somning's attempts to bring people to justice suggests that the lights and cameras donated by NGOs (and researchers) may do little if people's uncertainty is produced by fear and powerlessness. Andrew Mathews (2011) draws from his work on Mexican forest reform to term this inability to fully acknowledge state corruption a "public ignorance," wherein certain things cannot be seen or acknowledged, and therefore they remain invisible, protected from any public exposure and from censure by higher levels of political power.

In this chapter, I explore how the complex relationships between local authorities and rural people were reconfigured through land reform. The leopard skin land reform can be seen in part as the prime minister's attempt to wrest control over land distribution from local authorities in upland areas. In the face of growing protests over government corruption, Hun Sen presented himself as the country's benevolent leader by mobilizing student volunteers (rather than just government officials) to survey land. This allowed him to claim that he minimized corruption and to place blame for any further land conflict on local officials. But land reform is shaped by power tussles between local and central authorities. Local officials balked at the erosion of their control over resources and the idea that they were "considered inferior by the Prime Minister" (Kelsall and Kimchoeun 2014), and many local officials sought to use the reform to their own advantage. I detail the ways local officials and other elites managed to amass land and avoid direct confrontation with Hun Sen's student volunteers by clearing forest in expectation of the land reform and distribute land and money to loyal people in their constituencies to quell dissent. I explore these practices of "anticipatory land grabs" theoretically in collaborative writing in Work and Beban (2016); similar processes of the elite capture of land reform by local officials have also been noted in Southern Africa and South Asia (Jacobs 2009b).

But land reform does not have inherent qualities that produce homogenous effects; it is vested with particular dynamics depending on the balance of forces in any given place and time. Local officials' ability to benefit from the land reform was dependent on their access to patronage networks, forestland, and financial resources, as well as their relationships with local communities. In some areas, local people mobilized with the support of local officials to prevent elite capture of the reform. These diverse outcomes suggest the possibility of different forms of state-society relations that are not bound to neopatrimonial politics.

Relations between Local Officials and Land Claimants

When power flows through patronage networks, it makes any simple analytical separation between local and central state officials difficult, indeed misleading. Lower-level state officials in Cambodia eke out a living on low salaries (one village chief forlornly told me he makes "hardly enough to survive on"), and most opportunistically supplement their formal salaries by taking informal payments for services (such as signing documentation) and exercising discretion over land allocation through a proliferation of local modes of formal and informal land governance that is "quite at odds with the simplified and singular formality of land titling" (Dwyer 2015). It is pointless to entirely blame local officials for corruption, though; as Evans (1995, 40) puts it, "Personalism and plundering at the top destroys any possibility of rule-governed behavior in the lower levels of the bureaucracy." Hun Sen and the broader CPP depend on local officials to maintain control and party loyalty at the village level. This poses problems for the prime minister. On the one hand, he must maintain local officials' loyalty by allowing them latitude for enrichment through some control over natural resources, a portion of which they are expected to pass up the string to higher officials. On the other hand, local officials are problematic if they are overzealous and keep too much for themselves.

Lower-level officials are therefore "at the margins of the state but far from marginal" (Maclean 2013, 28). For the majority of rural people, the village chief is the most important node of access to state power (Ledgerwood and Vijghen 2002). In a 2011 study, for example, 81 percent of respondents said the village chief was the most powerful person in their village; this figure had increased from 33 percent in 2005 (Ojendal and Sedara 2011). The study's authors argue that this shows a "de-democratization," that is, a strengthening of authority in the person of the village chief. I suggest that this result is related to the increased inequality in rural areas. As villages become more divided between a small number of people who control land, resources, and external connections and a large number of people who find themselves excluded from patronage networks, local officials may be people's only link to higher authorities with greater resources and power (Hughes 2013). Decentralization (enacted with commune elections in 2002) has increased people's dependence on local officials, as officials' signatures are required for the basic documents—birth certificate, ID card, family book—that allow access to education, factory work, and migrant job opportunities (Eng 2013). Local officials also adjudicate in family grievances and land disputes. In this way, local officials have assumed much greater responsibility over everyday bureaucratic processes.

Local officials' ability to secure land and resources (either for themselves or for their constituencies) depends on their position within *khsae* networks. Village officials connected with military or politico-business networks command the ability to amass land and distribute it through their networks or to advocate on behalf of dispossessed villagers, while local officials who lack political connections, capital, or jurisdictional control over forests and concession land may themselves be alienated from circuits of official knowledge (Diepart and Dupuis 2014). The rise of opposition party (CNRP) officials created new networks for people in some areas to press their claims, but my study villages were all CPP-controlled, and the lone CNRP commune chief in the district was sidelined in meetings with higher officials.

These differences in officials' power and subjectivities create a pervasive sense of uncertainty for rural people, as people simply do not know whose side the local authorities are on or whether the local chief has the power to enact change. Village rumors frequently revolve around the characterization of various officials. Villagers repeatedly told me that some chiefs were crooked (*koit*, literally "broken"), as they "do not think about us at all; [they] just give land to people in [their] networks," and "People talk all about the foreign companies but look in this village: it's the local authorities!" Other chiefs were characterized as well-meaning but lacking the political networks necessary to help villagers. In an area where a military unit had confiscated half the village land for "training purposes" and blocked villagers from accessing their rice fields, one woman sitting with her two preschool-age children told me despairingly, "The village chief helps us but doesn't have much power. If we die, then the village chief will die too." She meant, I think, that local authorities without connections could do little in the face of military units that are connected with the powerful political elite, including Hun Sen himself. The village chief in this woman's village told me he had contacted land rights NGOs and even opposition party politicians to ask for support, but no one would touch the case due to the military's involvement.

Villagers said the potency of local officials' power was connected to their military connections, their age, and the land resources they controlled, as well as their familial connections with higher authorities. But some people told me it was impossible to tell which chiefs would or wouldn't be crooked. Srey Sophorn explained that it is hard because "it's a problem with the system":

> SREY SOPHORN: When we talked to one of the village chiefs, an old village chief, he told us that they literally put a gun to his head to make him sign [the property deals]. And when the new village chief came, he said the old village chief had done the signing, not him.
>
> ALICE: Are the older village chiefs more crooked than the younger ones?

SREY SOPHORN: No, I don't think it's any different. Sometimes the young authorities can be worse, because they want to rise up the ladder very fast. They have studied, they know a lot, so if they want to be crooked, they can do it very well.
ALICE: Are there any authorities that are in places with lots of forest that don't sell land?
SREY SOPHORN: It's hard, because it's a problem with the system. Maybe there are some, but I don't know. . . . In general, it's difficult. And they make the laws to protect the people with power.

For Srey Sophorn, it was difficult to imagine a situation in which a village chief in a resource-rich area would not be corrupt. But in her analysis, the fault lay with the wider system of upward accountability through *khsae* networks, which meant guns could be put to village chiefs' heads to enact land grabs.

The village chiefs themselves are often supportive (at least outwardly) of villagers' land claims, and some go to considerable efforts to take local complaints to higher authorities who may be able to help. Local officials frequently asked for my help and shared concerns about social problems in their communities. Commune officials in both Khang Cheung and Khang Leit dared to stand up to complain about land grabbing to ministry representatives at the roundtable meetings I held. The difficulty for rural people is that they are never sure whether this support is genuine or not, and the uncertainty over others' positions makes resistance difficult, as one farmer in his fifties described to me: "The commune chief and village chief help us. The commune chief supports the company too. When we have a meeting, the village and commune chief don't dare show their faces. They hide in the shadows. The real power comes from the higher authorities. When we need something signed, the commune chief helps, but he is two-faced." As this farmer notes, even the local chiefs that support the community are potentially two-faced, as they temper their support for their constituencies (who are also their family and neighbors) with their obligations to higher-level officials and other patrons.

Villagers' dependent yet uncertain relationship with local officials explains in large part why the majority of rural land titleholders do not officially register land transfers (which renders the national registry completely out of step with realities on the ground) but instead ask local officials to sign informal letters of land transfer (So 2009). Given the importance of relations with local officials, it makes sense for people to show their loyalty to local officials by making informal payments for state services rather than accessing distant provincial land offices (Hughes 2013). Furthermore, for many local people, these local agents of the state are their first—and often only—avenue for support when they face a land dispute.

CHAPTER 3

To understand people's support networks, I included a question in my survey asking people who had experienced a land dispute to note down everyone they went to for help; results are given in figure 8.

The results show the striking numbers of people who depended on local authorities to assist them when they had a land dispute. More than half of the respondents (51 percent women and 58 percent men) said they asked the village chief for help, and more than half of male respondents asked the commune chief for help (38 percent women and 52 percent men). Some men also accessed higher authorities (district, provincial, and Phnom Penh). Women were less likely to access higher authorities, including the cadastral commission, which was set up to arbitrate land disputes, and many people depended on talking with family and friends, settled the dispute informally, or did nothing.

It is worth calling out another peculiarity in this chart: the court—the place where many of us might imagine taking a land dispute if it progressed beyond

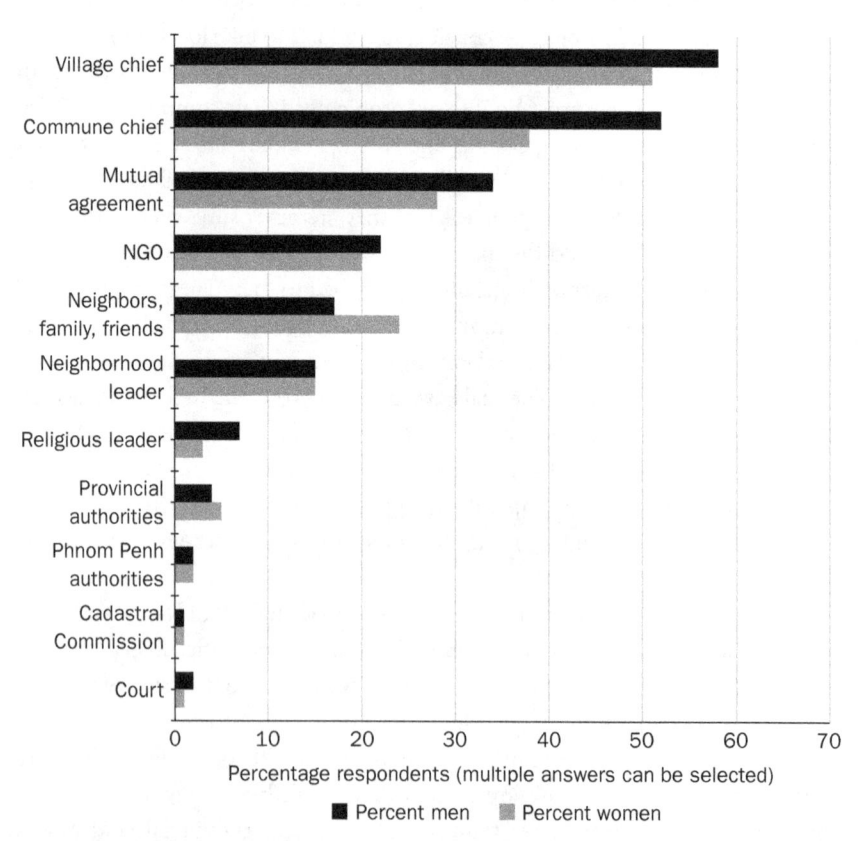

FIGURE 8. Who did you go to for help with your land dispute?

(Source: Alice Beban.)

the level of mutual agreement—is conspicuous in its almost complete absence. The law is seen as an impersonal, distant mode of government, and for poor rural people, it makes much more sense to invest in personal relationships with local authorities who may be able to protect them by connecting them with powerful patrons that can help with land claims. Caroline Hughes (2013) suggests that "even a clean and efficient cadastral court would be a second-best ally, since it cannot usher [the rural poor] into a wider world of patronage, protection and inclusion." Furthermore, most rural people see law as something used to suppress rather than as a potential mode of emancipation. Villagers are unlikely to take a case to court when a company encroaches on their land, but they may be subject to court proceedings if they exercise their rights on land claimed by concessionaires. This was the case even for those who received land titles. When I asked people facing land disputes whether they could go to court now that they had land title, many said that only those who have education and political networks can wield the law. As a woman activist told me, "some know that this land is really their land, but when they are told that the land isn't theirs, they are threatened by the authorities, they are not brave enough (*ot hien*) to protest. And the people who know about the law—the authorities, the people who come from far away to buy land—they suppress the villagers."

The court in Cambodia is reminiscent of Holston's (1991, 708) description of the Brazilian court, where elites launch bureaucratic maneuvers to tie up conflicts and use their power to control the juridical process. Even when people do try to take their cases to court, they are saddled with legal fees, and cases are rarely resolved. For example, of 157 land dispute cases involving agricultural land taken to Cambodian courts in 2013, only 29 percent of cases were partly resolved, compared to 42 percent of cases for residential land (NGO Forum, cited in Oldenburg and Neef 2014, 49). This indicates that courts are less likely to process complaints or lawsuits involving concessionaires. In this way, law in Cambodia is not separate from extralegal corrupt maneuvers but is implicated in the production of uncertainty.

Local officials themselves can also be censured through the use of law and discourses of anticorruption when Hun Sen deems it politically necessary. During the land reform, the prime minister reacted to angry, dispossessed farmers who brandished their land title documents outside his residence in Phnom Penh by accusing provincial officials of corruption.[1] Three local officials were charged with bribing the student volunteer surveyors, with images of their arrest splashed around national TV amid performative warnings from the prime minister to stay in line. Local officials therefore enjoy some flexibility to assert claims, but they may be subject to political censure if they go too far. In this context, local authorities' strategies to accumulate land and political control through Order 01 stayed away (for the most part) from the overt use of physical force, which might attract central state censure, and relied on the subtler processes of exclusion, coercion, capital, and political connections.

Local Authorities' Practices of Land Grabbing during the Order 01 Reform

With local officials' and other elites' authority to allocate land circumscribed by the presence of Hun Sen's volunteer student surveyors, stories abounded of their sidestepping the land reform. Officials in one of my study villages designated social land concessions (SLCs) to provide land for poor people in forest areas and then claimed this land for themselves. In another village, officials divided community forestland and persuaded the student volunteers to survey the land for them and their kin networks and political supporters. Some officials waited until the volunteers left and then redrew land boundaries or bought up land from land claimants in collaboration with higher authorities. Some officials with less access to powerful patronage networks worked alone to secretly clear and claim land before the survey teams arrived. But it was not only local officials who tried to use the land reform to their advantage. The requirement in Order 01 that land be cultivated led to a rush to clear forested areas before the survey teams arrived (Work and Beban 2016); in some villages where the word got out that the student volunteers were coming, all kinds of people rushed to clear the land. This was difficult, however, for poor households with few financial resources or little available labor, as one woman farmer with young children noted: "We were using the land a little, but not all of it, because we didn't have money to clear it. What if they don't measure the land that people use for growing? What will the people do without land to give to their children?" This statement reflects notions of what land is that are very different from Cambodian state policy and development agency discourse. For the state and donors, land is an input of production and political power; for smallholders, land is a source of household food, livelihood, and future well-being that people can claim and wait to clear until they need it and have the labor available. Order 01 revealed that many villagers with claims to unproductive forestland lacked the resources to either clear or cultivate their holdings. Those with large families or money or both could clear much more land than those without such resources, and the former already had larger holdings when Order 01 was announced. Villagers' primary concern was that they would lose land that remained uncleared.

Well-connected commune authorities and wealthy members of the village elite were also concerned when the students came. But the officials' question was not

"How can I clear my land?" but "How much land can I clear?" In one village, the village chief, commune council members, and other elite who knew about the campaign hired machinery to clear tracts of forest near the village before the students' arrival and put in boundary-marker sticks to cement their claims. It is difficult to understand precisely how much land local officials accumulated in anticipation of the land survey, or how many village- and commune-level elite were connected to higher levels of power, because maps and titles were not made public. My survey questions on land sales were also difficult to interpret, as many people were too afraid to talk openly in the context of a survey form about how they, or others they knew, were involved in land deals.

However, as I built longer-term relationships, people began to talk more openly. Land brokers (local people who buy up land on behalf of urban land buyers) were a rich source of information. I came to know well one land broker in Srai Saat commune. A weather-beaten man in his sixties named Lok Toeurn, he called me to his house one day to show me a map he said he had obtained from a contact within the Ministry of Land. I sat at a wooden table under Lok Toeurn's modest tin-roof house while he leafed through a plastic folder containing a pile of land documents to retrieve the tattered map. He carefully unfolded the large, A3-size paper and handed it to me, asking me if I could photograph the map in order to copy and plasticize it so that he could take it with him in the rain when he went to inspect land plots for purchase. As I inspected the map, I realized that it clearly showed the ways that particular powerful officials had benefited from the land reform. It also presented me with an ethical dilemma: whether to discuss data that was obtained under dubious circumstances and then given to me by a trusting informant for a different purpose. Given that state secrecy meant I was unlikely to obtain such information any other way, and since I am more interested in the general story the map tells rather than its links to specific individuals, I decided to tell the story of the map here, minus any identifying characteristics that could connect names or places.

The map depicted an area of approximately 300 hectares of former forest- and shrubland that lay between the edge of village cropland and the mountain range to the west of the village. This area is far from established roads and settlements, and villagers I spoke with said the land was considered communal land before the land reform, with no known private claims. Some families who were new to the area had attempted to clear part of the land by hand in the mid-2000s to cultivate rice, cassava, and mango, but the crops had died due to the poor soil ecology. Most people considered the area too far from the village to farm; local people used the land for grazing cattle, planting upland rice nurseries, collecting firewood, and gathering fungi and fruit. The map (which, according to Lok Toeurn, was generated from the Ministry of Land database after the land reform) showed that this former communal area had been divided into more than sixty individually titled land plots, a maze of geometric shapes with typed names indicating the owners of the plots. Overlaying this neat arrangement of lines and names, Lok Toeurn had made numerous handwritten additions to reflect the dynamics of land control that he saw on the ground: names were struck out, new names were written in pen, yellow highlights marked plots that the concession company had purchased, and orange highlights marked plots Lok Toeurn hoped to accumulate on behalf of investors.

The map told me two conspicuous stories. First, it gave weight to people's complaints that communal forest areas had been carved up during the land reform. Of fifty-eight named plots on the map, forty-three were typed, suggesting that the names were generated from the survey records at the Land Ministry. These typed names are likely for land plots that people claimed and cleared quickly before the Order 01 survey teams arrived, given that this area was under forest cover before the announcement of Order 01 and had no private claims that villagers knew about. The other names were scrawled in pen onto unnamed plots, or written over typed names, indicating that these plots were likely bought or grabbed after the survey teams had officially recorded land claims. Second, the map tells a story of elite capture. While the land reform policy prescribed a maximum 5 hectares land per person, I noticed that four names repeated again and again across the plots. In fact, of the fifty-eight named plots, forty were titled out to just four names. I later asked Puu Tanak and other friends whether they knew these names, and I found out that all four of these belonged to government officials at the commune, district, and provincial levels in Khang Cheung province. This distribution of former forestland to a handful of officials reveals the extent to which people with political connections benefited from the land reform in Khang Cheung.

While it was impossible for me to decipher the exact terms of the political economy of land distribution with officials and other elites during Order 01, it was clear that officials who had links to higher levels of patronage networks gained financially through their roles in land grabbing during the land reform. Lok Toeurn, the land broker, said that forestland claimed by local officials in connection with higher-level authorities was then titled in the names of higher officials or sold to the "Chinese company." He pointed out yellow highlights on the map and told me these were land parcels the concession company had purchased after the land survey. Seven of the eight plots highlighted yellow were large plots in the name of a single official. According to Lok Toeurn, the local authorities retained around US$20–$100 per hectare when they sold this land, depending on the land quality and sale price. Higher-level authorities also received a cut of the proceeds. In some cases, he said, local officials received a portion of the land to keep for themselves in place of financial benefits.

Others from the commune corroborated the information from the land broker's map. For example, Lok Tiim, a man in his sixties with whom I spent several afternoons drinking pots of strong coffee (with copious amounts of sweetened condensed milk) at the local coffee shop, leaned across the table one day and told me in a conspiratorial whisper that he was a former spy from the civil war period. He fought for government troops in the early 1970s and was dispatched to infiltrate Khmer Rouge platoons and assassinate troublemakers. This training, he proclaimed, made him a good observer, and he knew everything that was going on with land in the commune:

> The people with a lot of land here are the powerful people; there are more than ten people with large land areas, around 10 hectares or more each. Those are the people with money and power, the officials and the businessmen and military men from this commune. They already had land and they got more with the land titling, because they went and got all the forestland and claimed it for their own. Then there are the ones from outside who come to buy land, maybe thirty people or more, that have plots of up to 10 or 20 hectares. So there are hundreds of hectares in the hands of these big landowners.

Lok Tiim's claims about the numbers of large land claimants in the commune are greater than the land broker's map I discussed above, which covers only one village. However, they match well with my own observations from driving a motorbike around the foothills of the commune, where I observed many freshly planted mango, rubber, and cassava fields in the wake of the reform. These fields, which were forests before the land reform, had been quickly cleared and planted with cash crops.

This kind of elite capture was enabled in part by the control of information before the student volunteers' arrival. Local officials had access both to the changing guidelines for the implementation of Order 01 and to the powerful elites determined to take advantage of the results of the campaign. As one man complained to me, "The people in the village didn't know that the students were going to measure the forestland; they just knew about the measurement of the village land. So we couldn't go out and get a lot of forestland, but other people that knew, people that came from far away, they went and got a lot of forestland before the students came."

Not all local authorities benefited from the land reform, however. Those who lacked the resources (money or *khsae* networks with officials/elites who had the resources to clear land) were angry about the way they were sidelined and about the land grabbing in their villages. One village chief told me that all the forestland around the village was parceled out to the elite from the larger provincial town; "the land measurement has no justice." Another village chief agreed that the campaign had the effect of strengthening land control in the hands of the powerful: "The measurement is not about the company here; it's about the powerful people. If they just took the land maybe we could fight, but now they have the title too, so we can't do anything. They have the rights. They have the signatures of three ministries."

Similar land rushes occurred throughout the area, although they varied considerably with the situation of villagers and the strategies of local authorities. In one village, a woman who owns a small shop on the main road told me that local authorities held a meeting before the students arrived and offered forestland to some people in the community if they shared it with the authorities: "They gave the land to us before the students came. That is, they told some people they could go and clear the forest in a certain place. It wasn't everyone who went, only the people whose names got called by the village chief. Others were too afraid to go and cut when they didn't have their names called. They told us that if we cleared the land we could have it measured by the students when they came." It was not clear to me why certain people were selected to clear forestland with the authorities' blessing and others were not. One woman suggested that this depended on whether people were known supporters of the ruling party versus the opposition. The young village chief in this village justified his actions by telling me that he invited poor families to clear forestland before the students arrived so they would have "land for their future and our village would be better off." For him, the forest clearance was a village development strategy. I think he sensed my skepticism as we talked; he told me defensively that "it is the government's job to support rural villages, so we need to make sure the government policies help the people who need it in the village."

Beyond the attempts to make their claims legible to the coming survey team by grabbing and clearing forestland, local officials employed other strategies that used the survey and associated legal classifications as a cover to enact projects of accumulation at the local level. Recalling a planned SLC that was surveyed by the student volunteers but did not materialize, one man described how the landscape itself became illegible to him: "We were called to a meeting and drew lots for the social land concession land. I got a number and we saw the land; there was a stick with my number sticking in the soil. But then after the land survey when I went back to plant the land, there were no sticks, I couldn't find it. . . . I thought I was in the wrong place, but they told me that it's all been sold." A local activist drew a map to point out for me the SLC the man was talking about and complained that "this area was allocated to people before the land survey in lots of 1.25 hectares, but then it was sold off by the authorities. We didn't see any of it."

Many of the strategies to claim land were done in secret and completely excluded local villagers. In their discussions with me, land claimants often used the words "secretly" and "quietly" to describe officials' land allocations. A commune councilor representing the opposition party told me that the rest of the (ruling party–representative) council members held secret meetings to discuss the land reform and SLC plans without her; these processes are "done in secret; they wouldn't let the people go to see," she told me bitterly.

An Egg Can't Hit a Stone: Enrolling Villagers into Officials' Land Grabs

The authorities' strategies to maintain land control and accumulate land for themselves were not always secret from local people. In fact, villagers often went along with these schemes because of fear and a desire to maintain local relationships and to gain land and monetary payoffs. In four of five communes in which I spent time in Khang Cheung, powerful local players bypassed the official 5-hectares-per-household land limit in the land reform by offering money to villagers who would claim an area of forestland; in some villages, 50 to 75 percent of residents told me they received some money. The local elite then reportedly asked the villagers to thumbprint a deed of land sale and claimed ownership of the land for themselves. One smallholder rice farmer described these processes in his village:

> Before the students came, the authorities divided land that was designated as environmentally protected among the families, 5 hectares each. They said they would give them three hundred dollars [US] per plot to put their names on the title. They took copies of documents, so they have the correct name, identity card, and family information. So this is following the law; it is not illegal by the land law. They use the villagers as a step for their own benefit, all cooperating together among the village, district, and provincial wealthy people to get what they want.

Neither this man nor his neighbors who shared similar stories had any documentation for the land they described. They said that commune officials had the titles. They continued to wait, some hopeful that one day they may receive some money or land, others feeling hopeless. "I think it was a fake title," one woman lamented, while her neighbor said, "No, it was a sale certificate; it's because we can't read.... It said we would sell the land to them, and we signed it." I found that the payments people received for signing over land documents to the authorities varied widely: some families in the village received US$50–$100 of the promised US$300; others received nothing. The amount received did not appear to be clearly linked to people's kinship connections or political loyalty to the village authorities, although other villagers suggested that people who supported the opposition did not receive money.

Villagers justified their participation in these schemes by drawing my attention to their meager houses and lack of land and food. On one memorable afternoon, I sat with three middle-aged women who were weaving baskets in the shade. They spoke out in anger about the actions of officials:

> FIRST WOMAN: I don't have land now and I don't have anything to eat. One day, when I went out to cut grass, I heard the village chief say the land was being divided and we could get one hundred dollars [US]. I was so happy; I could make sure my children eat today. And then they didn't give the money. I went to see him; I wanted to hit him. He said, just wait awhile. And I went to see him again; he said another week. Another week, another week. And now there is no money.
>
> SECOND WOMAN: You wonder where your money has gone? Look at the village chief's new house. When they ask us to go and thumbprint something, I just do it. I didn't know what it was, couldn't read it.
>
> THIRD WOMAN: This bad stuff going on, Hun Sen doesn't know about this. When they give gifts, they don't give things to Sam Raimsy [opposition party leader] supporters. I got so mad, I couldn't go into the *wat* [temple] when they showed the land titles.

This conversation elucidates the difficult position that villagers find themselves in. Even if someone signs the papers proffered by the authorities, they may not get the money. They are then stuck—as the first woman is—furious at the village chief but resigned to wait endlessly, as she is a player in this scheme too and has no one else to turn to. Similarly, the third woman was palpably angry as she spoke, but she did not attend the land title display at the temple, which was officially an opportunity for land claimants to check the land survey and register appeals if the figures weren't right. She was so angry that she could not even bring herself to enter the temple. But she was not angry at Hun Sen directly. In her mind, the problems with Order 01 do not reflect badly on the prime minister as he "doesn't know about" the corrupt actions of local officials. This perception that the leader is benevolent and that crooked local chiefs are the problem is common among authoritarian regimes (O'Brien and Li 2006). Hun Sen and the CPP elite reproduce this sentiment by blaming corruption on wayward officials. For example, a government anticorruption unit set up with much fanfare has ignored high-level corruption and launched several politically motivated investigations against opposition parties and rights organizations (HRW 2017).

People who speak out about land grabbing to outside groups, such as opposition party representatives and NGOs, face threats, exclusion from state services and the spoils of development, or even physical retribution. In many cases, people worried that they would not get a land title or that their land title might be taken away from them if they spoke out. Some people were just happy to get something, even if only a small portion of their rice land was titled; even a small gift of partial land title represented the potential for protection and prosperity that a relationship with the state may grant. The Cambodian director of a local land rights NGO spoke bitterly about the ways that people couldn't see the land being taken around them because they were satisfied with their own small areas of land: "Before, the companies were too scared to come [here] because the people stood up to them. But with Order 01, people were happy to just get a little land and they forgot about the larger area of land outside their measurement; they didn't see what the village chiefs did. The village chiefs conspired with companies and rich people from outside to get that land. So the people are stupid; they are happy but they have lost their land in the long run. Order 01 is cruel."

People did indeed construe themselves as too "lazy," "stupid," or "not brave enough" to voice their complaints to other actors, as this NGO director suggested. People turned to me pleading for help in our conversations: "Please help us. I'm stupid; I'm just a farmer; I don't know what to do." One man asked me, "When will the students come back? Some people didn't get their land measured, because the people from the Ministry of Land said that it was too small, or had no shape. We didn't know where the people were from, the people measuring. We are stupid; we don't know much. And they never tell us anything. I guess we could go to the commune, but I'm too lazy (*kjil*)."

Although *kjil* is usually translated as "lazy," I don't think that's an accurate description. My research suggests that people's inaction does not emerge from laziness or stupidity; it emerges from fear and powerlessness. One woman who owned a local café shrugged her shoulders when I asked her why she didn't tell anyone about her land not being measured: "You know, an egg can't hit a stone. I know we won't win anyway, so why complain?" Some villagers imagined a day when the immoral acts of the officials would become public knowledge. One wiry man in his thirties gestured passionately as he told me, "They displayed the plots they had surveyed in the local temple after the survey, but when I went to see, it wasn't my name on the title. It was another name! But I couldn't do anything; I stayed quiet. Because even if I wanted to protest, where would I go? . . . I didn't say anything then; I bottled it up. But when they give out the titles, on that day, I am ready to kill someone. Everything will be made clear then, all the secrets of the authorities."

I never saw a day when "all the secrets of the authorities" were uncovered; at land title distribution ceremonies, most people were too fearful to speak out.

A Contrasting Case: Implementation of Order 01 in the Absence of Land Grabs?

One study village in Khang Cheung stood out for me due to the lack of elite land grabbing before and during the campaign, in contrast to surrounding villages (a case I discuss in detail in collaborative writing with Cambodian researchers Sokbunthoeun So and Kheang Un [Beban, So, and Un 2017]). In the village of Svay, in Phnom Mie commune, people told me they had few problems with corrupt and inequitable implementation during Order 01. One key reason for this difference is the geographic location. Svay is a long-settled area, and therefore land claims may be less contentious than in Srai Saat commune with its recently settled villages at the edge of the forest. Beyond this, however, conditions in this village and surrounding villages in the commune (and neighboring Srai Saat commune) were similar; all have extensive forest cover, and all share a history of conflict with the Pheapimex ELC. I believe that in Svay village, more equitable processes of land registration and distribution were due to strong community networks that had built up long-term relationships with key people in local government, informed community members about correct processes, and monitored the survey teams implementing the reform.

Although the strength of the community network has ebbed and flowed over time in Phnom Mie, the network is stronger here than in surrounding communes, due in large part to the efforts of local women who emerged as community leaders during the first wave of land activism in the early 2000s. At that time, Green Cambodia director Ming Tam deliberately recruited women when she worked with villagers to organize resistance to ELC expansion. Ming Tam told me that women are strong leaders in the network because they are "committed to the land. It is their family, their children's land, their whole life, so sometimes they are thinking about the land and not just thinking about making money." Other people echoed this idea that men are more likely to sell out and join land-grabbing networks, while women are more likely to think of the collective. I met several male community network leaders who appeared to be incredibly committed to their communities, such as Men Somning. But even Men Somning explained to me that he thinks the network needs women leaders because "women are stronger than men. . . . They don't think about fighting but about talking and being patient so they can have relationships with the community and with the authorities." This gendered construction of women as less violent and therefore more suitable as protest leaders is also noted in research on the emergence of women leaders in urban protests at Boeung Kak lake (Kent 2014) and in international areas as diverse as Israel and Nigeria (Sasson-Levy and Rapoport 2003; Ukeje 2004). In Khang Cheung, this construction of women as peaceable bodies is linked with the notion that women's exclusion from political spheres of power makes them more suitable community leaders, precisely because they are more likely to think of caring for children and the common good rather than personal gain.

The women leaders in this commune may have garnered respect from villagers because of their gendered subjectivities as peaceable, trustful community members, but their success in maintaining solidarity is due to the effort they put into the community network. Srey Sophorn and women community representatives from the other five villages in the commune meet most weeks to discuss land issues, and they hold monthly meetings in each village to spread information among villagers. While many people in the area migrate for work, these women leaders live full-time in their villages, and while none of these women are wealthy, all are from households that have access to enough land, livestock, and labor to maintain a living while also finding time to support their communities. Furthermore, the network in Phnom Mie has benefited from other NGO initiatives that bring groups of people together within the community, including a youth group, women's group, vegetable sellers collective, and community rice bank. The women leaders of the network are active in these smaller groups (often leading the groups and earning small per diem payments for attending trainings and facilitating meetings), and they use group meetings to talk about land issues and maintain connections with the community. My survey responses show how active the community network is in Phnom Mie. Similar numbers of people were aware of the community network in Srai Saat (46 percent) and Phnom Mie (47 percent), but in Phnom Mie, almost three-quarters (73 percent) of these people said they always go to meetings, and 96 percent said the network was useful. In Srai Saat, less than half of the respondents (47 percent) said they always attend meetings, and only 52 percent said the network was useful.

The women leaders in Phnom Mie have established relationships of respect with local officials in several villages. The commune chief in Phnom Mie regularly holds meetings in each village, and at these forums I was struck by the way in which villagers spoke up about their concerns, and officials listened and responded. In village meetings I attended elsewhere, government officials spent the majority of the meeting talking, while the audience sat in silence. (In one meeting in Srai Saat commune, a community activist took the microphone to pose a question about the land conflict, and the commune clerk jerked the microphone out of his hand and carried it back to the stage.) The village chief in Svay village, in particular, worked closely with community network leaders to support villagers and warn people about the risks of selling land for short-term cash gain.

During Order 01, the network in Phnom Mie used its contacts among villagers to spread information about the land survey before the survey teams arrived. Srey Sophorn told me that she first heard about the planned land survey from the Phnom Mie commune chief; she then met with community network leaders from the neighboring province (where the land reform had already been carried out): "When we met, the volunteers had already surveyed the land [in the neighboring province]. And the [network leaders there] told us that the authorities and companies grabbed land, and the students and authorities snuck off to measure land in secret. We got worried because the [NGO staff] who help us said they could not do anything during the survey, because the prime minister banned NGOs from being involved. So it was up to us to make sure we knew what was happening, and we informed all the villagers before the volunteers arrived."

Srey Sophorn and other community leaders from Phnom Mie commune agreed to go door-to-door to tell their communities about the land reform before the surveyors arrived. The network leaders also called on their village chiefs as well as the commune chief to ask for more information about what was planned and to request that the authorities assist the villagers during the land reform. Then the network leaders drew up schedules for monitoring the survey, with one or two representatives from the community network volunteering to follow the land survey teams each day and assist land claimants. In Svay, the community network was particularly successful at organizing a roster to accompany the measurement teams at all times during the implementation of Order 01 to encourage transparency in the process. As one farmer in his fifties explained, "[Community organizers] told us all about it before the students came. . . . They made a plan for who would follow the students and the land ministry people, and we had all the documents ready and waited at our land. The survey team was happy because the network knows more about whose land is whose than anyone else! We got all our land measured."

Srey Sophorn said that this plan of monitoring the survey worked better in some villages than others: "In some places we could have done better, because people put their names down to watch the survey but then they couldn't go. Or when we came on our motorbikes, the [survey team would] drive off to a different area. But we could still be there to help people. When the students went around, it was a group with the village chief and commune office people, and the Department of Land people, and they asked us questions about the land because we know the area."

Although Srey Sophorn noted that the community network's strategy of monitoring the survey was not always successful, my interviews with people in the commune (and particularly in Svay village) revealed that villagers in Phnom Mie reported less elite capture of the reform. Land claimants in Svay village mentioned land grabs or corruption during the land reform in only three interviews (out of thirty-four); at less than 10 percent of interviewees, this is much lower than surrounding villages in Phnom Mie and Srai Saat communes, in which approximately seventy people (out of seventy-eight interviews) discussed issues with corruption during the reform. I suggest this can be explained in part by the established relationships that people in this village have with local authorities. Several people described the local authorities as scared of the community network, which was something that I rarely heard in other areas. One woman told me: "I think it is different here because the authorities are scared of us. . . . They know that we are respected. When the students came, there were some problems and some people with more connections got more land, but not like other places. . . . Only a couple of people didn't get their land measured here."

It is worth dwelling on this woman's account to pull out the ways in which this narrative departs from other people's depictions of state-society relations at the village level. Many people I interviewed in Khang Cheung (particularly in Srai Saat commune) were either fearful of local authorities, uncertain about their intentions, or scathing of their inability to protect villagers' interests (as my previous discussion about the two-faced chief highlights). But in Svay village, several people used phrases such as "they respect us," "they listen to us," "they are scared of us," or even "they know we can kill them" (this last spoken by two women in their sixties who took part in protests against the Pheapimex concession in the early 2000s).

Village chiefs in Phnom Mie also described the ways community members demanded accountability through regular meetings with authorities and through the community network's extensive links with villagers. Local authorities were well aware that community members knew their rights, such as the village chief in Svay: "When [Order 01] happened, the people were very active in it, part of the process. Because they wanted the land, and because it was forestland, so they knew that if they didn't go along with the student team they wouldn't get the land. They were organized because they had the meetings first; they knew what they should get. I think the people here know more than most." This village chief's description of people's participation in local governance processes and their superior knowledge is striking in the way that he (as the official leader) does not claim any ownership over, or even a role within, this organized community. During our interview, he continually used the pronoun "they," placing himself outside the village meetings and knowledge sharing. He noted at one point that Srey Sophorn and other network leaders came to meet with him and "tell [him] what is going on and what the problems are in the village." This notion that villagers would tell the village chief what was going on was at odds with the situation in most villages, in which villagers would come to ask the village chief for help, and the village chief would then define what the problems were.

This relationship of accountability with local authorities does not mean the implementation of Order 01 was entirely free of problems in Svay. Some people still reported cases of forest clearance in advance of the land reform, and the community forest area was partially titled out to local villagers and elites (see chapter 6). The success of the land reform in Svay was also undermined a year later, when a massive irrigation scheme began construction in the area. This project involved decisions made by central government and investors who had almost no communication with village- and commune-level authorities, which meant that the relationships community network members had cultivated with local authorities were of limited use in resisting the project. This case suggests, therefore, that on the local level, well-organized, knowledgeable community members with a strong history of community mobilization and links to community leaders and supportive NGOs may be better placed to persuade authorities to work in a pro-poor manner, although they still face severe inequalities in power that limit their ability to push their case to a satisfactory outcome.

Conclusion: Politics of Relationships Rather Than Transactions

In this chapter, I have sought to show how the structure of political power in Cambodia creates a fraught relationship between rural people and their local government representatives. Local officials play a pivotal role in securing, or denying, people's access to state services and land. The officials reside in the same community as their constituents, have affective ties of kinship and friendship in their community, and may genuinely seek to act as a protective "father" of their "sons and daughters," but their own low incomes and desire for private wealth accumulation, as well as the necessity to pass resources to those in higher positions, mean they are often involved in resource grabbing. Rural people's narratives in this chapter suggest the multiple strategies local authorities and other elites used to grab land: clearing forestland in advance of the land survey, enrolling other villagers in schemes to claim land, and acting as land brokers on behalf of wealthy speculators. The differences in power among local authorities and their shifting, two-faced subjectivities create a pervasive sense of uncertainty for rural people, as they simply do not know whose side the local authorities are on or whether the local chief has the power to enact change.

More broadly, the various projects of elite capture among patrimonial networks during the land reform confound the assumption underpinning land titling reforms around the world that "the poor require emancipation from corrupt governance structures in order to participate as equals in a property regime characterized by contract" (Hughes 2013, 149). The land title in the Cambodian context is not a contract guaranteeing equal participation in the property regime; governance in Cambodia continues to focus "on relations rather than transactions" (155) and, in most communities, the land reform worked to deepen these patrimonial relations. The case of Svay, however, illustrates that while rural people are often marginal to neopatrimonial networks of power and authority, people with established relationships within communities and with local authorities can work to hold politico-business networks accountable. This different kind of power relation has emerged through women activists' decade-long efforts to defend their land and build trust and collaboration in their communities. To be sure, this case did not show the cessation of land grabbing; however, in addition to mitigating the worst effects, Svay highlights potential for new forms of state-society relations: a shift from fear of authorities to greater political engagement.

It is important to recognize that the local authorities are bit players in a larger political game. While some village and commune authorities managed to amass land and wealth through Order 01, the land titling reform acted on a broader level to place land control more firmly in the hands of the central state—specifically, in the hands of the prime minister. In the following chapter, I argue that the prime minister's ability to sidestep local/subnational officials and gain the trust of rural land claimants depended on the mobilization of the volunteer university-student land surveyors.

4
YOUTH VOLUNTEERS TO THE FRONTIER

The Student and the Governor

I first met Sokha, an earnest twenty-year-old economics student, in the cramped office of his university's student association just a few weeks into my field research. Sokha recounted his adventures as a volunteer in the Order 01 land reform. Between May 2012 and May 2013, more than 2,700 young people were recruited directly from student associations and universities, as well as from Buddhist temples in Phnom Penh, to serve as Order 01 land reform volunteers.[1] Sokha led a team of twelve university students to survey land in Khang Cheung with the assistance of local officials. To my surprise, Sokha finished the interview by offering to accompany me back to Khang Cheung to help interview officials. "If it's just you, they might not talk with you, but if I'm there, I can get an interview with anyone you want," he said confidently. I wasn't so sure. Several officials had turned down my requests for an interview because the Ministry of Land had warned them not to talk with researchers.

But two weeks later, Sokha and I were shown straight into the spacious office of the district governor, a broad-shouldered man in his sixties. "Hi, Uncle," said Sokha casually (using the familiar term for uncle, *Puu*). My research assistant, Sokun, and I exchanged glances; age is a dominant marker of social hierarchy in Cambodia, and normally a young man would be expected to address an older man—particularly a senior government official—politely by title and honorific (Jacobsen 2012; Ledgerwood 1996). However, the governor spoke openly during the interview and even asked his secretary to photocopy a number of classified documents and maps for us. My preconceived ideas about the dominant social position enjoyed by older men in Cambodian society vis-à-vis younger men became further unsettled as the interview went on. At one point, Sokha and the governor disagreed over whether the student volunteers should have surveyed land that was not being actively cultivated. Sokha cut the governor off midsentence:

> ALICE: Was there any land that could not be surveyed?
> GOVERNOR: Well . . . some people didn't get the land that they weren't growing on, you see—
> SOKHA: (*cutting in*) There were eighty-one titles, 343 hectares, that couldn't be given to villagers because that land was forestland under the control of the Forestry Administration.
> GOVERNOR: But you see, Cambodian people have a custom of cultivating some land, and having a wider area around their land for their cattle to graze, and for hunting. . . . This is Cambodian tradition.
> SOKHA: They don't use this land every year. . . . We can't measure it if they don't use the land.

The governor continued to plead the case that villagers' grazing and forested land should have been surveyed, but Sokha spoke over him, dismissing this as "traditional thinking" that was outside the scope of the land reform.

In this chapter I argue that the unusual—though contingent—power of Sokha and other volunteers to make decisions and bypass local officials lay in the volunteers' position as the prime minister's youth. The volunteers' power arose from their "in-between-ness" (Ní Mhurchú 2015), not only because they were volunteers (and therefore neither full state employees nor outside the state) but also because of what this category signified: they were youth—young, uncorrupted, and in need of protection—and they were soldiers—with the technological sophistication and militarized garb to clarify the political power and threat they embodied. Both roles were clearly tied to the personal power of the prime minister. This subjectivity allowed the volunteers to gain the trust of rural villagers while disarming local officials, making the volunteers more effective in carrying out the state's reform agenda and bolstering the power of the prime minister as the benevolent leader who donated land titles to people. Essentially, the volunteers provided the labor necessary to carry out the project in a short time, they embodied a positive image of Cambodian development before the national election, and they enabled the central government to bypass local officials and other elite who control the distribution of property in many rural areas and whom rural people often see as corrupt and untrustworthy.

To analyze the ways the volunteers reproduced social categories, I combine feminist literature on intersectional oppression and land tenure with works on the politics of land reform. Feminist political ecology scholars working through intersectional analyses connect the racialization of development processes that present the global south as different and inferior (Escobar 1995; Ferguson 1994) and argue for a postcolonial intersectionality that recognizes how gender and race are critical categories in shaping development (Mollett 2012). I use this insight to analyze the racialization and gendering practices of Cambodian land policy, which privileges certain liberal ontologies of land as modern, certain land users as legal, and particular agricultural forms as development. Most of the volunteers were male, and they saw their work in highly masculinized ways that stressed their authority and control. When they encountered land claimants in rural areas, their demeanor and actions reproduced gendered and racialized notions of the good subject that placed Khmer men above women and indigenous people, such that indigenous women were at the bottom of the hierarchy. The volunteers promised to provide private land titles that would extend the state's protection from foreign land-grabbing companies, but only for those whose land use patterns and notions of property fit with the volunteers' understandings of legitimate land claimants. As such, the volunteers both "represent[ed] the state to the people and the people to the state" (Wolford 2016, 80) as they enacted decisions that had lasting material and discursive implications for who can claim state protection through land title.

Essentially, then, the volunteers were transformed into development agents. The volunteers were sent to upland areas that were previously excluded from state and donor land titling efforts. They offered a mechanism for the state to curb dissent among rural people tired of land conflict and to bring the edges of state territory under the purview of the prime minister and in line with neoliberal capitalist conceptions of property. The Order 01 reform reimagined these spaces as communities where the extension of private land title would allow both agribusiness companies and entrepreneurial smallholder farmers to prosper. The volunteers became the vanguards of this imagined space, tasked with not just measuring land but also transmitting the promise of this imaginary to rural people.

On the ground, however, this modern blueprint was much more difficult to implement than the volunteers anticipated. They encountered land claimants who argued or refused the survey, officials and local elite who tried to reassert their power over land distribution, and company representatives who felt that their claims were valid. The chaos was heightened by the rushed implementation of Order 01; the students arrived in the field barely trained, and the rules kept changing as the Land Ministry responded to problems in the field and sent out new—sometimes contradictory—additions to the order. This resulted in highly diverse decision making on the ground. Sometimes the volunteers used their authority to push through land measurements for those who they felt were deserving candidates; at other times, they avoided making decisions and deferred to the trained land officials. Given this, I argue that the volunteers were not passively absorbed into the state; rather, they drew on their own ideas about property and legitimate land claims. These ideas were shaped by their own backgrounds, their training, and their encounters with rural people.

In this chapter, I draw on eighteen interviews I conducted with student volunteers, some over multiple sittings, in city cafés, rural temples, and university offices to understand how the encounters between volunteers and land claimants shaped the land reform outcomes. The interviewees included fourteen men and four women (women made up about 20 percent of volunteers), some recruited from student associations at wealthy universities and some poorer students recruited from youth associations affiliated with local Buddhist temples. I also observed two volunteers while they surveyed land and verified titles, and I spent a week with one volunteer (Sokha, from this chapter's opening vignette) with whom I conducted fifteen interviews with provincial officials. I relied on both opportunism and the snowball method of acquiring interviews, as many of the volunteers were warned not to talk with media or researchers, making open recruitment difficult.

Mobilizing Youth to Build the Frontier

Youth mobilization is a key component of state-making, and the "youth question" in Cambodia—where almost two thirds of the population is under thirty (United Nations 2015)—is critical for the ruling party.[2] Indeed, young people everywhere are a potentially dissident social group (Comaroff and Comaroff 2005), but they can also be mobilized politically as vanguards of new systems (Shepler 2005, 131). Youth can be politically co-opted through state institutions such as schools, youth associations, and sports clubs (Raffin 2012). In Cambodia, two institutions—the family and the Sangha (Buddhist community)—have traditionally shaped the lives of young people, but the rise of state-sponsored youth associations and sporting groups is certainly not new (Ledgerwood 1996). Anne Raffin (2005) shows how the French colonial state mobilized youth through clubs and paramilitary groups in Cambodia, Laos, and Vietnam, with the goal of inculcating conservative and patriotic feelings in youth and channeling these toward the regime.

In the postcolonial period, leaders in Cambodia have repackaged youth groups into pillars of support for their own militaristic projects, and these groups have become important elements of state formation (Raffin 2005). In the 1950s, King Norodom Sihanouk mobilized thousands of youth in sports and cultural groups, forming the Royal Khmer Socialist Youth (RKSY) in 1957 to consolidate his power with an ethic of agrarian nationalism (Raffin 2005). Under Hun Sen's rule, youth associations have sprung up in most universities, schools, and temples. The majority of these are politically affiliated with the ruling CPP party, although some do belong to the opposition parties (Ryerson 2010). The CPP's control of many large school and youth groups, including the Scouts, Red Cross Youth, and university and temple associations, has helped the party control the youth vote[3] by "tying the youth to the party so they toe the party line."[4] What I suggest in this chapter is that the political mobilization of youth can reshape individual patron-client relations and other social categories (including gender and race) but also sits in tension with these existing relationships. This tension leads to opportunities for both change in social structure and entrenchment of existing relations of power and authority.

The Cambodian state's recruitment of the youth volunteers in Order 01 was celebrated as "one of the only policies of its kind in the world,"[5] but it had precedents in King Sihanouk's use of youth volunteers to travel around the country assisting with the modernization of agriculture in the 1950s (Raffin 2012) and in Thailand's use of volunteer schoolteachers, village headmen, and students in the early 1970s to "clear a backlog of 50,000 land certificates" due to a shortage of state officials (Larsson 2012, 124). It is also reminiscent of many states' attempts to send youth to frontier areas, such as China (Rodriguez 2011), the Soviet Empire (Shulman 2012), the Peace Corps in the United States (Hoffman 2000), and Project Rondon in Brazil (Rosenbaum 1971). These state projects often focus on frontier sites that challenge the project to build a unified, modern state (Hall 2013; Tsing 2005). For example, in World War II, the Chinese state mobilized Han Chinese youth volunteers to perform "frontier service" (*bianjiang fuwu*), with an agenda to gain the trust of ethnic groups on the frontier and build a unified, modern China (Rodriguez 2011, 356). These projects of state formation can transform the socioecologies of the frontier. Under Mao's Down to the Countryside movement in the 1960s–1970s, approximately 17 million young urban Chinese were sent to strategic border areas to open "wasteland" for state rubber plantations. In the process, they radically changed the ecology of the frontier areas and the ways of life of indigenous ethnic minorities, who were faced with an influx of people and new policies (Shapiro 2001, 142).

Similarly, the Cambodian state has long sought to reconstruct the uplands and in particular its indigenous groups—seen as backward and potentially dissident. Investments in infrastructure, education, large-scale natural resource extraction projects, and the promotion of cash crops and settled agriculture aim to reduce poverty and modernize indigenous groups. The prime minister told a group of indigenous people in Khang Leit that if they took up cash cropping they would no longer need to practice shifting cultivation and making wood handicrafts; instead, they would "turn the wood basket into rubber" (Hun Sen 2012d, 1). Order 01 built on the state's modernizing efforts by spreading particular conceptions of private land rights and state protection into indigenous areas, with their history of communal land tenure regimes, and into upland rice-growing areas, where Khmer peasant land tenure systems allowed for common grazing areas and uncultivated forestland held in reserve for future use.

Recruitment and Training of the Youth Volunteers

In July 2012, the dean of Cambodia's Royal University of Agriculture (RUA) made an unexpected visit to nineteen-year-old Sophea's class. As she told the story: "He said 'the government needs volunteers to go around the country right away and measure company land to give to poor farmers.'" Sophea was one of approximately 350 volunteers recruited directly from the RUA's degree program in land administration, effectively shutting down the program for several months during the volunteers' deployment.

Beyond the RUA program, the majority of volunteers were recruited from student associations, including two of the largest youth associations—the Union of Youth Federations of Cambodia (UYFC) and the Pagoda Children's Intelligentsia and Student Association (known popularly as "the Pagoda Boys").[6] The UYFC began in 1978 with close ties to the CPP and has chapters at most universities. Many of the UYFC members who volunteered in the land reform studied at high-ranking universities (such as the National University of Management [NUM]), and they represented Cambodia's new urban middle class. They saw their participation as a form of civic engagement and a potential door to a government position upon graduation. One volunteer from NUM told me that the leader of his UYFC chapter called a meeting and encouraged members to sign up in order to "help the poor people get their land back from the companies." He added that volunteering would increase his chances of getting a job at the Land Ministry, because "if you don't have political connections, then you can't get a job; it doesn't matter if you have the skills or not. So I wanted to do the volunteering and then try out for the ministry."

While the UYFC volunteers I spoke with were mostly born in Phnom Penh, Pagoda Boy volunteers were mainly from the rural provinces. The Pagoda Boys comprise more than four thousand young men, primarily poor boys from rural areas who reside in Phnom Penh's pagodas while they attend school in the city. They receive free accommodation and food largely funded by the ruling party. The Pagoda Boys are at once an asset and a threat to the national government.

Buddhist temples are precarious zones for the government because the Buddhist clergy is a powerful alternative authority. Historical events have shown that monks who support the government help legitimize state authority, while monks who oppose the government can mobilize public support (Gyallay-Pap 2007; Harris 2007). Thus, Pagoda Boys are potentially dangerous to the regime; unlike the middle-class students from elite universities, they are from poor families who know the hardships of recent years, and they live in the urban space of the Buddhist temple where moral authority can permit political dissent (Work and Beban 2016). The recruitment of volunteers from the temples therefore fulfilled a dual purpose of amassing labor and neutralizing young people whose growing numbers and frustrated aspirations represented both promise and threat to the ruling party. One volunteer from Phnom Penh's largest temple explained to me how student leaders called a meeting and encouraged the boys to volunteer, "even offering CPP hats for us and talking about how it would be good for our future." As with many of the volunteers from both the UYFC and the Pagoda Boys, this volunteer said he signed up because of a genuine desire to help his country resolve land conflicts and "help the poor people instead of the companies," alongside the hopes of having an adventure and winning a coveted government job.

After signing up, things moved quickly. The volunteers received just two days' formal training on *Koh Pich* (Diamond) island in Phnom Penh, an area of the city that is itself a symbol of Cambodia's rapid urban development. The volunteers received training in the use of handheld GPS units for marking coordinates and learned how to complete application forms for land title. They listened to speeches by Hun Sen and Land Ministry representatives, which stressed the volunteers' service to their country. Hun Sen congratulated the volunteers with a lavish dinner and said that their work "would bring both economic development benefits and would improve the lives of poor rural people by giving people private land title. . . . This would allow people to take out loans and invest in their land, and secure their land so companies could not seize it" (Hun Sen 2012a). The volunteers also received a training manual that laid out the legal orders stipulating which land should be surveyed. The dominant message during training, as one female volunteer recalled to me in an interview, was that the volunteers' job was to help the people by getting land back from the companies so they could use it and that doing so would develop the country. This message focused, as other volunteers recalled, on the benefits of private land title for protection, as well as the ability to use the land as collateral for loans and gain a higher price for sale.

Following training, the volunteers were organized into teams of twelve and transported to rural areas to work with provincial land officials for up to six months at a time. The selection of which land to excise from ELCs and state land areas appears to have been made by officials in the prime minister's office and the Ministry of Land in conjunction with high-level provincial officials, rather than at more local levels of government. The student volunteers and land officials then arrived in these areas with maps provided by the provincial government. They asked land claimants to come to the village temple to show their identification documents and fill in claim forms. Then the volunteers made decisions on the ground about which land plots would be surveyed and titled.

In the field, the volunteers generally lived in the villages where they worked, lodging at people's houses, temples, or community meeting houses. They were encouraged to interact in the community and get to know villagers; indeed, Hun Sen praised those who "do not wait just to measure land; if you have free time, you can help the people and do good works for them" (Hun Sen 2012a). Hun Sen singled out one team who "put together a house for a widow whose former house had burned down" (Hun Sen 2012c, 1) and another team that wrote a brief history of a village that would be "kept as a heritage" (Hun Sen 2012b, 2). While some volunteers told me that they kept to themselves and some said they were treated with suspicion, others recalled going to local dances, helping in the fields, and even repairing the roof of one widow's house after it was damaged in a storm.

Some volunteers developed strong emotional attachments to the places they worked, and stories of relationships with local village youth and marriage were common. For example, one day Sokha took me to visit his girlfriend, whom he met during his volunteer deployment. She is the daughter of the village chief in the area that Sokha's team was stationed. Sokha told me that they planned to marry after he completes his studies. The family joked about shedding tears on the day the volunteers left the village, and Sokha laughed as he remembered, "When I left Khang Cheung, some people cried. Some said, 'You have been here so long, why do you leave me?' And I didn't know what to do; I cried with them." The youths' in-between roles as volunteers—part of the state but not "of" the state—facilitated their daily lives in the villages and their work tasks, as I describe in the next section.

Hun Sen's Heroic Youth Soldiers

In Hun Sen's public speeches during the land reform, his language drew on the conception of the volunteers as youth who needed to be looked after; he urged land claimants in rural areas to help the volunteers, protect them, and support them in their task as "our sons and daughters."[7] "I thank the sons and daughters of the nation. Some volunteers call me and my wife mum and dad. And my wife frequently calls the teams; yesterday she called eleven teams" (Hun Sen, July 2012 speech at land titling ceremony). Hun Sen frequently mentioned in his speeches how he, his wife, or his son Hun Manit (who officially headed the initiative during its second phase) personally phoned the volunteer teams to check on them, and each team leader reportedly had a special cell phone with a direct line to the prime minister (Hun Sen 2012a, 2012b). During interviews, a variety of land claimants, officials, and activists frequently told me about this direct phone line; it represented the volunteers' ties to the prime minister in a society in which power works primarily through one's connections to the political elite.

Hun Sen used the language of protection and familial ties—which drew on an image of the volunteers as youth—alongside the language of military service. When addressing the volunteers at training sessions in Phnom Penh, he described himself as their commander in chief and the minister of land as the chief of staff, and he pronounced that "all governors must look after their land management soldiers" (Hun Sen 2012a). The volunteers wore military uniforms with the Ministry of Land logo on them and drove to villages in military trucks. The prime minister further instilled this masculine militaristic image through frequent comparisons between Order 01 and his own war exploits during the Khmer Rouge period, as in these remarks during a speech to the volunteers: "I remember when I was eighteen years of age and I had to part from my family to live in the forest as a soldier. Even though we have sorted out everything for you from head to toe, you must still undertake this mission under rain, wind, and heat, traveling across forest and rivers. This brings back memories from the old days; you have my sympathies" (Hun Sen 2012a).

Both of the volunteers' subject positions—as youth and soldiers—were clearly tied to the personal power of the prime minister. As soldiers, the volunteers carried the technological sophistication and militarized garb to clarify the political power and threat they embodied. As youth, they helped out around the village; they were trustworthy and distinct from local officials and line ministries. This in-between subject position explains why rural villagers generally held the volunteers in high regard and why local officials felt marginalized. Among the hundreds of upland and lowland villagers I interviewed, the vast majority characterized the volunteers as trustworthy and committed to their country—in stark contrast to the way people spoke of government officials. In some cases, people said the students gave them food and money; one woman in Khang Cheung told me: "The students helped us a lot. I won't forget. They gave us small things; altogether they gave us fifteen thousand riel [US$3.50] and helped give food and things to us. From their own hands." Similarly, Grimsditch and Schoenberger's (2015) report on seven provinces found that the majority of rural land title recipients surveyed (88 percent, n = 420) thought the youth volunteers were helpful and respectful. One female volunteer suggested that the students blocked corruption because their tie to Hun Sen effectively turned them into watchdogs: "Having the students helped. Because some people from the department of land are corrupt, they would accept money from people, and they would want people to pay to have their land measured. But . . . there was always the students, and if we saw anything, the prime minister told us to contact him."

This suggests the volunteers' position as both of the state but not in the state—they temporarily occupied a high rung in the state's political patronage networks with their access to Hun Sen, but they were perceived to be new and therefore outside the systemic corruption that plagues the Land Ministry. One male volunteer from a top university in Phnom Penh suggested that the students were well regarded in the village because the volunteers' wealthier backgrounds allowed them to refrain from corruption, in comparison to the land officials who were understaffed and underpaid:

> VOLUNTEER: If you think about it, the students go to university and most of them are not so in need. We are new; we tend to not be so corrupt. So I think that using students might show a better image, something that is politically, politically . . . well, it's doing something that is political but not in a political way.
>
> ALICE: And you think it was successful in that sense? Politically, in terms of winning the support for the government?
>
> VOLUNTEER: Yes, because if we had used the government officers, the people would not be happy; they would not be happy at all. The officers would not have enough pay, and they would have problems with corruption. In Order 01, the intention was to help people without taking money, but with the officials it would have turned out the opposite way.

In contrast to this volunteer's narrative, my research suggests that there clearly was corruption during the survey, including demands for payments and land grabbing. This was often orchestrated by local officials and other elites, but several reports suggest the volunteers also took bribes, used pressure, and made threats (Rabe 2013; Focus on the Global South 2013). However, I found that people tended to have positive attitudes toward the volunteers even when they were highly critical of the land reform. Land claimants got angry at land officials who were said to have tampered with the records after the students left, or they blamed local elites who cleared forestland in anticipation of the students' arrival. Even people who did admit to giving money or produce to the volunteers assured me that this was not corruption; one woman in her fifties who owned a small plot of rice land in Khang Cheung told me she gave the volunteers "small gifts," such as cash or a chicken, whereas the land officials demanded "bribes" (see Work and Beban 2016). It is not clear whether these gifts were intended to sway decisions or whether this woman just wanted to make the students more comfortable. The woman's distinction between the volunteers and the corrupt officials may also reflect a fear of retribution for speaking out in the interview because of the volunteers' ties to Hun Sen. However, when I asked this woman why she gave the students gifts, she said that she "felt sorry for the youth, because they work hard and they are away from their parents," suggesting that the volunteers embodied an entirely different subjectivity that evoked pity and maternal care, in contrast to people's feelings about the land officials' bribes.

While the volunteers as youths were therefore generally well regarded by villagers, the volunteers as Hun Sen's personal soldiers had the effects of unsettling traditional ideas of generational hierarchy and marginalizing local officials during the reform's implementation. Several volunteers said the authorities were scared of them. One male volunteer proudly told me, "The authorities listened to the students, because they were worried that these were Hun Sen's students." Similar sentiments were a marked feature of many interviews with village and commune chiefs; one village chief in Khang Cheung told me pointedly: "The students get directives straight from Hun Sen—like his grandchildren—not reporting to village head or district. The provincial head is scared of the students." Another village chief in Khang Cheung compared the power of the volunteers, who surveyed land within the concession boundaries, to the power of the land officials, whom he saw as lacking the power to stand up to the concession company: "The land officials and students both came to measure here at the same time. The land officials measured the house land, and the students measured the parts that the land officials wouldn't go. The land officials wouldn't measure the land with the company; they didn't dare. But the students would, because they are sent from Hun Sen; they have the directive to measure the land that is in conflict with the company."

While village chiefs, including this man, respected the students' power, they also said they resented the students. Several village chiefs complained to me that local authorities were not remunerated for the extra work of looking after the volunteers, but the student volunteers received healthy stipends for their work. One junior-ranked official at the Khang Cheung Provincial Department of Land told me his superiors even asked him to put in his own money as a donation for the students' food. One commune chief complained, "I had to work all the time, every day, when the students came, and I get nothing extra. Sometimes I want to cry because there are so many documents to sign." Other local authorities told me they had no input into survey planning, and two village chiefs told me the students left to survey new areas without telling the local authorities where they were going.

But although the volunteers held power over local officials due to their links to Hun Sen, this power was limited when they encountered higher authorities and corporate concessionaries who manipulated the volunteers. Rumors abounded about companies that provided the students with food and drink and the local elite who gave large donations to volunteer teams and entreated them to survey the land in the elites' favor. Volunteers told me that "some people just talk to the high-ranking officer and make arrangements so we don't know what is happening," and "sometimes the provincial authorities or the company people just tell the government officials doing the land measuring with us to go and measure without the students." These strategies to exclude the students had to be done with care, as Hun Sen made public examples of officials accused of bribing the volunteers by convicting the officials and throwing them in jail (Hun Sen 2012d). A more common strategy was for local officials and elites to bypass the volunteers by grabbing land in advance of the survey or after the students left, as I discussed in detail in the previous chapter.

Uncertainty on the Ground

The volunteers' power to gain the trust of villagers and marginalize local officials was facilitated not only by the volunteers' subjectivity as Hun Sen's heroic youth but also by the confusion on the ground. In this section, I discuss how the rushed volunteer recruitment and unclear rules of Order 01 provided the space for volunteers to make decisions that were incredibly diverse from team to team—and even within teams—as the volunteers were guided by their own understandings of the rules; by broader notions of morality and fairness; by race, gender, and class norms; and by their encounters with land claimants. Many volunteers criticized the speed with which the land reform was developed, such as one volunteer who exclaimed: "It was very confusing! Because it was all a last-minute thing you know. It was, right, we are going to have the election soon; we want to win. How will we do it? Right, policy. (*laughing*) I think it was very last minute. I think people do not have the correct knowledge about how you . . . do all kinds of things. And then they deliver these incorrect ideas to the people in the village."

The volunteers said the training was so fast, they felt ill equipped to use the GPS units, "because when you go to the field, there's all kinds of things that you don't expect." These unexpected issues included having to use older GPS models that the volunteers had never seen and having to perform more advanced operations, such as deleting data points. One volunteer explained, "If the villager says, 'Oh I was wrong; I thought this was the corner of my field, but actually this is the corner,' you have to delete it. But we didn't know how to delete it! So then we deleted everything, and sometimes we input the wrong numbers. Sometimes we get completely lost!"

The volunteers received one afternoon's instruction on how to help land claimants through the written application process, but this was also very different in the field. One female volunteer remembered that "it wasn't that easy to know where [on the form] we should fill in the details, and where they should fill things in. . . . At first it was quite messed up." Beyond the inadequate preparation of the volunteers, the instructions about which land to measure changed frequently, leading to confusion and inconsistent implementation on the ground. This had real material outcomes for people; indeed, I suggest that this is a large reason why a recent survey of ten provinces found that approximately 75 percent of people were awarded title to only part of their land under Order 01, and the titling of uncultivated and disputed land varied widely from province to province (Grimsditch and Schoenberger 2015). This confusion over what the rules were allowed the prime minister the flexibility to sidestep blame for any problems and strengthened the power of Hun Sen's oral pronouncements to guide policy. I explore two examples of this in detail below: the 10 percent rule for community land provision, and the measurement of disputed and uncultivated land.

The 10 Percent Rule

A prime example of uncertainty on the ground was the confusion surrounding a provision to retain 10 percent of land for community use. I first began to hear people refer to the 10 percent land rule in discussions with community activists. At a community network meeting in Khang Cheung, activists told me they had heard volunteers discussing this rule, but they were not sure what it meant. I asked volunteers about this 10 percent rule during interviews. Seven volunteers had heard about it, although they interpreted it in different ways: some said that the 10 percent was "land we measured out for the community to build schools and temples," while others said it was to create an SLC "for poor people and for when people get married." Some said they had never heard of this provision, and one student laughed loudly when I described it, saying: "That's ridiculous; I never heard it. I think it is those people getting land for their own purpose. . . . It may be a way to expand the land concessions."

This example illustrates how Hun Sen's oral utterances guided policy that may not exist in written form. The prime minister did in fact refer to the 10 percent land rule in a 2012 speech, in which he said that "the purpose of the land reform is to create the leopard skin landscape, plus leave 10 percent land for future population growth" (Hun Sen 2012d). However, I could not locate this stipulation in any of the multitude of written instructions produced during the land reform, and when I asked a lawyer at the Ministry of Land to clarify, he said he had not heard of this provision either.

Disputed and Uncultivated Land

One of the most contentious aspects of Order 01 was whether disputed land should be measured. When Hun Sen first announced the order, he said that disputed land would be measured, but this abruptly changed two months into the campaign; instead, he asked the volunteers not to measure disputed land and to refer problems to the land officials (RGC 2012). This meant that many people in active conflict with ELCs were excluded from the land reform. Some people who lived on land that the plantation company was already using for cassava cultivation told me ironically that the problem was already solved in their area, as one man said wryly: "In this area, they didn't measure because the company already planted the sugarcane three years ago. So there is no problem now, because the land is already gone." In these cases, the land reform legitimated the land grabs that had already taken place.

In the midst of this confusing and emotive shifting of rules, the volunteers drew on their own ideas and beliefs to make these decisions. Some volunteers said they avoided dealing with disputes; they referred disputed land to the officials, asked people to sort the dispute out themselves, or just left the area, although some had misgivings: "We didn't measure when there was a dispute; we kept going to other areas. But it was hard; sometimes I wanted to measure for people but we couldn't. The villagers would ask us, 'Why aren't you measuring my land?' But sometimes, we had to just go away." Other volunteers saw it as their role to try to solve disputes. This was particularly the case for the two team presidents I interviewed, both of whom were also upper-middle-class urbanites from top universities. They were emphatic that if disputed land was not measured, this would betray the spirit of the initiative: "It's hard, but we have to decide.... Because as the president [of the volunteer team] I had to know the way to do it.... It is like mediation. I think this role is wrong for me because I study economics! But I think it's important.... We have to find a solution. We shouldn't keep it and try to solve it later; that's not good."

Volunteers' decisions were also shaped in the moment through their encounters with land claimants. The emotional intensity of interactions added to the volunteers' confusion; several volunteers recalled people who became angry, started crying and screaming, offered monetary and food bribes, pleaded, and recounted stories of poverty and desperation. The volunteers were quite unprepared for this; one exclaimed that he "didn't know what to do." One male volunteer became visibly upset in the interview, shaking his head as he told me, "This is so difficult to solve; people get upset when they can't get the land they want. Either way, it is difficult—if we measure this [forest] land, this is against the law. If we don't measure the land, the people are angry; it's so hard."

Faced with unclear instructions and complex claims, the volunteers had many different ideas about what to do. Some volunteers said they went "by the law" and only titled "peaceful" cultivated land; some said they titled land if they could see that it had been used for agriculture in the last four to five years; yet others described their decision making as much more holistic, depending on their judgment of the individual's character, particularly his or her propensity for using the land in the future: "We look at the potential of that individual; what are they doing, what will they do with the land. When we see the case of the outsider who just wants the land title, we think that maybe he will just request a loan and not use the land or just sell the land, so we don't measure. But with the people that actually live in the village, I think they will improve the land more. Because they are living on that land, and they want to do something more than just betting on the land."

Essentially, the volunteers' ambiguous subjectivities and the confusion on the ground allowed them to transcend age-based hierarchies in their dealings with local officials and make decisions. For example, during a wide-ranging conversation in a local coffee shop, Theara, a university student living at one of the sprawling temples in Phnom Penh, described the ways he navigated the rules to measure uncultivated land:

> THEARA: In the case of people not using the land, the government officials didn't want to measure it. . . . I think for rich people it shouldn't be measured. But not for poor people. So sometimes, we measured the land anyway . . . if we could see that they are poor, that they want to improve.
> ALICE: Right, so it's based on whether you think they will use the land?
> THEARA: Right, we had to decide; we had to think about their character, their potential.
> ALICE: So with those kind of things, you had the power to make the decision?
> THEARA: Yes, we could do it. When there's paperwork involved it's harder, and it's the officials that have to do it. But when it's the decision there on the ground we can do it. We think about the people.

Other volunteers similarly told me how they made their own decisions on the ground and found ways to bend rules and solve disputes. Seven different volunteers shared stories of how they found ways to measure land for people when paperwork was unclear or ownership was disputed by using their moral judgment to help people they felt deserved to have their land surveyed. But when the volunteers met difficult cases, many were also quick to say that they were "just students" without the authority to do anything. In this way, the volunteers invoked different aspects of their somewhat ambiguous positionality. They drew on their authority as Hun Sen's soldiers to transcend age-based hierarchies in their dealings with local officials, and they also drew on their status as inexperienced young volunteers to avoid blame for mistakes or difficult decisions. At the same time, the depiction of the initiative as a masculine, militarized campaign and the volunteers' privileged urban ethnic Khmer backgrounds ultimately meant that the campaign entrenched gender, race, and class hierarchies, which I turn to in the following section.

Transcending and Entrenching Social Hierarchies

Although the student volunteers' decisions about whether to survey people's land or not seemed to be based on individual ideas and negotiation with land claimants, I wanted to understand whether I could discern any patterns of disadvantage. Were women land claimants less likely to have land surveyed because entrenched gender roles meant women had less political connections and social power? Were Khmer people more likely to have land surveyed than indigenous people because some indigenous people did not want individual land title or due to racism among surveyors? I also had hunches that people with more wealth and political connections might have been able to influence the survey process and that older people and those who had been living on the land for longer would be able to stake greater claims to the land. I surveyed land claimants in my two study provinces to explore these questions.

My survey included 270 households (198 in Khang Cheung and 72 in Khang Leit), and was carried out one year after the volunteers had surveyed land (see preface for more details about the survey process). The survey sought to understand whether there were any discernible patterns that determined whether people had their land surveyed during the reform. Given the small sample size and the challenges I encountered while administering the survey, broad conclusions from the survey should be treated with caution. But the data does include a relatively even spread of land claimants who reported having at least some of their land surveyed during the land reform (60 percent) and those whose land was not surveyed (40 percent), and the story it tells helps to give context to the qualitative data from my field sites.

To analyze people's likelihood of having their land surveyed, I constructed a binary-dependent variable measuring whether the respondent had at least some of their land surveyed (1) or none of their land surveyed (0) during the land reform. I then constructed a logistic regression model using explanatory variables that I found to be theoretically or substantively related to having land surveyed. Along with variables that were relatively easy to measure (such as gender, age, ethnicity [Khmer and indigenous], education, family size, and settlement history), I examined political networks by asking people whether they held any official roles in the village (such as village chief, police officer, commune council) and whether they participated in village affairs (for example, whether they belong to NGO programs or village committees). Wealth was difficult to measure, as most people did not have a steady income; therefore, I collected information on assets (including farm machinery and means of transport such as bicycles and motorbikes), house materials, livelihood activities, food security, and land size. Finally, I also explored whether growing different crops on the land or the location of people's land (close to roads or isolated from road access) mattered.

I created a multivariate logistic regression model using variables that I found to be significantly correlated with having one's land surveyed at the bivariate level. Table 1 reports the logistic regression output, including odds ratios, standard error (in brackets), and significance level (*). Due to the different context of the land reform for indigenous people, I ran the regression model first without an ethnicity variable (Model 1) and then with an ethnicity variable (Model 2).

The first point to note is that the model explains one-fifth of the variance without the ethnicity variable (Model 1), and over one-third of the variance with the ethnicity variable (Model 2). Around two-thirds of the variance is left unexplained, which suggests that beyond systematic discrimination, the confusion of changing, unclear guidelines and the student volunteers' personal beliefs, values, and specific encounters with different land claimants shaped their decisions.

The survey data suggests that several factors significantly increased the likelihood of having one's land surveyed, including education level (in the first model, each extra year of education meant a person was 17 percent more likely to have their land surveyed) and whether people cultivated rice on some of their land (people who cultivated rice were 80 percent more likely to have land surveyed, which may be due to rice fields being more clearly defined than upland fields and claims over rice land carrying more weight than uncultivated or swidden land). People who claimed land far from roads were less likely to have their land surveyed than those with land close to roads; this may be due to the volunteer surveyors having difficulty accessing remote land. People who belonged to community networks were also less likely to have land surveyed; however, this variable was not significant when people's ethnicity was considered, and it likely reflects the

TABLE 1. Logistic regression analysis predicting relationship between land survey and demographic and wealth factors

	MODEL 1 (WITHOUT ETHNICITY)	MODEL 2 (WITH ETHNICITY)
Ethnicity		**0.051** (0.03)**
Gender	**0.852* (0.282)**	**0.403* (0.183)**
Food security	0.919 (0.048)	0.985 (0.063)
Grows rice on land	**1.808* (0.594)**	1.320 (0.577)
Land received from authorities	**2.321* (1.026)**	1.451 (0.700)
Owns at least one bicycle	**6.431** (2.901)**	**2.846* (.1657)**
Education	**1.169** (0.0593)**	1.039 (0.066)
Number of people in household	0.901 (0.055)	1.019 (0.082)
Age	1.001 (0.000)	1.000 (0.000)
When moved to land	1.213 (0.147)	1.026 (0.152)
Land size (ha)	0.949 (0.038)	0.928 (0.043)
Location (near small road)	0.539 (0.201)	0.621 (0.292)
Location (no roads nearby)	**0.352* (0.197)**	0.412 (0.262)
Network membership (organizations)	**0.384** (0.141)**	0.341 (0.194)
Network membership (authorities)	1.340 (0.996)	1 (omitted)
Constant	0.302 (0.290)	2.205 (2.86)
Overall Pseudo R^2	0.222**	0.361**
Overall Log likelihood	–130.1683	–97.568
LR Chi2	LR Chi2(14) 74.33	LR Chi2(15) 110.32
N	270	270

NOTE: * = $p < 0.05$, ** = $p < 0.01$.

indigenous community network members who refused to join the land survey as they did not want it to affect their communal land title claims.

Three factors are significant in the final model. First, the odds of an indigenous person having their land surveyed were only 5 percent of the odds of a Khmer respondent having their land surveyed. This is not surprising since, as mentioned, some indigenous people in my study areas refused to join the land survey; conversely, some indigenous land claimants (particularly women) told me they wanted to join the land survey but the volunteers didn't come to their part of the village or didn't survey their shifting cultivation land. It is notable that my Khang Leit survey in indigenous majority areas included eight Khmer respondents, all of whom had their land surveyed during the reform.

Once ethnicity is controlled for, two other variables are significant. First, gender: women were 60 percent less likely than men to have their land surveyed (discussed in depth in the next section). Second, households with at least one bicycle were almost three times as likely to have their land surveyed as households that did not own a bicycle. Due to my survey methodology, this result is difficult to interpret because I only asked about current asset ownership, and I don't know whether people bought their bicycles before or after the land reform. It is possible that people with land titles were able to leverage the titles to access loans in order to buy bicycles. But this is unlikely as my survey found no difference in lending behavior between those whose land was surveyed and those whose land was not surveyed during the land reform (see chapter 5). It is more likely that bicycle ownership signals greater household wealth and mobility in rural areas than not owning a bicycle and that wealthier households were more likely to have their land surveyed. In my study areas, 83 percent of households owned a bicycle, but the poorest households tended not to own any form of transport. During the land reform, households with more financial resources were able to press their claims by clearing and planting crops on their land, and they likely had more social status that allowed them to negotiate with land surveyors. It is also possible that people with bicycles were better able to monitor the survey team's location and bike quickly to their agricultural land plots in order to negotiate their land claim with the surveyors. Land claimants told me that, since the student volunteers moved slowly around the commune over weeks or even months, it was time-consuming to wait for their land to be surveyed; I met some claimants who did not have their land surveyed because they could not make it to their agricultural land when the surveyors arrived or because they had to return to factory work in the city.

Gendered Encounters in the Lowlands

Land titling programs can undermine the position of women, especially in contexts where property is titled in the name of the male spouse rather than under joint land title, as researchers have noted in areas as diverse as Sub-Saharan Africa, Mexico, and India (Agarwal 1994; Hamilton 2002; Jacobs 2009a; Pedersen 2015). My survey results, which show that women were 60 percent less likely than men to have their land surveyed, are striking, though, considering that gender empowerment is one of the pillars of Cambodia's land administration program. The bias toward male land claimants having land surveyed at higher rates than women (in my survey) suggests that volunteers' decisions about which land to survey were likely shaped by a combination of their maleness, their training, and their urban, educated notions of what it meant to use the land productively. Of course, these decisions were negotiated in encounters with land claimants. Male land claimants were likely more able to draw on *khsae* networks to a greater extent than women in order to find powerful people to back their claims if needed.

And given that the surveyors were mostly young men, social norms made it difficult for women to speak up and press their claims.

The physical appearance and characterization of the youths as soldiers projected a militarized masculinity, which accentuated the social distance from women land claimants and encouraged a gendered division of labor within survey teams. One male volunteer in a study by the nonprofit group Focus on the Global South (2013) reported feeling "excited when my boss told me that the youth volunteers would wear a military uniform. For me as a man, I must serve this military obligation. Then, I will become a real, strong man." Other volunteers alluded to the exciting danger of their work. One male volunteer told me that "the police went with us too, in case there were any disputes with villagers, for our security. We wore the soldier's clothes when we went out, but no weapons—just the GPS!" The volunteers' stories had a sense of adventure; for many volunteers, this was a rare time away from their parents' surveillance, and several volunteers described their sense of freedom, particularly in terms of being able to choose their own romantic partners. (Indeed, in one speech in Sihanoukville province, Hun Sen [2012b] celebrated Team 100 for breaking records for engagements, with five engaged couples so far, including two couples within the team—quite a feat considering there were twelve volunteers per team!) Romantic songs and poems reminisced about the heroic mission of the team and tales of love in the countryside: "On the first day of his mission, the student measurement volunteer met the beautiful woman who lives in the countryside and fell in love with her immediately. He gives all his love to her; please love him in return. Love at first sight."[8] However, this sense of adventure was tinged with a sense of masculine entitlement. One male student became engaged to a young village woman during his mission and boasted to me that "if one of the volunteers wanted to marry a local girl, then the marriage had to happen."

While there certainly were women volunteers, there was a strict gendered division of labor within the volunteer teams. Women comprised approximately 20 percent of the youth volunteers; they were primarily recruited from the Royal University of Agriculture's land management degree program. The four women volunteers I interviewed all said work tasks were highly segregated; the male volunteers surveyed land while the women helped people fill out claim forms and cooked and cleaned. This gendered division of labor was framed by several volunteers as necessary due to women's lesser physical ability and reflects broader cultural notions of women as physically weaker and in need of protection (Ledgerwood 1996). One male volunteer suggested that this was a natural breakdown of work roles: "I think they are not very physically capable of doing it. Sometimes, the places, we are up in the mountains, we have to go all the way up and down, all the way up and down, and they are not very capable (*laughs*) of doing that. And sometimes in the forest and all of that, you know, and it's hard for them to do that, to go all the way like that." This construction of the terrain as physically impossible for women to traverse was recounted frequently in interviews; indeed, volunteers' descriptions of their tasks often sounded like macho adventure stories, as they navigated rainy-season floods, mountainous terrain, and forests to complete their task. "The routine was that we had to go to the forest, and we had to climb, climb, climb"; "Sometimes I got up at 4:00 a.m. and had to walk from the district to the villages because the truck for the student team was being used and there was no transport"; "I think the measurement was very difficult because it was the rainy season, so sometimes we had to swim to measure the land for people."

The women volunteers I interviewed noted that even if they did not take part in the task of surveying land, their participation in the mission was a challenge to their families. One nineteen-year-old student said her parents would not let her join the volunteer team until she asked her university professor to convince them. Another woman suggested that the task of surveying was not physically impossible for women, but the labor division was a gesture of "gentlemanly behavior' by the male volunteers: "Usually the women did the paperwork. It's not that they weren't allowed to go . . . but the boys, they're gentlemen. They wanted the girls to not have to work too hard. And it was hard work to do all the walking and the swimming to do the measurement."

The gendered division of labor during the survey meant that after the initial forms were completed, local people's interaction with the students was largely restricted to the young men in the teams. Some female land claimants suggested that this had implications for how the land was measured, because they did not feel as comfortable talking with men. One woman in Khang Cheung told me, "It is better if we deal with women because women understand each other." The effect, in some cases, was to exclude land that is largely women's domain. For example, several volunteers said they privileged paddy rice land and cash crops rather than home gardens, orchards, or shifting cultivation land that was, according to one male volunteer, "not well cared for and had large trees in it." Some volunteers also said they did not survey land held in reserve for children to inherit or for cultivation when the labor power became available, because it was not currently cultivated. One woman in Khang Cheung told me that the volunteers "did not understand about how the land we are saving for our children is our land. They wouldn't title it for us but that's what we do." In this way, two key domains of women's labor and decision-making power were excluded by some volunteers: home gardens, which are generally cared for by women (often older-generation women in Khang Cheung) and land held in reserve, which is distributed when children marry.

A further example of decision making that entrenched gender hierarchies is the volunteers' decisions about whether to survey land held jointly by a husband and wife if one spouse was not present. Many Cambodians—particularly men from my Khang Cheung study sites—work in Thailand and Phnom Penh, and it was quite common for one spouse to be away when the student volunteers came to title land in Khang Cheung. Order 01 explicitly privileged joint land title for married couples; both partners had to be present to sign the title application. This led to a great deal of ambiguity over what to do when a spouse was not there. The following four quotations from volunteers suggest four different ways this was handled:

> In cases where people said that the man had gone off with a new wife, or was in Thailand and couldn't come, we couldn't measure. They have to have the documentation.

> [If the spouse was away] we would measure for them and put both names. But only measure. Not deliver the certificate.

> Actually, I think it is unfair for the woman. Because actually, (*laughing*) I've never seen a certificate that says the husband has gone. . . . Sometimes I think it is very difficult for them because they do not have enough money to issue the paperwork.

> I think it would be a no [we can't survey the land]. . . . But you know, when you sign the papers, for measuring, you actually have to stamp your right thumb, like this (*motions stamping thumbprint on a paper*) . . . but there are ways, you know, you can do it like this (*motions stamping his other thumb on the paper*) and do a fake [print], and then it goes through.

The decisions made by these four volunteers are remarkably diverse—ranging from emphatically not measuring land for people whose spouses were away to actually faking the husband's thumbprint so that the woman land claimant could put in her application. Most often, volunteers opted not to survey the land, which meant families with one or more adult family members working away from the province missed out. This confusion sometimes worked in women's favor, as when the volunteer faked the thumbprint, but it more often worked against women receiving land title, because it is more common for men in the area to work in Thailand while women find employment in the nearby garment factories or maintain the house and raise the children. Some women told me that their husbands had not come back for years and were not sending money home to their families. Yet, even if the spouse was unlikely to come back, the women could not claim land title without documentation showing that the couple was separated. In my time doing interviews, I only met one woman who had managed to gain a document from the commune clerk to certify that her husband was not coming back. This means that women in both cases were subjugated—women with husbands who worked away from the area were either excluded from the land survey altogether or their land was registered in joint title, which may inhibit their ability to formally sell or mortgage their land later with no formal divorce certificate.

Of course, just as the volunteers had agency to negotiate on the basis of their understandings of the rules and their notions of right and wrong, land claimants told me of ways they worked to bend the rules. Some women made meals for the volunteers to win them over, such as by slaughtering a chicken. Others told the volunteers their stories of hardship, hoping to make the volunteers feel sympathetic toward them. One young woman told me she took the volunteers inside her house to show them the lack of food rations for her children. One woman in her forties, whom I knew to be married but whose husband worked away in Phnom Penh, was cagey at first when I asked her about her land title, and she declined to show it to me. When she eventually pulled it out, I noticed that her marital status was marked "Widow" and that she had been awarded individual title to the land. I murmured apologies, assuming her husband had recently passed away, but she said, "He's not dead; I just told the commune that he died in Phnom Penh, and I had people here back this up, and they signed the widow paper for me so I could get the land myself."

While these examples show that some women did manage to use the confusion on the ground to their advantage, these were exceptional cases. Most people I interviewed said they were helpless to respond when they were told that their land could not be surveyed. Rural women were doubly subjugated by their gender and their class. They had much lower education levels on average than men in the village, and they were far less likely to hold official positions in office or to have networks with men who held these positions. And with high rates of cash poverty, women whose husbands had left them felt they could not approach the commune clerk to get a certificate of marriage dissolution, even if they may have been eligible. Several people also said that they did not feel they could argue with the volunteers. The volunteers' militarized appearance likely contributed to land claimants' reticence to press their cases. Villagers certainly noticed the volunteers' uniforms and the military trucks that delivered the students to their field sites. I did not meet any land claimants who said that the uniforms made them fearful of the volunteers, nor did I meet anyone who believed that the volunteers were part of the military. But many people mentioned the uniforms when I asked about the volunteers:

"Oh, the volunteers? You mean Hun Sen's volunteers with the army uniforms?" The uniforms were a potent symbol of the volunteers' relationship to the prime minister and the power (and potential military violence) that he embodied.

Racialized Gendered Encounters in the Uplands

In indigenous-majority upland areas, the land reform reflected not only gendered and classed but also racialized elements, as the volunteers, who were all from Cambodia's majority Khmer ethnic group, saw indigenous people as less modern and in need of development. My survey analysis shows that many indigenous people's land was not surveyed, but this is due in part to my survey methodology. I was unable to conduct the survey in two of my planned study villages, where high numbers of indigenous people received land title, because village authorities threatened me and I was forced to leave (see chapter 2). In the villages I did survey, many people refused to have their land surveyed in order to wait for communal title claims. In Sai Tong commune, indigenous elders spoke out against the student volunteers and instructed people to wait for communal title; consequently, the uptake of land claimants during Order 01 in this commune was low.

Some volunteers were genuinely confused about why indigenous people might not want private title but preferred to wait for communal title. The discourse of racialized modernity, which assigns indigenous peoples to a backward category of the other that must be developed, is so naturalized in Cambodia that these volunteers suggested people were "too uneducated" or "too traditional" to understand the value of property (Ashcroft, Griffiths, and Tiffin 1998, 171). "The problem is that [the indigenous people] just don't understand what's important for them. They think [the titles] are not important, but the truth is that land title is the most important. They don't understand, but when we have title, then we have control over the land. It's because they don't have school; they are still traditional" (volunteer surveyor in Khang Leit).

Beyond these racialized ideas, the volunteers' understandings of proper land use were guided by ecological considerations of what it meant to use the land well, which often privileged cash crop cultivation. When I asked one volunteer how he felt Order 01 might have affected shifting cultivation practices, he somewhat defensively suggested that those practicing good agriculture would benefit:

> ALICE: Do you think the titling has changed the agriculture systems of the indigenous people?
> VOLUNTEER: I think there are some villages that do good agriculture.... They have cashews, they do rice, they can do cash crops. They use their land well, and they can get title for that land.

For this volunteer, "good agriculture" meant cash crop cultivation. Other volunteers found ways to survey shifting cultivation land, even if they felt that this was outside the bounds of Order 01: "Most of the time, most of the people who own the land next to the forest, they are indigenous. So sometimes we actually measure for them. Because the thing is at the end of the day they will just burn down the forest and plant rice (*laughing*), you know. So we measure for them, but we talk to them about planting other crops too, crops that will be better for them."

In the uplands, then, the students embodied a position as agents of development; in similar ways to missionaries and aid workers, they sought to benefit the lives of indigenous people by protecting them from rampant corporate concessions through commodifying their land (Li 2007; Stirrat 2008). Essentially, the volunteers' mission in the uplands was not just titling land but selling the idea that land's value emerges through its commodification as private property. Indigenous people who applied for private title in upland areas were asked to thumbprint a contract (in Khmer language) that included a declaration stating that they were "really willing to live as private individuals outside the indigenous community" (MLMUPC 2014). In many communities, some people decided to take the private land title, while others opted to wait for recognition of their communal lands. This had the effect of not only redrawing property lines but also radically shifting local ecologies as well as people's social relationships with land and within their communities (as I describe further in chapter 6).

Soon after Order 01 implementation began, an independent Cambodian newspaper caused a stir by suggesting that indigenous people were being forced to take private titles.[9] The minister of land denied this, but in April 2013, one Land Ministry spokesperson was quoted as saying, "We have to push all the minority people to register for private land titles to protect their land and stop the disputes with economic land concessions."[10] The volunteers I spoke with, however, said that they did not use outright threat or coercion but rather deployed a range of strategies of persuasion that drew on their presence as youth living in the community to build trust with people. These strategies included enrolling brokers (elders in the community and village chiefs), "hanging out" (*dtau dau leeng*), doing good deeds for local people, using peer pressure, and being seen conspicuously in public spaces helping villagers to fill out private title applications. These strategies are worth discussing in detail because they illustrate the ways in which policy implementation is not just a series of bureaucratic moments or formalized encounters with state agents but also the slow process of trust building, persuasion, and pressure, which in this case reproduced the racialized gendered state. This was made possible by the volunteers' constant presence in the village and their status as trustworthy youth, and it often took place through intimate encounters in village spaces with the assistance of trusted village leaders.

ENROLLING BROKERS: ELDERS, CHIEFS, AND STUDENT VOLUNTEERS

Theara remembers that it was not until he was in the back of the army truck, rumbling slowly out of Phnom Penh city, that he learned his team would be stationed in Khang Leit province. For young urbanites like him, the upland provinces represented wilderness and adventure, but when he arrived, "it was much harder than I thought; we couldn't speak the language, and they didn't trust us." Moreover, many indigenous communities were in the process of applying for communal land title (CLT) and stood to lose access to communal forestland and shifting cultivation plots if they accepted individual titles (Rabe 2013). Only ten people in the village asked for their land to be surveyed in the first two weeks, and that made things difficult for the volunteers and land officials, as "it was hard to just measure one plot, and then not measure the ones that border it. We needed to have all the neighbors come to witness the surveying and they didn't come." Theara's team started to use its authority as Hun Sen's volunteers to persuade traditional village leaders to help:

> THEARA: So what we had to do was to go through the authorities—start from district, commune, village. . . . Make sure the authorities understand, and they can ask the villages to come to a meeting. I talked to the traditional leaders in the village and asked them to persuade people to meet with us. At the meetings we explained why the titles are important.
>
> ALICE: What did you say?
>
> THEARA: We explained about how there are two big things. One is that without title, your land doesn't have value. When you have title your land has value. So when the land has value you can sell it and you can use it as collateral to get a loan. And the second thing is that it saves the land from the companies.

Another student agreed that "the important thing was to contact people through the province first, then the district and the commune down to the village, so the authorities could tell the people to cooperate." Trust could be built "if the villagers see us walking with the traditional chief and elders."

The language barrier was an important aspect of the need for brokers. Several volunteers said that some indigenous women did not speak Khmer, so the volunteers asked the village authorities or people's neighbors to translate. In one case, the volunteers asked "the authorities to go beforehand, to tell the villagers what to do." This reliance on village authorities as brokers is a common strategy for outsiders who wish to access upland villages, be it NGO staff, researchers, government officers, or company representatives, but it is intensely problematic. During my research in upland Khang Leit province, for example, I organized a series of community meetings and household surveys with the assistance of the village chief in each area. Several days later I was in the provincial capital when I met a man from the village who had attended one of the meetings. He told me, "It was no good, because the village chief told us first what to say. . . . That always happens when people come to the village." I suggest that this use of male elders as brokers is particularly worrying for the land reform, because the voices of indigenous women—who are potentially most vulnerable in this land commodification process—were mediated by men in positions of authority. Thus ethnic women were doubly subjugated: they were pressured to choose individual property (which put their membership in larger communal property claims in doubt), and their lower levels of education and Khmer language ability meant that their voices were mediated by men.

HANGING OUT: LIFE IN THE VILLAGE

The strategy of enrolling local chiefs and elders did not always work. Volunteers complained to me that some village elders "did not understand about the title" because "they had old ideas" and that "some people do not listen to the elder that we asked to help us because they listened to other elders in the village." The volunteers said that another strategy was to hang out in the village and talk with people one-on-one to convince them of the benefits of private title. Because the students usually lived in the villages for one to six months and were encouraged to interact in the community, volunteers noted that they had ample opportunities to talk with villagers about the benefits of land titling and persuade people to apply for title: "One of the things we did was hanging out sometimes. You know we did not just work all the time; sometimes we talked with them. And you know, the second month there, we spent whole days there just talking with them. We danced, ate with them. And we tried to convince them to think about what they should do, to think about the future. . . . You know we tried to explain it to them in a diplomatic way."

The volunteers explained to me how they tried to find people who were willing to work with them, so "when the neighbors see us, the . . . rumor will spread and people will talk." The key was to "know about peer pressure. . . . Like, that person is doing it; why don't you?" The spatiality of these encounters was also important, meeting not only at people's fields far from the village but also in the domestic spaces of the communal well or meeting house, "the places that people cluster together and are willing to meet . . . so then other people will see and will start to trust you, and it spreads."

When I asked the volunteers what they said to people during meetings and conversations to persuade them to accept individual title, most volunteers said they talked about the ability to easily take out loans and protect land against land grabbers. However, one volunteer noted that in indigenous communities, "they aren't interested in loans, so I have to talk about how this will be your land, just yours to share with your children and grandchildren." In indigenous communities, the CLT mechanism potentially allows communities to maintain their land holdings in the face of distress sales and land grabs, as much larger areas of land can be included in the title (including spiritual land and forest for shifting cultivation), and decisions must be made communally; but ironically, the volunteers tried to persuade people of the benefits of private title by citing the insecurity of the CLT. One volunteer became quite agitated during our interview when he told me why he encouraged people to apply for private title: "Look, in theory, the [CLT] is perfect, we don't argue that the idea is not perfect. But if you look at the practical side . . . with how slow it is, and the paperwork you have to do . . . and then even if you get communal title, you do not have the people to enforce it. So in that case, you know, the individual land title is best for them."

In some cases, these persuasive arguments contained ominous warnings of land loss if people did not join the survey, as suggested by one volunteer's recounting of what he would say to convince people:

> Think, if you want to wait for the government to do that communal title for you? It's not going to happen. And then who will join? The communal land should be all together, not one here, one there, with some people private, some people communal. . . . So now I think it won't work to wait, to have the communal, because you are not all together. So I think you should do the private title now. You will have the rights to own the land now, and you can also pass on to your children. . . . But if you wait, then the company can come.

These techniques of persuasion matter because the results were a very high uptake of individual land plots in some indigenous communities (Milne 2013) and a proliferation of new tensions about the future of communal land title that are not yet resolved (see chapter 6).

The Youth Volunteers after Order 01

Given that an important implicit aspect of Order 01 was to win support for the prime minister and his ruling party before the national election, I asked the volunteers what they thought of the campaign and whether their attitudes toward the policy and the government more generally had changed at all due to their time in the field. The majority of volunteers supported the campaign and told me that they "saw how happy the people were when they had their land measured." The volunteers asserted that "now the villagers can have easier relations with the people in the village and authorities" because "when we measured the land, they had to find a compromise with their neighbors over the land boundary so they could have their land measured, so now they get on better." Others suggested that people would use the land more efficiently: "They will plant something worthwhile and build more permanent houses," and "They will develop the Cambodian economy."

Several volunteers, however, were more critical. They suggested that there were many areas left untitled, that many problems with companies were still unsolved, and that the policy was too short-term to be effective. Several volunteers had stories about corrupt volunteers who colluded with company management, and local authorities, and land officials to claim land. Indeed, all the volunteers I interviewed had stories about other teams that took bribes from land claimants, although none admitted doing this themselves. The volunteer recruitment took place in two waves (mid-2012 and 2013), and volunteers told me that corruption was much more pronounced in the second wave: "Now the campaign deviates from where it first started, day by day. . . . It's going sideways. Many things are not clear. And I think now the government has shifted their attention from this project to other projects. Leaving it behind without putting any amendments in, without putting the wrong things right."

A university lecturer in land management reflected that this apparent increase in corruption might have been due in part to the wider pool of universities and graduated students recruited in the second wave or to the loosening of some regulations (such as a higher cap on how much land one person could claim). One male volunteer who participated in the first wave of the campaign said that the volunteers in the second wave were more corrupt because they did not have such good intentions as the first volunteers, and this attitude began to creep through the campaign: "There were more people that were lazy, and there were more issues. You probably heard about the people that cut down precious trees to take back to the city with them. . . . I think they came with a different intention. They didn't come with good intentions; they came with the intention of making a profit."

Another volunteer suggested that when the campaign began, many people thought that it would be hard work with no reward, so only "brave people" volunteered. Later, people who had hung back realized that they could gain financially. His description of the corruption of second-wave volunteers reinforces the notion of the purity of the first volunteers by linking financial and sexual corruption: "The villagers loved the students. When I went, the villagers loved us; we didn't get money from them or cheat them in the first stage. But now the students get chased out; they ask for money from the villagers, and they do things like sleep with the virgins in the village."

Despite these rumors of corruption, however, most volunteers were enthusiastic about the success of the project and its contribution to national development. The volunteers' encounters in the field have not only shaped their ideas about the Cambodian state but also altered their broader life trajectories in significant ways. In the wake of Order 01, more than six hundred volunteers—including Theara and three other volunteers I interviewed—passed the state examination and began work with the Ministry of Land. Two volunteers from Phnom Penh are now stationed full-time in the uplands working at the land department, and one of these volunteers told me he is getting much better at surveying and dealing with people now that he has time to learn from others in the department. "We got training properly when we joined the ministry, after we passed the exam," he said. "Now I can operate the total station, which is a more accurate way of doing the land survey than the GPS units we used before as volunteers."

Sokha was still undecided about his career trajectory when I last spoke with him. He was working for a private real estate firm at the time, and he said that his experiences as a volunteer had put him off joining the ministry. He worried about the sustainability of the land reform: "Making it happen is one thing but keeping it alive is another thing. . . . Some people sell the land without transferring the title; they just give the title to the new person but don't go to get the name changed. So I think that if we just put the focus on making it happen but not keeping it up, then it does not really work. And we see that the people with power try to use it to their advantage, try to make it a political thing." Sokha said he could see that the Land Ministry "is all corrupt, and you have to be like that to be part of it. . . . But helping people is my thing; becoming part of something that is about the party, that is not my thing." One of the women I interviewed also said that she did not want to join the Land Ministry because of the "unfinished problems that we couldn't solve." Instead, she was employed at a land rights NGO in Phnom Penh.

I called at the large temple where I had previously met two of the Pagoda Boy volunteers and found them still living at the temple, sitting outside in the sun under a shady tree. One laughed when I asked him whether he was hoping for work in the Ministry of Land. "I can hope but they haven't called me; I just work at the ministry of the temple," he said wryly, meaning that he did not have a job at all. He said that some young people from the temples had found jobs in the Land Ministry, but in general he felt that the selection processes discriminated against people like him, who came from the provinces. "Most of us tried and we didn't get it," he said. "But the students from the good universities, they got accepted and now they have a good government job." It seems that the volunteers' ambiguous subjectivities, their "in-between-ness," was fleeting; some are now absorbed into the state as full-time employees while others have rejoined the swelling ranks of urban young people—although they carry with them (and many like to tell others) their memories of being part of Hun Sen's youth.

Conclusion: The "In-between-ness" of Volunteers

My focus on the volunteers in this chapter contributes to scholarship on everyday state formation by foregrounding actors whose very subjectivity challenges analyses of state and society as either two distinct, impermeable spheres or an inseparable whole. The volunteers' status as Hun Sen's youth enabled them to be seen both as more trustworthy than state officials because they lay outside of established state structures and as more powerful and potentially threatening due to their close ties to the prime minister. The volunteers were able to exploit the ambiguity afforded by their roles to wield a surprising amount of agency on the ground in relation to local power brokers. Overall, though, the students were not in a position to systematically resolve entrenched disputes between farmers and state-capital interests, and they tended to reproduce in their work hierarchical modes of authority based on class, gender, and ethnicity.

My analysis of the land reform volunteers confirms that the reform was no simple technical exercise in land registration and titling; rather, it intersected with a series of contested political fault lines, including questions of loyalty to the regime, neoliberal ideas of tenure security, and the concoction of classed, gendered, and racialized hierarchies in play in contemporary Cambodia. My survey results—showing that just over half of land claimants had their land titled—give weight to my contention that this titling reform was never about creating a legible rural landscape. The opaque, secretive reform details, the rapid policy changes according to Hun Sen's oral pronouncements, and the rushed training for volunteers led to widespread confusion on the ground. As the volunteers navigated this confusion in their encounters with land claimants, their status as Hun Sen's volunteers reinforced the notion that the land title was a personal preelection gift from the prime minister rather than a shift to a bureaucratic mode of property administration. Ultimately, then, the volunteers reproduced Hun Sen's place at the apex of the system.

This chapter also draws out another productive aspect of uncertainty for the state: the ability to deny responsibility for mistakes and push blame onto others (Roy 2016). For most of the volunteers, their participation appears to have successfully reinforced nationalist ideologies that posit foreign companies as the cause of Cambodia's land issues. Some volunteers did voice doubts about the success of Order 01, telling me that "we still have the problem of the companies" that "come to Cambodia and are crooked." But even these critical volunteers argued that the government could not bear responsibility for these problems because government officials could not see what was happening on the ground. As one volunteer said: "When the government provided the land concession they didn't see the problems; they didn't know how many people lived inside the concession." This tendency to divert blame away from the CPP was also evident in the ways people blamed local authorities for land grabbing during the land titling reform rather than the more distant state elite (discussed in the previous chapter). The obfuscation of economic and political connections between state elite and international companies, land speculators, and local state officials enables blame to be apportioned to others and the state to gain a greater sense of authority.

This analysis of the gendered, racialized implementation of the reform raises a new question: How did this shape people's lives after the students left? In the following chapters, I turn to the aftereffects of land reform. In chapter 5, I ask what difference the land title makes to people's daily lives in these spaces of land violence. My analysis reveals how the production of subjectivities through land titling deepened the cleavages of class and gender relations in rural areas.

5

LIFE IN THE LEOPARD SKIN

The Company Is All Around Us

I chanced upon the house in figure 9 while navigating my way around the perimeter of the Pheapimex concession on my motorbike. The house was nothing special—simple, one room with a tin roof, perched off the ground just high enough to store firewood and fishing gear underneath. But it stood out to me because it was the only dwelling left in an area surrounded by cassava plantation. I sat on the steps with the owner of the house, a woman in her fifties, and we watched her young grandson dig in the dirt and shriek with glee when he unearthed ants and they fled from his poking stick. The woman told me other villagers used to live nearby, but most people left when the company moved into this area two years prior. She shook her head emphatically when I asked her why she stayed. "They didn't offer enough compensation to buy anything else if we left here," she complained. "And I didn't want to end up in the city with nothing. So I said I'm not moving." She said she received land title for her land during the land reform, but she is still worried. "Most people are scared here," she told me. "Because the company is all around us, we are scared of them taking our land; I can see them coming closer."

While previous chapters have focused on the broader politics and implementation of Order 01, it is equally important to ask, What happens after people receive land titles? This perspective, which I examine over these final chapters, contests state recognition (through both individual and communal land title) as an analytic endpoint. The expectation that the leopard skin land reform would

FIGURE 9. This small home is the only dwelling left in an area surrounded by a cassava plantation.

(Photo: Alice Beban.)

provide tenure security and reduce poverty depends on all land being equivalent, a fungible commodity that can be represented by geometric lines on a land title and a simple price tag. But the idea that land title provides land tenure security obfuscates the reality of living in the leopard skin landscape. The leopard skin is relational: it is specifically about the promise of situating smallholders within and around large concessions. Therefore, analysis of the land reform must understand what the quality of this relation is: What does it mean to live within a land concession?

In this chapter, I examine how the land reform shaped people's livelihoods and relationships with land and to what extent its promises were borne out. I focus on four key benefits that the land title was expected to provide, according to the discourse on land titling from international agencies and the Cambodian Ministry of Land—tenure security, poverty reduction, women's empowerment, and plantation employment. I analyze my survey results through a comparative lens examining the trajectories of land claimants who had land surveyed versus those who did not have any land surveyed during Order 01. I find that Order 01 did not provide rural landholders with tenure security, nor did people who received land title manage to move out of poverty or find employment on nearby plantations. The relationship between land title and gender empowerment is also complex, as entrenched gender norms limit women's ability to escape from abusive relations. I then move to a broader analysis of the ways the land reform shaped social relationships within my study communities. Order 01 deepened class and gender-based inequalities, as communal land enclosure and coercive land sales in the reform's wake ultimately effected another layer of exclusion. In the final section, I contend that we cannot understand people's continued tenure insecurity without attending to the affective dimension of people's lives inside land concessions.

The Leopard Skin Promise: Tenure Security, Wealth, and Women's Empowerment

Perceptions of Land Tenure Security

Tenure security has both a perception component and practice component. This means that beyond the possession of a formal land title, what matters is how people perceive tenure. One way to assess this is to ask people about how worried they are that their land will be taken (Broegaard 2005). It is also important to understand people's practices of using land title to enhance credit access and land transfer, as well as people's shifting patterns of land use (Akram-Lodhi et al. 2007). If the land title is indeed a means of providing tenure security to people within leopard skin areas, I would expect people's perceptions of tenure security to be higher among those who received a land title during Order 01, and I would expect people to access credit markets and land markets and to make long-term investments in their farming systems.

I assessed perceptions of security first through two linked survey questions: a recall question—"Before the land titling campaign, were you afraid that someone would take your land?"—followed by a question about current experiences: "Now, are you afraid that someone will take your land?" In Khang Cheung and Khang Leit, 60 percent (n = 270) of survey respondents said that before the land titling reform, they felt afraid someone would take their land (figure 10, left bar). Most other respondents said they were not sure whether someone would take their land. Results were similar across provinces. In other words, the vast majority of survey respondents did not feel secure in their land tenure before the land titling reform.

When asked about current perceptions of land tenure, I found no significant difference in tenure security between people who received land title and people who did not receive land title during the reform (figure 10, middle and right bars). Around 10 percent of people who received a land title moved from the Insecure to Not sure category, suggesting that land title contributed to perceptions of security for some recipients but did not provide full tenure security. Among land claimants who did not receive a land title, insecurity slightly in-

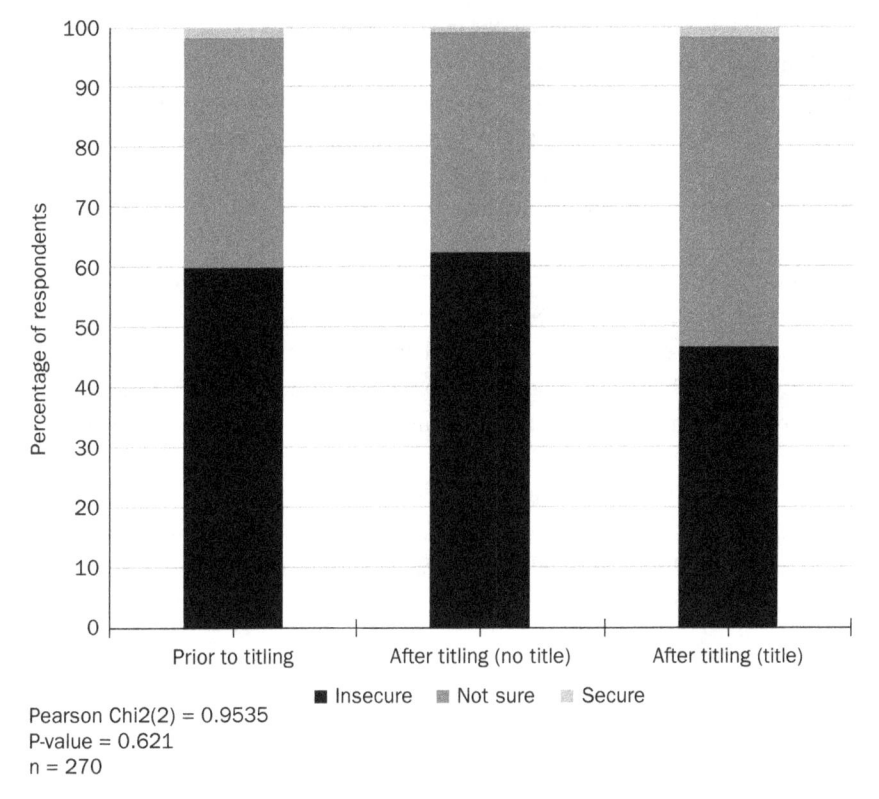

[Chart showing percentage of respondents categorized as Insecure, Not sure, and Secure across three groups: Prior to titling, After titling (no title), and After titling (title).]

Pearson Chi2(2) = 0.9535
P-value = 0.621
n = 270

FIGURE 10. Perceptions of tenure insecurity (possession vs. no possession of land title).

(Source: Alice Beban.)

creased following the tenure reform. This is commensurate with my ethnographic findings that people who did not receive a title are now deemed illegal settlers and may be at greater risk of land dispossession, a risk that is also noted in studies in Thailand and Laos (Hirsch 2012).

Use of Land Title to Access Loans

Beyond people's perceptions of security, land title theoretically increases tenure security and reduces poverty by enabling access to credit, which people can invest in their farms or off-farm economic ventures (de Soto 2000). However, loans can also be a cause of insecurity if people become indebted and must sell their land to repay their debts (Akram-Lodhi et al. 2007; Akram-Lodhi, Haroon, and Kay 2009). A central question, then, is how the possession of formal land title affects people's credit access and loan behavior.

140   **CHAPTER 5**

Very few survey respondents in the indigenous-majority province of Khang Leit had any loans; therefore, I only used responses from Khang Cheung for this question. I suspected that those with land titles might have taken out more loans, as many rural people told me that the land title was important as a source of collateral. However, in Khang Cheung I found that people who possessed land titles were no more likely to have loans than those who did not have land titles (figure 11).

Land title holders had slightly higher loans (mean of US$902) than those without land title (mean of US$841) and were more likely to borrow from a formal microfinance institution (MFI) rather than from informal moneylenders (75 percent of titleholders held loans from MFIs, compared with 64 percent of people who did not have a land title). Contrary to the notion that formal institutions offer better conditions for borrowers, interest rates were no different for people with title than those without title.

These responses suggest that a lack of access to formal lending institutions was not the issue in this area; people already faced high levels of indebtedness. A separate question in my survey backs this up; when I asked people to rank sources

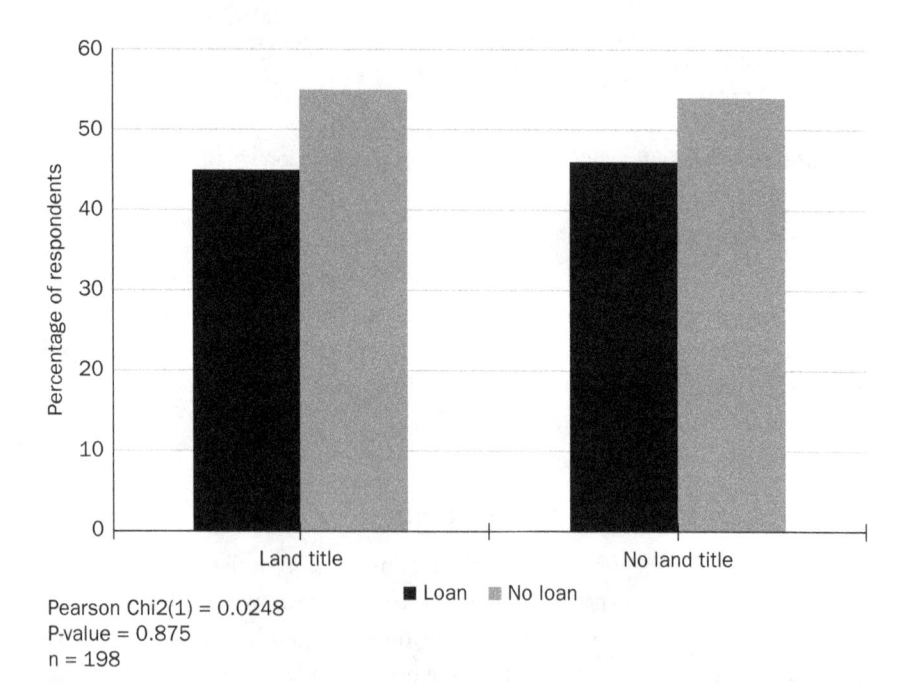

Pearson Chi2(1) = 0.0248
P-value = 0.875
n = 198

FIGURE 11. Loan behavior (possession vs. no possession of land title) in Khang Cheung.

(Source: Alice Beban.)

of insecurity, not one respondent said that insecurity was due to a lack of loan access. Rather, in interviews, several people described the influx of MFIs into their villages and the presence of what one farmer evocatively described as "motorbikes that drive around all day, coming with their suits on to check up on our loans." Predatory MFIs regularly issued loans with no collateral and then forced people to give up their land or other possessions. This situation led Anton Simanowitz and Catherine Knotts to argue in the UK's *Guardian* newspaper on 6 March 2015 that "Cambodia's Poor Are Drowning in Debt" due to the lack of regulation and oversupply of credit. I recall a conversation with one of my neighbors in Khang Cheung, a man in his thirties named Chana who worked as a loan officer at the ACLEDA Bank MFI for five years. He became visibly agitated when we were talking and said he recently quit because "I wasn't comfortable with what they asked us to do. Sometimes we had to try to sell people more loans, even if they already owed money. And if they don't pay, we go and talk to them, we talk about taking their land, and sometimes they cry." Chana said that his MFI managers instructed him to procure evidence of property ownership from people taking loans, whether the prospective borrower had a land title or not. It was easier if they had a title, but sometimes Chana took people on the back of his motorbike to visit the commune office in order to obtain a letter stating that the land (or livestock) belonged to the borrower, or he would write a statement himself and have the borrower thumbprint it.

It is important to note that the incidence of loans in Khang Cheung is likely not representative of the national context. In more remote areas, lack of access to formal credit markets has reportedly been a larger issue (FAO 2019). However, in Khang Cheung, where improved infrastructure and proximity to the regional capital have facilitated the presence of loan sharks, I found that land title was not the key driver of loan access (although it was discursively seen as important by both land claimants and lenders); nor, conversely, was land title the key driver of indebtedness, because predatory lending was already widespread before the land reform. This might be changing, though. On a visit back to Khang Cheung in 2019, I found that many people had lost their land after using their titles as collateral to take out loans (primarily for health and food shortage crises) that they could not pay back (see the conclusion), and some people told me that mortgaging the land title enabled them to get multiple large loans. This suggests that more research is needed on the long-term effects of land commodification in the context of Cambodia's unregulated loan sector.

Land Markets after Order 01

Along with the theoretical expectation that property title increases access to credit, economic theorists also suggest that property markets will become more buoyant, allowing rural people to reap the benefits of higher land prices and secure market transactions (Feder and Feeny 1991; de Soto 2000). In Khang Cheung, just eight people in my survey (n = 198) said they had purchased land since the land reform, and twenty-six people said they had sold land. But in casual conversation, people frequently talked about selling their land, and some local authorities told me that almost everyone in their village had sold land following the reform. One district chief said that "225 people [of 320 households in the village] sold their land after they received the title." I believe this discrepancy between survey and ethnographic results is due in part to people's embarrassment at having sold land. Several people told me they felt forced to sell their land after the reform, and twelve survey respondents who sold land (out of twenty-six) said they were extremely unhappy with the sales they made after the reform. One woman described in an interview how middlemen forced her to sell her land after the land survey but before land titles were distributed: "I sold my land. I had land in the middle of a lot of people that sold to a powerful person from Phnom Penh. Now it's all cleared and he is planting a plantation there. I got one hundred dollars [US] per hectare. If we waited for land title maybe we would have got five hundred dollars [US]. But we were forced to sell because the neighbors all sold and the middlemen forced us to sell. I didn't want to sell but I did."

Other people concurred that land sales rose after the land reform as urban investors came from Phnom Penh to buy up large tracts of land, such as one woman in her forties who said sadly, "Now the wealthy people have bought all the land here with titles. They did everything by the book. They came here once the students had left and asked everyone to sell. So now we have no land to share with our children." This woman suggests that wealthy buyers preferred titled land in the wake of the reform, while a land broker in Srai Saat who worked on behalf of a wealthy Phnom Penh businessman told me that the land reform created a price differential between titled and untitled land:

> ALICE: Was more land sold before the students came or after?
> LAND BROKER: Most land after. Because then people had titles. The land that had the land titles sold for more, and the land that didn't get land title sold very cheap. But they all got sold.

Of course, selling land can be positive if people want to sell and if the sale enables people to pursue other viable livelihoods. However, many people said they felt forced to sell because everyone around them had sold to urban investors. A second land broker in Khang Cheung described to me how he tried to persuade groups of landowners to sell so that absentee buyers could develop plantations on large, contiguous blocks of land: "Normally if some want to sell, then all will sell. If they don't want to sell, I explain to them how it will be hard if they are the only one ... and the plantation is all around them.... So usually they will sell when I talk with them. Sometimes the buyer offers to give them a plot of the same size in a different area instead." He proudly told me that he had already managed large land purchases for five urban investors since the land reform, and he had a 100 percent success rate at persuading people to sell their land. He put this success down to his kind manner with people. Other people who had sold land through him, however, said they were scared because he told them that if they didn't sell, the land would be taken anyway, as one woman noted:

> We are scared, and we don't have money. So we sell. We had land in the middle of a lot of people that all sold, so we were forced to sell.... He said we would lose the land anyway.... Then the [wealthy buyers] rent [the land] out again to people to use. The people here used to do rice on the land.... But now people run out of money. If they have equipment they can [log] wood, but there is less and less wood now; it's all cut down. Now they have to go and sell their labor in the Chinese company or the mango plantations for very low wages.

This woman's narrative eloquently connects land sales to coercion, a lack of other meaningful work opportunities, and the creation of a laboring class in her village—people who labor on the same land plots they formerly owned. This potential for land formalization to result in a social divide between those who accumulate large plots and those who become landless laborers is noted in many studies on land reform (Borras, Kay, and Lahiff 2008; Cleary and Eaton 1996; De Janvry and Deere 1979). From the point of view of neoliberal economics, the ability of people to leverage their land titles to exit from agriculture and the accumulation of land into more efficient farm units is a sign of success (Li 2009). Certainly, land sales are not always distress sales, and people don't always want to stay in rural areas or to farm. But in Khang Cheung, most people told me they sold land due to fear and poverty, not economic opportunity.

Relationship between Land Title and Changes in Farming Systems

If people are more secure in their tenure and able to access credit, it follows that people will be able to invest more in their farms (such as in soil fertility or more lucrative cash crops that may take longer to establish) (Deininger, Ali, and Alemu 2009). Deininger (2003) cites work from Southeast Asia showing that investment and output per hectare are higher on titled land as farmers invest in more lucrative crops and farming methods that take time and capital to establish. However, in my survey, only two people (of 198 in Khang Cheung) said they had changed the way they used their land in the year since the land reform. These were both wealthier farmers who planted mango, a crop with fluctuating and (at the time) depressed returns but one they said they were cultivating defensively to make sure others didn't take their land. Other farmers, whether they received land title or not, said that they did not have the resources to invest more in their land. Their rice farms were a carefully balanced part of a broader livelihood strategy that included urban migration and off-farm labor. One farmer in his fifties said, "We just do what we always do. Why would we change? We don't have the money for growing other crops, and there's no water this year anyway. The rains were a month late! And my children are in the city so they aren't here to help." Another farmer, in her forties, said, "I have land but I'm not growing on it at the moment, because I don't have any markets, and I don't have money to grow."

Many farmers talked to me about their future plans for their farms, and they spoke in depth about the problems they faced. But they did not see land title as a mechanism that would enable them to improve their farming systems. These sentiments are illustrated by a conversation I had with Puu Tanak as we transplanted his paddy rice. He was already stressed; the rains had come late again, and farmers were more than a month behind with their transplanting, but he said that his problems were more than just the weather:

> The weather is one thing. . . . It's changed, definitely. But it's also the market. People here can only sell rice for eight hundred to one thousand riel [US$0.25] per kilogram. But if we think of the fertilizer, the seed, we don't make any money. And all the good land goes to companies and they ruin the land. They are taking everything. . . . They will take mine too. Any that's left, people have to sell because they can't make a living. But what else can we do? We don't know how to do other jobs. We want to work on the land. But the government doesn't help us with market, training, anything like that. So we make a loss, and then we have to sell the land cheap. So what do land titles mean? In a few years, there will be no land left.

Puu Tanak's narrative connects the increasingly erratic flooding and droughts in Khang Cheung with unequal market opportunities, a lack of state support, and the influx of agribusiness companies that squeeze farmers onto small, unproductive plots and degrade surrounding land and waterways with chemical-intensive production. For Puu Tanak, as for other rural people, Order 01 was a land reform in the absence of broader structural agrarian reform. As one farmer said to me, "The leopard skin should mean that the government actually supports small farmers as much as they support the concessions. But we never see the government helping us; they have abandoned us."

Gender Empowerment

Alongside claims that the land reform would enable land tenure security and poverty reduction, the Cambodian government and academics claimed that women with joint (husband-wife) land title would be empowered to gain greater control over land and household decision making and to escape abusive relationships (Mehrvar et al. 2008; MWA 2008). I felt this was an important claim to investigate, not least because Cambodia has high rates of gender-based violence toward women (MWA 2008), and recent studies suggest that domestic violence rates may increase when communities are embroiled in land conflicts with agribusiness concessions (Kent 2014). Many Cambodian women are economically dependent on their spouses or other family members, and a central reason women stay with abusive partners is to avoid the financial hardship and stigma of being divorced (*memae*) (Mehrvar et al. 2008). Holding property title jointly or in women's names theoretically empowers women to escape abusive relationships, as the title ensures that property will be divided between partners when the marriage is dissolved and women will not be left destitute (Agarwal 1994, 2003). In Agarwal and Pradeep's (2007) study of five hundred women in Kerala, India, for example, women's property ownership was associated with a dramatically lower incidence of intimate partner violence compared with women who did not own land. However, it is vital to interrogate this assumption of a simple causal relationship between land rights and women's well-being in a context where enduring gender constructs view women as family homemakers and condone gender-based violence against women for the well-being of the family unit (Brickell 2011; Mehrvar et al. 2008).

I found this relationship difficult to investigate, in part because the complex relationship between land title and gender empowerment is related to the varied use of formal legal channels for marriage and divorce in rural Cambodia. In order to be legally married, couples must apply for permission from the commune, hold a public announcement period of ten days, have a ceremony, and then register their marriage at the commune, which issues a marriage certificate. The majority of couples do not complete the registration. Strictly speaking, then, the vast majority of people in Cambodia are not legally married, although they are recognized by their communities as married couples. It follows that most people who wish to divorce do not complete formal divorces, which must be recognized in a provincial or municipal court to be formalized. Instead, most people obtain a de facto divorce letter from the commune office, which is usually thumbprinted by both husband and wife. I knew of only five couples who had paid to have their marriages formally recognized and one couple who had a formal divorce through the courts. The commune clerk in Phnom Mie confirmed the commune office's role in divorce cases: "In Cambodia, when people divorce, they don't often go to the court to do the official divorce. So we normally organize it at the commune office level. We have the right to try to help the couple to work things out together, and if they want to separate, we can informally acknowledge that. And then we can say to them how they should divide the land." As this commune clerk notes, the commune office is the key mediator in marriage disputes in rural areas. This begs the questions of how applications for marriage dissolution are treated at the commune level and whether the possession of a land title makes any difference in the distribution of marital property.

The commune clerk in Phnom Mie allowed me to photocopy the commune dispute log, which contained details of all disputes brought to the commune between 2012 and 2014 (i.e., both during and after the land reform). Of a total forty-one cases recorded, twenty-three involved a marriage dispute in which one or both partners wanted to separate. The reasons given for separation included physical violence (ten cases, all brought by women), alcohol abuse (seven cases, all brought by women), verbal abuse (four cases, two brought by women, two by men), money management (four cases, all brought by women), adultery (three cases, all brought by women), and mutual agreement that the partners "no longer love each other." The council suggested reconciliation (usually with the thumbprinting of a contract) in fifteen of the twenty-three cases and separation in eight cases:

- fifteen cases: commune suggests reconciliation (nine brought by wife; five by both; one unclear)
- eight cases: commune suggests separation (two brought by husband; one by wife; five by both)

The numbers are obviously very small here, and generalizations should be treated with caution, but these cases do reveal gendered ideologies and practices that have real consequences for women's and men's land control and their power within marital relationships. The case summaries (generally one to four pages) mention that the husband has brought the case to the commune council in only two instances; both of these instances were resolved with separation. The wife brought the case to the commune council in ten instances; nine of these were resolved with reconciliation. Reconciliation was even counseled in cases involving ongoing domestic violence accusations. For example, a case in 2012 stated,

> Commune previously saw this couple and reconciled them. Now they are back. Wife said: I cannot stay with husband anymore because he drinks, destroys property, is violent and never helps with housework. Husband said: I go to the forest to collect wood and ask my wife for rice to take with me, and she says bad words to me. I don't want to divorce my wife.

> *Resolution*: The couple thumbprinted a statement, saying that the husband would no longer abuse his wife, that they would treat the children well, and that they would have better communication.

In another 2012 case, the commune council drew up a similar contract with the couple:

> *Wife's conditions*: 1: Husband stops drinking; 2: Husband helps with domestic work; 3: No violence in family; 4: No other women.
> *Husband's conditions*: 1: My wife stops saying bad things to me; 2: My wife keeps an open mind.

Compare this detailed contract signed by both parties to the simple summary of another 2012 case, which was brought forward by the husband and resolved in favor of separation:

> Husband divorces from his wife. Because he says he does not love her anymore.

These differences in the grounds for reconciliation or divorce reflect deeply held gendered notions of women's place as the protector of family harmony. "Good" women hold the family together; their duty to their husband (as to their nation) is to maintain harmony. The commune office in Phnom Mie said that the office's aim is always reconciliation, and they can then informally acknowledge separation if reconciliation is unsuccessful. "Usually we can work it out," the clerk told me. The Phnom Mie commune chief told me that he reminds the couple how they "made promises to stay together and love each other. . . . We have children to care for; we have to remember these promises." He said that women are "skilled at getting their husbands to change," and he felt that reconciliation is good for women because "divorced women have a very hard life. . . . They don't have their husbands to work and they can't feed the kids. So it's better for the women to keep the couple together." Implicit in the commune chief's narrative is the notion that it is women's duty to keep the family together; the corollary of women's skill and promises is that women in abusive relationships have forgotten their promises and do not have the skills needed to maintain family harmony. In other words, this narrative subtly places blame for abuse on women.

The commune office's focus on reconciliation also meant that in cases of physical and mental abuse, the commune office made rulings that perpetuated gender-based violence. In my interviews with women in Khang Cheung, more than twenty mentioned domestic violence, and five said they had asked for separation from their abusive husbands but the commune didn't help them. I found these interviews shocking; I had to walk around the back of the house to cry after talking with one woman. She told me that she had separated from her husband of thirty years just three months before our interview: "I didn't go to the authorities; I went to the police post to file a complaint that I wanted to separate. Then I left. He was so bad with me. He would go away for a year or more, and then come back and get drunk and beat me and have fights with others. We went to the authorities three times and they made contracts with him, but that didn't stop him." At this point in the interview, the woman showed me scars on her left arm and the side of her head where she said her husband had beaten her several months earlier. Then she went on: "We have five children. Three are with my husband now. I wanted my children to go with my husband so they could have a better life than I could give them, but the two youngest are with me. My husband got all the land, 1.5 hectares of rice land. Maybe I could have got something, but I don't want to go through the authorities to get the divorce. I tried that already. It is better now that he is not here. When he was with me, I was always scared."

One theme that runs through this woman's story, and similar stories I heard from other women, is her repeated attempts to get help from the commune council and the council's focus on reconciliation. While marital reconciliation is likely appropriate in many cases, the consequence here was that women ended up leaving in desperation, without any property settlement from the commune. Given that the commune office counseled reconciliation in the majority of cases, the question of how land title might enable women to escape from abusive relationships seemed less relevant. Even in cases where the commune did counsel separation, the logbook gave little mention of how property should be distributed between husband and wife. However, the commune clerk assured me that the commune did not let men take all the land or property. Whether there was a land title or not, he said, the commune's position was that land should be shared: "When the people separate, it is only the commune chief who can make decisions about how the land is to be divided. The people are not allowed to do this themselves. We say that the land has to be divided equally, we stipulate that. If they have the land title we look at that, and if they don't have the land title, we know that the land is for both of them. We can do that. And if there are children, then what matters is the land for the children."

Although this clerk described the equal division of land between husband and wife, the commune logbook showed that the commune office most commonly divides land in favor of the partner who will look after the children. As a female commune councilor explained to me, "the person who is looking after the children needs to get the land, but not for themselves, for the children. Like, if they have three land plots, the husband might get one and the wife two because she has to divide with the children." Because gender constructions in Cambodia typically assign women the role of primary caregiver, the commune's practice of dividing land in favor of the caregiver means that women may actually gain more land than men when the marriage dissolves. However, as this commune councilor explained, this land is ultimately divided for the children. This potentially means that the mother must divide the land she received when the children marry, while the father keeps all the land he was granted when the marriage dissolved. In any case, the possession of a joint land title has little bearing on the outcome of these cases, where decisions are underpinned by deeply held gender ideologies.

Shifting Land Tenure and Livelihoods in the Wake of Order 01

The previous section argued that the promises of land title were unfulfilled two years after the leopard skin reform. This comparative lens (analyzing people with land title against people without land title) is important for challenging the promises of land titling on the proponents' own terms; it suggests that land title cannot always be equated with tenure security, gender empowerment, or poverty reduction. But this comparative analysis is inherently limited. It does not capture the way the land reform engendered broader socioecological shifts in rural communities. In this section, I broaden the analysis to explore the ways in which Order 01 shaped livelihoods and land tenure along class and gender divisions in Khang Cheung.

To give a sense of how the land reform intensified change in patterns of livelihood and land tenure, tables 2 and 3 sketch out the main shifts I observed in land tenure and livelihoods for households in Tmor Muoy village. I constructed the tables from my ethnographic observations and interviews in the village, as well as from survey responses on livelihood and wealth. I grouped households roughly into poor, medium, and rich, based primarily on my estimation of assets (house size and construction materials, landholding, transport, farm machinery). The sharply delineated rows and columns in the tables appear static, but I want to stress that Order 01 was a moment within ongoing processes of plantation expansion and enclosure of communal land. The land reform intensified livelihood and land tenure changes rather than initiating them. In the tables, I stress continuity as well as change by repeating aspects that continued across the columns and italicizing aspects that show change. Tables 2 and 3 outline the land tenure relations and livelihoods, respectively, within the village before and after the land reform.

The tables show that one of the biggest shifts in Tmor Muoy village after the land reform was the enclosure of the remaining forest- and grazing land around the perimeter of the village. This enclosure of commons has been a feature of land

TABLE 2. Land tenure before and after Order 01 land reform

	LAND TENURE BEFORE ORDER 01	LAND TENURE AFTER ORDER 01
Poor (Small house plots, tin roof, flimsy walls, limited road access to house/farm plots; no motorbikes/machinery)	No farmland or very small farm plots (less than 1 ha); no land title Access to forestland around village and in protected area	No farmland or very small farm plots (less than 1 ha); *land title to some plots* *Largely excluded from forestland around village and in protected area*
Medium (Medium-size house, tin or tile roof with strong pillars; bicycles and possibly motorbikes; mix of cattle and hand tractors)	Some farmland (0.5–10 hectares; most around 1 ha); no land title Access to forestland around village and in protected area	Some farmland (0.5–10 ha; most around 1 ha with some increased sizes); *land titles to some paddy/crop fields up to 5 ha; bifurcation as some people sold land during and after Order 01, while a few purchased or claimed land* Access to forestland far from village in protected area (*but must pay increased fines*)
Rich (large house, tiled room, strong pillars; cars and/or multiple motorbikes; hand tractors)	Village elite with large farmland (10–20 ha); handful of landowners with land title Access to forestland around village and in protected area	Village elite with large farmland (10–20 ha); most with land title *Absentee landowners from Khang Cheung town/Phnom Penh with large farmland (10–100 ha) on former forestland, most with land title* Access to forestland around and in protected area *and cleared and claimed former forestland around village*

NOTE: *Italics* = change in livelihoods after Order 01.

privatization efforts from colonial regimes through today, when land deemed vacant and available is claimed by individuals, with disastrous implications for the poor who depend on commons land (Geisler and Makki 2014; Weaver 2003). Much of the former forestland around Tmor Muoy had already been subject to enclosure before the land reform; valuable timber was gone, and the soil was sandy and prone to drought. But the commons land was still an important source of grazing land, firewood, and food for poorer families. Order 01 provided impetus for local officials, other elite, and urban businessmen to claim the remaining land. Two women in the community network described these changes and their impacts on people's livelihoods and social reproduction:

> In the early 2000s we could get food and earn up to seven hundred dollars [US] per year from collecting fruit, fungi, vegetables, firewood, and animals from the forest. But with Order 01 the villagers just received a small amount of land that was their rice land. They are happy to get that, but they lose access to the forest. Order 01 opens forestland to the company.

> In this village, the poor families lack food about three months of the year. In the past they lacked food about one or two months of the year, but could get food from the forest. Now they are less food-secure, after the land reform, because the forest was divided.

As these two women suggest, the leopard skin reform intensified an ongoing process of deforestation. Medium-wealth households that own a hand tractor can still access a distant protected forest area for logging (approximately 15 kilometers away), but this is now too far for poorer households who have only nonmotorized buffalo carts. As Puu Tanak noted, "The company was already cutting the trees here. But before, there were still trees on some of those mountains. But after Order 01 they are all gone. Now the trees are thousands of hectares up the mountains. Some high-ranking people and people from the city clear forestland and pay people up to one hundred dollars [US] per month to look after the land, to guard the land to make sure other village people don't get it."

Puu Tanak signals another shift: the influx of absentee urban landowners to the area. Urban landowners claimed and cleared forestland before the land survey in conjunction with local officials and other elite, and they also bought up land after the survey. This has led to a mango boom around the village. Mango is cheap and easy to establish from saplings, and although it takes time to mature, it offers a more secure tenure claim than rice or cassava production, as it is a permanent crop. Some large landowners have also developed rubber, corn, cassava, and sugarcane plantations. One woman spoke bitterly of these new plantations and their role in turning the villagers from peasants into wage workers:

> Now, after the land titling, there are people with large plantations getting all the land. Ten-hectare or twenty-hectare farms. They plant sugar cane, corn, mango, and rubber. Those new people don't stay here; they hire people to watch the land. In a couple of years, all the people from here will be working for them. And we get paid just enough to live on. On my land, we grow just enough rice to eat with nothing leftover. The idea of leopard skin doesn't allow any of our land around the rice field (*kbal dae*) that wasn't planted in rice. They took everything except a little rice land.

This woman's reflections reinforce the idea that the leopard skin is spatially incompatible with people's farming systems. While the *kbal dae*, or "headland," around the rice field is necessary for grazing cattle that then provide manure and labor for the rice field, the land reform only surveyed the rice field itself. Many farmers told me they had sold or planned to sell their buffalo because they could no longer access grazing land. Instead, those who could afford it bought hand tractors

TABLE 3. Livelihoods before and after Order 01 land reform

	LIVELIHOODS BEFORE ORDER 01	LIVELIHOODS AFTER ORDER 01
Poor	Non-timber forest product (NTFP) collection	*Very limited* NTFP collection far from village
	Firewood collection and charcoal production	*Limited* firewood collection far from village
	Fishing (at Tonle Sap)	Fishing (at Tonle Sap)
	Migrate to Thailand or Phnom Penh	Migrate to Thailand or Phnom Penh
	Wage labor on concession and piecemeal work for larger local farmers	Wage labor on concession and piecemeal work for larger local farmers *Wage labor on new local plantations for absentee owners*
	Some paddy land rental from medium or large landowners	Some paddy land rental from medium or large landowners
	Watching buffalo for medium or large farmers	Watching buffalo for medium or large farmers
Medium	Paddy rice production (with upland rice nurseries)	Paddy rice production (*no upland rice nurseries due to enclosure of nearby forest*)
	Crop production (fruit trees, home vegetable gardens)	Crop production (fruit trees, home vegetable gardens)
	Livestock raising (chickens, pigs, buffalo, cows)	Livestock raising (chickens, pigs; *very limited buffalo and cows due to shift to hand tractor and no grazing land for cattle*)
	Small-scale logging (if owning a cart or hand tractor)	*Very limited small-scale logging (if owning a cart or hand tractor), and must pay increased fines*
	Migrate to Thailand or Phnom Penh	Migrate to Thailand or Phnom Penh
	Own small business (e.g., food stall)	Own small business (e.g., food stall)
	NTFP collection	*Very limited* NTFP collection far from village
	Firewood collection and charcoal production	*Limited* firewood collection far from village
	NGO village liaison representatives (do not receive regular wage, but do receive per diem payments for meeting and training attendance)	NGO village liaison representatives (do not receive regular wage, but do receive per diem payments for meeting and training attendance)
	Official posts in local Buddhist temple clergy	Official posts in local Buddhist temple clergy
	Public servants (e.g., teacher)	Public servants (e.g., teacher)
Rich	Logging (medium scale or large scale in connection with regional military or politico-business elite)	Logging (medium scale or large scale in connection with regional military or politico-business elite)
	Paddy rice production (using hand tractor and HYV seeds)	Paddy rice production (using hand tractor and HYV seeds)
	Some limited plantation production (mango, corn, rubber)	*Expansive plantation production, especially mango, also rubber, corn, sugar cane, cassava*
	Wood storage/logistics (brokers for small-scale loggers)	Wood storage/logistics (brokers for small-scale loggers)
	Former military commanders, some active in military	Former military commanders, some active in military
	Official posts in local administration (village and commune council)	Official posts in local administration (village and commune council)
	Land brokerage	*Expanded land brokerage (getting kickbacks from new absentee landowners; facilitating land deals for companies/absentee owners)*
	Remittances from children in city or overseas	Remittances from children in city or overseas

NOTE: *Italics* = change in livelihoods after Order 01.

for plowing their rice fields and more chemical fertilizer for maintaining soil fertility in the absence of manure.

The influx of absentee plantation owners has opened up opportunities for some villagers to work as security guards and agricultural laborers. Many of the villagers I talked with, however, were bitter about the low wages offered (as the woman's narrative above attests). Those who gained most from the influx of urban land buyers were a small group of male village elites, including the village chief and deputy chief as well as a former military commander (who now has a stake in the logging industry) and two other local businessmen. These men acted as brokers for the urban owners, overseeing land purchase, consolidation, crop production, and labor in exchange for monetary kickbacks.

This inequality in labor opportunities illustrates the ways in which the land reform intensified structural conditions of insecurity along class lines in Tmor Muoy village. Those who lost most were people who could not lay claim to any land because they were landless already or people whose claims were not recognized because they lost access to common land use areas that were grabbed during the campaign. Those who gained most were people who had connections, resources, and information and people who embodied the subjectivity of modern-citizen farming commercial agriculture.

Reshaping Gendered Livelihoods and Land Tenure

Not only did Order 01 reshape class relations between households in Tmor Muoy; the campaign also reshaped gendered livelihoods and land tenure relations. Table 4 shows gendered work (for production and reproduction) before and after Order 01. I have coded activities that are most often gendered male, female, or both. There are always exceptions to the rule. (For example, in women-headed households, where either men were away working in Thailand or women were widowed or unmarried, women performed firewood collection, plowing, and small-scale logging, activities that are generally gendered as men's work.) This table therefore gives an approximation of gender norms, based on my ethnographic observations of who generally performed labor and on my interview questions and survey questions, rather than on any definite dividing line.

Table 4 shows that the land reform reshaped work within and outside the home. The forest enclosure during Order 01 made it more difficult for women to collect NTFPs, which are both a food source for the family and sold at the local market. Firewood collection, generally a male activity, is also more limited in the wake of Order 01. This loss of forest livelihoods for men and women puts pressure on poor families to make ends meet and interacts with other factors (including the prolonged drought and the expansion of migration networks) to increase

TABLE 4. Gendered livelihoods by social class before and after the land survey

	BEFORE ORDER 01	AFTER ORDER 01
Poor	NTFP collection	**Very limited** NTFP collection far from village
	Firewood collection and charcoal production	**Limited** firewood collection far from village
	Fishing (at Tonle Sap)	Fishing (at Tonle Sap)
	Migrate to Thailand for construction or plantation work	Migrate to Thailand for construction or plantation work
	Migrate to Thailand for factory work	Migrate to Thailand for factory work
	Migrate to Phnom Penh for construction work	Migrate to Phnom Penh for construction work
	Migrate to Phnom Penh/Khang Cheung town for garment work or service work	*Migrate to Phnom Penh/Khang Cheung town for garment work or service work*
	Wage labor on concession and piecemeal work for larger local farmers	Wage labor on concession and piecemeal work for larger local farmers
		Wage labor on new local plantations (crop maintenance)
		Wage labor security work for absentee landowners; land clearing for new plantations
	Some paddy land rental from medium and large landowners	Some paddy land rental from medium and large landowners
	Watching buffalo for medium and large farmers	Watching buffalo for medium and large farmers **(limited as less buffalo raising)**
	Home garden	*Home garden* **(limited access in some cases)**
	Caring for children and elderly	*Caring for children and elderly* **(mainly older women, as women of working age increasingly migrate)**
	Housework, food purchase and preparation	*Housework, food purchase and preparation* **(mainly older women as above)**
Medium	Paddy rice production (with upland rice nurseries)	Paddy rice production **(No upland rice nurseries due to enclosure of nearby forest)**
	Crop production (mango, fruit tree, banana)	Crop production (mango, fruit tree, banana)
	Livestock raising (Men take cattle to graze; *women tend home gardens and chickens or pigs*)	Livestock raising (*women tend home gardens and chickens or pigs*) **Very limited buffalo and cows due to shift to hand tractor or no grazing land for cattle)**
	Small-scale logging (if owning a cart or hand tractor)	**Very limited small-scale logging (if owning a cart or hand tractor)**
	Migrate to Thailand for construction or plantation work	Migrate to Thailand for construction or plantation work
	Migrate to Thailand for factory work	Migrate to Thailand for factory work
	Migrate to Phnom Penh for construction work	Migrate to Phnom Penh for construction work
	Migrate to Phnom Penh/Khang Cheung town for garment work or service work	*Migrate to Phnom Penh/Khang Cheung town for garment work or service work*
	Own small business (e.g., food stall)	Own small business (e.g., food stall)
	NTFP collection	**Very limited** NTFP collection far from village
	Firewood collection and charcoal production	**Limited** firewood collection far from village

	BEFORE ORDER 01	AFTER ORDER 01
	NGO village liaison representatives (primarily women, some men)	NGO village liaison representatives (primarily women, some men)
	Official posts in local Buddhist temple clergy	Official posts in local Buddhist temple clergy
	Public servants (e.g., teacher)	Public servants (e.g., teacher)
	Home garden	*Home garden **(limited access in some cases)***
	Caring for children and elderly	*Caring for children and elderly **(mainly older women, as women of working age increasingly migrate)***
	Housework, food purchase and preparation	*Housework, food purchase and preparation **(mainly older women as above)***
Rich	Logging (medium scale or large scale in connection with regional military or politico-business elite)	Logging (medium scale or large scale in connection with regional military or politico-business elite)
		Expansive plantation production, especially mango, also rubber, corn, sugar cane, cassava
	Paddy rice production (using hand tractor and HYV seeds)	Paddy rice production (using hand tractor and HYV seeds)
	Some limited plantation production (mango, corn, rubber)	Expansive plantation production, especially mango, also rubber, corn, sugar cane, cassava
	Wood storage and logistics (brokers for small-scale loggers)	Wood storage and logistics (brokers for small-scale loggers)
	Former military commanders	Former military commanders
	Official posts in local administration (village and commune council)	Official posts in local administration (village and commune council)
	Land brokerage (getting kickbacks from new smallholder settlers; facilitating land deals for companies and absentee landowners)	**Expanded land brokerage (getting kickbacks from new absentee landowners; facilitating land deals for companies or absentee owners)**
	Remittances from children in city or overseas	Remittances from children in city or overseas
	Own small business (such as moneylender, shop)	Own small business (such as moneylender, shop)
	Caring for children and elderly	Caring for children and elderly
	Housework, food purchase and preparation	*Housework, food purchase and preparation*

NOTE: Regular type = male; *italics* = female; underline = both male and female; **bold** = change in livelihoods after Order 01.

rates of labor migration among poor and medium-wealth households. This in turn means that as more women (and men) of working age migrate for work, the childcare and housework (including food cultivation, preparation, and production) is performed by older women. Essentially, grandmothers are caring for grandchildren, a pattern that has been noted in many parts of the world as labor migration increases (Kelly 2011). Home gardens have declined in some households, both because women left at home do not have time to cultivate the gardens and because gardens farther from people's houses were counted as part of the headland that was not titled in Order 01, and these areas were subsequently sold to middlemen or abandoned. Among rich households, the generational shift in care work is not occurring to the same extent as in poorer households, in large part because wealthier households in Tmor Muoy are less likely to migrate for work (a phenomenon also seen in other Cambodian studies [Molyaneth 2012]).

As deforestation and land enclosures cut off people's access to the forest, the "male work" of finding and claiming new land and small-scale logging is only available to men who have the wealth and political networks to participate in the logging sector or plantation expansion. Masculinity in this context becomes increasingly militarized. The forest clearance in the plantation is undertaken with bulldozers; something that many people told me is more violent to the land and offensive to land spirits. The jobs available in the logging industry are high-risk. Small-scale loggers are often fined or threatened by government officials, military personnel, and concession company workers. Some local men from poorer households have managed to find work as security guards patrolling the ELC plantation boundary. I met one of these security guards while I was riding a motorbike around the perimeter of the plantation. I got caught in a rainstorm and took shelter in a small hut, where I met a man in his sixties. He said he was from Phnom Mie, and he worked at the plantation as a security guard. He took me inside to show me the rifle he keeps on a small desk. His voice broke when he told me that if he saw people's cattle or buffalo wandering into the plantation, he was supposed to shoot them in the leg. "They told me not to kill them; they want them shot in the leg so they can limp back out and then it's a warning to the villagers not to let anymore cattle in." He looked furtively outside the hut, before telling me, "But I don't do that. If I see them, I just yell at them, I chase them out. . . . I don't want to shoot anything." This man is essentially policing his own community, having to choose between maiming his friends' and neighbors' cattle or potentially losing his job. The fact that he shoos away the cattle rather than maiming them shows his care for his community and the ways he navigates the boundaries between being a member of a targeted community and a company employee, despite the contradiction (and potential retribution from the company management) that this creates.

Livelihoods and Relations with Agricultural Companies and ELCs

The leopard skin imaginary assumes that smallholder farmers will find employment within land concessions. But with the exception of some laborers, such as the security guard I described above, I found that most local people in Khang

Cheung and Khang Leit did not work regularly on the plantations. This was not the case when I began research in 2012, however. When I first arrived in Khang Cheung, I estimated that around 80 percent of local households sent at least one member of the household to work in the plantation, with male workers (around 70 percent) employed to clear the trees and plant and harvest the cassava and female workers (around 30 percent) employed to plant and weed the cassava. People from other villages in the area also came to the plantation; every morning, I saw a stream of people on bikes and on foot heading to the plantation, as well as a handful of minivans that brought laborers from more distant villages.

But when I arrived back in Khang Cheung in December 2013, most local people had stopped working on the plantation. Out of 198 people I surveyed in the area, 48 said they previously worked at the "Chinese company," and only 5 of these people said they still worked there. The main reasons for this dramatic shift were threefold: first, the plantation's labor needs declined significantly after the trees were cleared and the company mechanized harvesting; second, the company hired migrant laborers from elsewhere in Cambodia rather than hiring local people; and third, locals quit working at the plantation because they felt labor conditions had worsened. The latter reason was what former laborers most often articulated to me, such as one man in his forties who worked at the plantation for nine months before quitting: "In this village, one or two people from every household worked at the company last year. But now, many of us have stopped. It's too hard. And we don't get paid regularly, maybe once every couple of months. They oppress us."

When people such as this man described the reasons they quit working at the company, they didn't just talk about pay or the difficulty of the work involved; they described a basic lack of respect for workers' dignity. I heard the same story from ten former laborers: The last straw was the day the company cut down a stand of trees that had provided shade for workers on their lunch break: "We left because they don't pay on time. Sometimes we are short of food. And the main thing, the most important thing, was when they cut the shade trees down in the fields. Now we can't even rest. That was when we quit." Several became physically agitated (raised voices and a sharp tone) when they recalled the removal of the shade trees.

Within these responses was the notion that the company was destroying the village—the forests, streams, animals, and even the health of the people—and yet, the company was so powerful, people felt that there was little they could do. One man said, "The work at the Chinese company keeps getting harder but the salary is the same. There are lots of chemicals and this poisons the streams. We get sore stomachs, and we have had buffaloes die. They don't pay a regular wage to workers. If you complain, they chuck you out. So we don't dare complain. Young people have killed each other in the company. If anything happens they don't call the police; they try to solve it themselves. They are like their own government. They do whatever they want. We have no power." Villagers concurred that the company was dangerous, as this man suggests—"They are like their own government." I frequently heard stories about people being killed in the plantation and fights among workers and one grisly story about a body in a sack repeated over and over. This story had the quality of an urban myth that I could not find any basis for, but it was a powerful reminder to people that the plantation was a violent place. Several people told me that the land spirits in the plantation area were angry and pointed to evidence of machinery that kept breaking and mysterious illnesses striking down workers. In these stories, it seemed that only the land spirits had any agency to punish the company for what people saw as morally corrupt treatment of the land.

Some people pointed out, however, that at least the company provided some job opportunities in a place where there were few other options. One village chief said that the company provided employment without discrimination: "The company is good for our village. We don't have any other jobs here, so the people are happy. And it's equal for everyone. Anyone, man or woman, fifteen or older who has the strength to do it can work in the Chinese company. Old people can work too."

The village chief from the neighboring village had a different story: "The company doesn't want to hire people from here. Because if we go to work in the company, our families can bring us food, or we take food with us. But when they have people from far away, the wife of the manager sells them food. So they want the people from far away. And if they hire us, they hire us to work far away so we have to stay over there. Now they have stopped asking us to work in the company." This is particularly interesting, because its logic is opposite to classic literature on plantation-smallholder relations, which suggests that peasant households are useful precisely because the burden of social reproduction falls on the household (including the unmarketed labor of women in the home preparing food [Stoler 2002]). More recent literature on land grabs and migrant labor suggests that corporations often prefer migrant workers because they are easier to control, as they work, eat, and live within the plantation boundaries and may have restricted mobility beyond their workplace (Li 2011). One woman said she actually lied about her residence and told company management she was a migrant from Kampong Cham because the company would not hire local workers: "When the villagers put their names down to work, they ask them where they are from. And if they say they are from here, they say they don't want them, they want people from far away. So I said I was from Prey Veng so they would hire me."

This woman was one of only a few local people working at the plantation when I returned for my second round of fieldwork. People seemed embarrassed to tell me that they worked at the plantation, and most of the workers came from poorer households who were desperate for cash, such as one woman with a small baby who had sold all her land to pay for her sick mother's hospital bills: "My husband and I work at the Chinese company when it's not rice season, and we help my siblings in the rice season. The work in the Chinese company is difficult. The people who work there are the people who struggle. The people who have no choice. I'm poor.... I don't have cows or buffaloes. I don't like to talk about it with the other villagers; I'm embarrassed."

Similarly, in Khang Leit, many people said that the ELCs preferred to hire migrant labor from other provinces. Some indigenous respondents also said that ELCs did not want to hire indigenous workers because the managers were Khmer and preferred to hire other Khmer. Also similarly to Khang Cheung, some people also said that local people who had found jobs at the plantations quit because the conditions were so bad. One man told me, "Now in some villages, the villagers used to work in the company but now they quit. Now there are mainly Khmer and Vietnamese people working." Many of the complaints from people in Khang Leit were similar to those in Khang Cheung—the company does not pay on time, the conditions are tough and keep getting tougher, and the company prefers to hire people from outside. One elderly man in an indigenous-majority village next to a rubber plantation told me bitterly that plantation labor was slavery: "Now many of the indigenous people don't work at the plantation; they don't want to be slaves of the company. Some go, but hardly any. They want their time; they know that losing their land, losing their culture, and becoming wage laborers is just becoming slaves."

Similar to the notion I heard in Khang Cheung that "the company oppresses us," the idea this man articulates—"we are becoming slaves"—reveals a relational subjectivity that is at odds with the state's notion of prosperous smallholder and wage worker households in rural areas. For people in Khang Cheung and Khang Leit, not only were the promised jobs not forthcoming (see Li 2011), but the work conditions and plantation activities were socially and ecologically damaging to people's sense of self and community.

Affective Life in the Leopard Skin

In this chapter, I have argued that tenure insecurity persists, and for some has increased, following the land reform. My explanations have emphasized the interconnected realms of the economic (e.g., the unregulated loan sector, the lack of decent plantation jobs, coercive land brokers), the political (e.g., people's dependence on local authorities, lack of state support for smallholders, state-sponsored

ELC expansion), and the ecological (e.g., severe drought, deforestation). But this misses a dimension. We cannot understand tenure insecurity unless we also understand the affective dimension of people's lives, particularly how fear and uncertainty shape everyday life for people who live in and around land concessions.

Fear

People's fear of the state elite and plantation companies taking their land emerges from layered fears: the memories of civil conflict, state repression, and racialized fear of outsiders. Many people in Khang Cheung and Khang Leit expressed fear that the concession company would eventually take their land whether they had a land title or not:

"Even if I have the certificate, I am still afraid! I am afraid for my land here, and also for the land in the forest because the company could still take it."

"I am afraid. I am afraid and I am happy at the same time. I am afraid of someone taking my land even if I have title, because I have don't have power. I am under them."

One community activist articulated the contradictions of achieving tenure security within a land concession area as "creating a prison," because the land reform locked people into small areas of land while legitimizing forest clearance in surrounding areas. "Now the company gets more land," she said, "as people now have no right to protest over the other land outside their measured plots. They just wait and watch the company clear all our forest." Similar metaphors of living in a prison or cage or being stuck were repeated frequently in my interviews. Even in villages beyond the boundaries of the ELC, people talked about conflicts in nearby villages and expressed concern that these problems might come to their village at any moment: "I'm very worried about the companies coming in the future. Now they are in the next village, so I think in the future they will come here."

This constant worry was not something people could ignore; everyday life was marked with the physical presence and symbolic threats of the companies. Tensions increased as plantations encroached onto forestland near villages and moved closer to people's fields. In Khang Cheung, the plantation company closed off farmers' access to grazing land by digging a deep trench that prevented cattle from crossing onto ELC land (figure 12). The shrubland and streams villagers used to graze and bathe their cattle, collect water, and gather firewood and NTFPs all lay on the other side of the trench on the edge of the cassava plantation (in the figure, the area to the right). In Khang Leit, people with small plots of rice land lost road access to their fields when the company that owned the surrounding land put up razor wire fences around the fields and installed security guards. In these

FIGURE 12. Trench separating concession land from village farmland in Khang Cheung.

(Photo: Alice Beban.)

physical ways, people's former sense of land ownership as fluid—seasonally shifting from private rice paddies to communal grazing areas and forest around the village—now had to conform to fences and permanent physical boundaries.

One day while I waited with my children at the market near Srai Saat for our motorbike to be fixed, a woman with a small baby wrapped to her chest started crying quietly as she told me about her fears: "I'm worried that someone will take my land. The army is one side and the Chinese company on the other. I don't want to sell my cows and buffalos but I might have to, because now there is no land for them. In the past we used to help each other. Now we just help ourselves."

I often heard sentiments describing the moral lapse this woman articulated—"now we just help ourselves"—a sense that this was not just material enclosure but also a rupture of community solidarity. This sense of insecurity was also gendered. I noticed this particularly in a village in Srai Saat commune, in which the military confiscated villagers' land to use for a military training unit and rubber plantation. While both men and women were afraid to use that land, several people said they needed men in the household to enter the area, and one woman told me she "didn't dare to enter because I don't have any sons." Another farmer told me that she did not dare to enter her own fields, but she asked her adult son to "live on the land, to stay in the hut there all the time, so they won't take it." In this case, the conception of the wild, untamed forest as the domain of men was extended to former paddy rice fields now perceived as the wild, dangerous domain of the military.

Uncertainty

People's deep fear of a violent future is interwoven with uncertainty about leaders' intentions. Here, I want to return to my discussion of the land title as a political gift to suggest that land title recipients' continued tenure insecurity is bound up with distrust of what the land title represents. When I asked people what the land title meant to them, many people paused, taking a long time to answer and sometimes shrugging their shoulders or quietly saying they weren't sure and asking me what I thought. These three statements are representative of comments that I heard often in Khang Cheung and Khang Leit:

> KHANG CHEUNG WOMAN: I'm not sure, because maybe at the moment the title gives us protection but, in the future, maybe the government will change the law and it won't mean anything anymore.
> KHANG CHEUNG MAN: Title is not so important. If they want to take the land back in the future they will. That's what they do. They can just make another law and overthrow this one.
> KHANG LEIT WOMAN: The thing I'm most worried about is the land title. It all depends on the higher people in government. If they don't think the land titles have a value to them, then they will get rid of them. We can't trust the laws in our country.

These statements reveal a profound uncertainty about and distrust of the government and national law. What the land title signifies is whatever the higher people in government value at the time. As in Sarinda Singh's (2012, 8) study of uncertainty in Laos, where "policy is negotiable for those in positions of authority," people's skepticism toward the law is born from years of conflict, multiple regime changes, and personalized politics that foments fear and distrust. And this fear was actively stoked by the actions of land surveyors and land brokers during Order 01. In both Khang Cheung and Khang Leit, people told me that the government may take back the land title after five years if farmers do not maintain productivity. Some said they heard this from the student volunteers, such as one woman in her forties:

> ALICE: Do you feel you have security now you have the land title?
> WOMAN: I don't know. If we haven't used the land in the forest in five years, they will take it back; that's what the students said. They surveyed the land for me even though there were some shrubs; not all was in rice. But they said we have to plant. . . . But it's hard because we don't have much time or money to prepare the land. . . . We're afraid they will take it back.

In this woman's case, the student surveyor apparently bent the rule requiring that only cleared land be surveyed and then said that she needed to plant within five years in order to legitimize his actions. In other cases, land brokers and local officials warned villagers that the state would take back the land title in order to coerce people into selling land. I saw this strategy one day when I was interviewing a woman at her home garden and a local monk stopped his motorbike outside her gate. I knew the monk from my previous meditation sessions at the local temple, and I gave him a wave. He smiled hello and walked over to the woman. "I hear that you have some land you might sell?" he asked her. "Maybe," she said. "Who is buying the land?" He explained that he was working as a land broker for a wealthy politician (*aekadom*) from the city, who was looking to consolidate large land parcels after the land reform. "I don't know," she said, looking down at her garden. "I don't have much."

They stood talking for a while, and then the woman called out to her husband to get the land titles down from a shelf inside the house. She spread the titles out on the ground and the monk looked over them carefully. "I have three hectares, about that, of rice land," she said, "and about five hectares of forestland up on the hill that I got from my parents." "Look," said the monk, pointing to the plot outline on one title. "They didn't measure that forestland. See? This is just 0.7 hectares and another 0.5 hectares here. . . . So most of it isn't measured." The woman grabbed the title. "But it's still my land," she said. "I got it from my parents." The monk shrugged his shoulders. "Look, you're better off to sell your land to me now. Because if you don't plant all that land within five years, they will take the titles off you. Then the company can get all the land. You can either sell it now, or you will lose it all." The woman's young son ran up to her at that point and started weeping. "Mom, don't sell the land; you can't do that!" She picked up her son and told the monk she would think about it.

A few days later, I went to see the monk at his temple and asked him about the five-year provision for taking the title back. "Well," he said, "that's what I was told." He was evasive when I asked him who told him about it. Then he interrupted me: "Anyway, it's better for her to sell, because the land is too steep and she won't be able to plant it all. And she has small children. She is better off taking the money now."

What I find particularly disturbing about this encounter is that monks are treated with great respect in rural Cambodia, often seen to be more trustworthy than state institutions (Harris 2005). This was the only time I met a monk working as a land broker (that I knew of), but the Buddhist sangha does control a huge amount of land and social power in Cambodia. Here, the monk/land broker drew on this respect to legitimate his coercion.

Conclusion: Anticipation and Foreboding

My argument in this chapter extends a temporal dimension to the notion of "in situ displacement" (Feldman and Geisler 2012, 974), the ways that people are "displaced in place" through the loss of entitlements, social exclusion, and alienation. Feldman and Geisler's (2012) concept recognizes violence beyond the moment of acute dispossession, but methodologically, the focus remains the material loss of rights, entitlements, and communal land access. Here I recognize that beyond material losses, it is the constant reproduction of fear and uncertainty that shapes people's everyday lives and their relationships with land and with each other in land-conflict areas. Fear is the "institutional, cultural and psychological repercussion of violence" (Krujit and Koonings 1999, 15) that fundamentally affects people's social relationships, material abilities to earn a living, and sense of self. The uncertainty and fear with which people perceive life in the leopard skin landscape infuses everyday life with a strange temporality. People continue to live and labor on the land, neither dispossessed nor fully confident in their ability to maintain their rural foothold. Many people's lives in this context are in a state of "lost or absent futures, of time standing still, waiting" to see if the company would come (Brigstocke 2016). This temporality of foreboding needs to be contrasted with the temporality of anticipation (High 2014; Singh 2012), the desire for development and the uncertain potentiality of state power that I have suggested is so productive for Hun Sen's government. People moved between these emotions; some remained hopeful and expectant that they could hold on to their land, some had given up all hope and said it was just a matter of time before they would have to leave, and many seemed to hover between an expectation of development and a profound fear.

This fear imbues the land title with particular meanings. My survey findings suggest that Order 01 provided rural landholders with neither tenure security nor the ability to move out of poverty; rather than being a document that secures people's rights to land, the land title in the context of the leopard skin is a gift that can be taken back if people do not perform their roles as productive, modern citizens. Going beyond the temporal uncertainty of not knowing when the company will come or when the state might take the land title back, the rural landholder asks a deeper question: How will the land title protect me when someone tries to take my land? In the following chapters, I consider the ways in which land titles both open channels for people to press their land rights and narrow the field of resistance.

6

COMMUNAL LAND STRUGGLES IN THE WAKE OF THE LAND REFORM

The Origin Story of the Community Network

I arrived at Srey Sophorn's house as the sun was setting. The promise of the first wet-season rains hung in the air, and Srey Sophorn's neighbors were already out in their fields preparing the land for plowing. I was surprised to see Ming Tam, the head of the NGO Green Cambodia that supports the community network, sitting on a bench under the house with her legs crossed, frowning intently at an old laptop resting on her lap. "Good," she said, waving me over. "You're here. What do I write?" Ming Tam explained that one of Green Cambodia's funding organizations, Oxfam, wanted her to write the history of the community network. "What should I tell them?" Ming Tam asked, visibly troubled at the thought of creating a linear narrative from the turbulent history of fifteen years she had been working to build up the community network. "Do I put in all that stuff—that internal stuff? Like the problems between the funders and us? The problems with the community forests?"

This chapter takes up the challenge of making sense of this story that Ming Tam tells. I step back from analysis of the land reform to take a longer view of how struggles for communal land in Khang Cheung and Khang Leit have evolved and how Order 01 shaped these struggles. For Ming Tam, the "internal stuff" was a constitutive element of the struggle. One story could not be told without the other. I had little advice for Ming Tam. I told her I imagined the funder wanted to hear a success story they could put on their glossy reports and distribute to their supporters: the clean version of history. But of course that is never the whole story, and as Wendy Wolford (2010) points out in her research on the Brazilian Landless Workers Movement (the MST, *Movimento dos Trabalhadores Rurais Sem Terra*), being attentive to the messy pieces—the internal conflict, disconnections, failures—is an essential part of building a stronger movement. Ming Tam handed me the laptop. "I'll talk and you write it down," she said, and began immediately:

> In 2001, Pheapimex ELC started. We got hold of maps and documents about Pheapimex's plans and told all of the villagers. Because of our work, the company couldn't enter between 2001 and 2003; the villagers held strong against them. But one night in 2004, bulldozers and tractors came. The villagers had no warning; the first they knew was the sound of bulldozers crunching trees. The company tried to do it secretly; they hired people from other provinces. When the villagers saw the trees cut, they cried. I cried. We knew we had to do something that brought everyone together; the communities couldn't protest one by one. We organized two thousand people from eleven communes around the Phnom Pich mountain. . . . We blocked the national road. The police tried to arrest the leaders, but the people stood strong. They were not afraid to die. While we were sleeping, a bomb went off and injured nine people. They tried to scare us, but we didn't give up. We stopped the company.
>
> This was ten years ago. Now the people have stopped their activism. They have to migrate for work, they have to feed their families, they have to get through the day. We had problems with people cheating each other, and with other NGOs. People argue; the NGOs fight with each other. And the officials threaten people.
>
> The company came back in 2010. They began growing cassava. Now the company has the land and the forest is gone. We try to keep going, we work on the community forest. But it's hard, the officials always say we have to get another signature, another map. And then we don't have the resources to make sure it's protected. And then Order 01. Order 01 was cruel. People lost more forest, and the wealthy people have taken the best rice land. The community forests, they got titled out to people; we don't know what is happening with them now.

In this chapter, I expand on two connected points in Ming Tam's story of the tensions inherent to social movements organized by and with NGOs and focused on a politics of state recognition. First, NGOs bring financial resources, networks, and information that can mobilize people beyond localized movements, but NGOs are themselves dependent on a political economy of development funding that leads to competition for scarce funds. Since the 1980s, as donors sought to bypass corrupt states, NGOs have taken on the role of service deliverers channeling state and donor funding to communities, and NGO practice and discourse have become increasingly professionalized and depoliticized, with community leaders often transformed into NGO workers and managers (Esteves, Motta, and Cox 2009). Local-level community networks made up of rural smallholders are often organized and funded by registered NGOs. In turn, these NGOs are funded by larger NGOs, who are themselves funded by international donors. While donor agency staff I interviewed emphasized their commitment to community-driven programs (rather than donors' agendas), donors must report results to their own ministries or governing bodies, and funding is usually tied to specific projects in line with donors' priorities. The Khang Cheung community network, for example, is organized and funded by Green Cambodia, which is a registered NGO funded by four different organizations, with short-term cycles of funds earmarked for land rights, conservation, and livelihoods projects. During my fieldwork, Green Cambodia lost two grants because the funders had shifted from land rights to climate change projects, and the NGO had to let go six of its nine staff. These organizations' need to compete for scarce funds can discourage solidarity between communities (as NGOs claim particular communities as their villages) and forces their accountability upward to states and donors rather than to the communities they serve. These concerns are nothing new; scholars have raised similar critiques about the NGO-ization of development funding since the 1990s (Edwards and Hulme 1996). But these critiques remain relevant, as increasing numbers of NGOs competing for more scarce funding must ensure they attract continued support from upstream donors (Banks, Hulme, and Edwards 2015).

Second, due to this funding structure and the potential for the state to shut down NGOs that are deemed to be antigovernment, NGOs often direct resistance to methods that are less likely to cause official rebuke. At the extreme, NGOs dependent on state and donor funding for their survival may end up colluding with the state to delegitimize radical action, even cooperating in the criminalization of social movements and justifying the deployment of force against them (Petras 1999). Most commonly, though, NGOs and donor agencies seek to focus land advocacy on working through legal channels to gain state recognition of land rights rather than through overt protest or other forms of activism. Scholars working within feminist and indigenous studies have demonstrated that the politics of state recognition is fraught with paradoxes (Brown 2002; Coulthard 2013) and risks delegitimizing broader structural change by making selective concessions that preserve hegemonic social relations (Esteves, Motta, and Cox 2009). Social movement theorists point to the risks in centering activism on state recognition, when claimants align with state actors who can define the limits of what is considered acceptable or appropriate activism (Hale 2002).

Critiques of the limits of state recognition are articulated concisely by Glenn Coulthard (2013, 13) in his discussion of indigenous recognition in Canada: "The core problem [with the focus on state recognition], of course, is that the structural and discursive settings within which recognition claims are articulated and assessed are by no means neutral: they are profoundly power-laden, and almost always to the detriment of indigenous claimants. As such they have the ability to mould how indigenous people think and act, not only in relation to the topic at hand (the recognition claim) but also in relation to themselves and others." Coulthard's insight here is that in the process of gaining legal recognition of land rights defined and controlled by the state, other ways of understanding land and life on and with the land are undermined; thus, "land claims processes produce Aboriginal property owners whose territories, and whose very identities, become subject to expropriation and alienation." In Cambodia, the struggle for state recognition of communal land is a particularly weak advocacy tool because the government has effectively thwarted the process through obfuscation, bureaucratic delay, and overcomplicated procedures. In rural Khang Cheung and Khang Leit, most communal land claims languish under bureaucratic delay and confusion. This means that Order 01 did not destroy fully functioning communal land tenure systems and unified social movements, but it did further undermine communities' tenuous claims to communal land.

The point here is not to label NGOs as regressive forces for peasant and indigenous communities; this does not do justice to the complex links between NGOs, community movements, and state actors. In Cambodia in the 1990s, NGOs fought to include communal land rights in the law to challenge the dominant paradigm of private property and agribusiness development. Now, a diverse range of NGOs work to bring people together to formalize communal land to protect it from encroachment. This effort has brought funds and focus to communal land struggles. But it has also had the perverse effect of taking funding, creativity, and effort away from strategies that seek land justice beyond partnership with the state and markets. This is the limitation at the heart of state recognition, which Brown, borrowing from Gayatri Spivak, suggests makes rights "that which we cannot not want"; they promise to secure a relationship with the state based on liberalism's "sunny formulations of freedom and equality" while concealing ongoing "un-emancipatory relations of power" (Brown 2000, 231).

My comparative discussion of struggles for communal land in Khang Cheung and Khang Leit in this chapter reveals the limits of a politics of recognition, both in the state's ongoing production of uncertainty over the claims process, which leaves communities languishing for years and breaks solidarity, and in the state's articulation of land itself—the notion that people's land use can be neatly sectioned into private or communal ownership in order to be recognized by the state belies the way land is used and managed in both indigenous and rural Khmer communities. In the national imaginary, the backward indigenous who practices subsistence-focused shifting cultivation and recognizes the land's spiritual agency is the other to the modern Cambodian nation of entrepreneurial rice farmers. This idea shapes land law and NGO programs. To be eligible for communal land title, indigenous land claimants must perform an indigenous subjectivity that excludes many people whose farming systems do not fit with the traditional model; to be eligible for private land title, Khmer farmers must perform a commercial smallholder subjectivity that denies their diverse livelihoods. As I discuss in the next section, this has the effect of reproducing these binary identities, undermining broader understandings of land, and separating the advocacy efforts of indigenous and Khmer communities rather than considering how these communities can share with and learn from each other.

NGOs and Subject Formation in Indigenous and Khmer Peasant Communities

When I spend time working with agricultural NGOs in Cambodia's lowlands or talking with indigenous farmers in the uplands, I am always struck by the diverse ways people relate to land. I remember working with a very frustrated Cambodian NGO in the mid-2000s. The NGO was encouraging farmers to grow export certified organic rice, and my job was to help farmers ensure that their fields weren't contaminated with chemicals from neighbors' fields. But this was almost impossible! Everyone's fields were inundated with the same water in the rainy season as the whole area flooded, and the fields became communal cattle grazing areas in the dry season. Indigenous farming systems are not straightforward either. Indigenous Cambodians have long histories of intricate systems of communal land governance and use. Many communities remain rooted in communal governance for managing areas of reserve land, fallows, and forest, but private plots for cash crops have become widespread. Some indigenous farmers work cash crops into their shifting cultivation systems on communal land. It is not surprising, then, that not every indigenous farmer supports communal land title, nor does every Khmer farmer support private land title. But the legal, static categories of private and communal land tenure require communities to either prove private tenure or make themselves visible to the state and NGOs as worthy of community designation in ways that reflect the Cambodian government and NGOs' racist assumptions about traditional models of indigeneity and "Khmerness" and deny the fluidity with which indigenous and Khmer communities use land.

Shifting rice cultivation, for example, has traditionally been central to indigenous farming systems. In Khang Leit, 45 percent of my survey participants practiced shifting cultivation to grow a diverse range of rice mixed with root and vegetable crops. Khmer farmers in Khang Cheung also practiced shifting cultivation. In Phnom Mie commune, twenty-three households I spoke with regularly planted shifting rice nurseries in forestland at the start of the rice season (a technique called *bonkeur*). People cleared a small area of forest near the village each year. They roughly leveled the land but did not bother to take out stumps or trees. Then they broadcast rice seeds when the rains came. In all cases, people did this in addition to cultivating a lowland rice nursery (*somnab*) on their paddy land. Seedlings from both nurseries were then transplanted into people's rice fields after approximately twenty-five days, as one woman explained to me: "*Bonkeur* is similar to *somnab*; it both takes about twenty-five days. But *bonkeur* produces slightly taller rice plants that can survive better if there is heavy rain when the plants are first transplanted. So people might do both, and then when they transplant, they transplant the *somnab* to not-so-flooded parts of the field, and *bonkeur* to more flooded parts."

This woman explains the technique as a way to increase system resilience. But these practices are invisible in government agriculture and in NGO and donor agencies' discourse. In fact, I have not once seen this practice mentioned in NGO reports about lowland agriculture. When I spoke with a Department of Agriculture extension officer in Khang Cheung, he said this technique was practiced in several parts of the province: "Yes, people do the upland nurseries. They cut the forest and use it for one year, maybe two or three years, and then they cut somewhere else, so they can get more flood-resistant seedlings. I have seen it in [three districts] here." I asked the extension officer why none of the state or donor reports mentioned *bonkeur*, and he shrugged: "I think it's small; it's not important. They don't talk about it in the government." But while the state official declared this practice unimportant, farmers said this cultivation is widely practiced in Khang Cheung and becoming even more important due to harsh droughts and floods in recent years that require tough seedlings from upland areas.

The forest- and shrubland near rural villages is also a central part of Khmer farming systems. Farmers graze the cattle that fertilize their fields on communal shrubland, and many families depend on nearby forestland for gathering wild fruit, fungi, and root vegetables for eating and selling. Small-scale logging and charcoal production also supplements farmers' livelihoods, especially in villages with small land plots and poor soil. But I found that these latter livelihood practices were problematic for agricultural NGOs who wanted to present peasant farmers as ecological stewards of the land, so people's dependence on forests was often omitted from NGO reports on Khmer communities.

State and donor discourse that ignores practices of *bonkeur* and small-scale logging helps to construct Khmer farming systems as (exclusively) private land use systems. This construction makes the idea of the leopard skin landscape of small farms dotted around plantations possible—private small farms can only coexist peacefully next to large agribusiness concessions if both are spatially and temporally bounded. But few farmers in Khang Cheung fit this model of the Khmer entrepreneurial rice farmer whose farming system is contained within private rice fields. And those who do fit this model tend to be the wealthier farmers who can purchase tractors and chemical fertilizer (and therefore don't require cattle for plowing and soil fertility) and who rarely need to collect forest products to cover food shortages and make ends meet. The majority of farmers in Khang Cheung depend on farming practices that may be more ecologically sustainable but are invisible in the idea of the leopard skin and in the discourse of both the government and the NGOs.

Government and NGO discourse in Khang Leit also privileges certain conceptions of being indigenous and silences others. Communities that apply for CLT must prove their indigeneity; essentially, they must occupy the "tribal slot" by showing that they retain traditional land use and governance methods (Baird 2013b; Li 2000). The first step in a CLT application is registration as an indigenous group whose members "manifest ethnic, social, cultural and economic unity; practice a traditional lifestyle; and cultivate lands under customary rules of collective use" (RGC 2001, art. 23). The burden of proof is demanding and creates tensions within villages. The construction of indigeneity through land use practice and governance is particularly problematic in areas in which Khmer migrants have moved into indigenous communities or where people no longer practice shifting cultivation but still depend on communal forest areas for food security and spiritual well-being and therefore still desire CLT. One Khmer district official in Khang Leit laughed when I asked about CLT. He told me that some communities "can't get the communal title because they are not even doing shifting cultivation! They are just like Khmer.... They're not real indigenous; they're just pretending!" I heard racist statements like this from senior officials many times; they give a sense of the difficult position indigenous Cambodians find themselves in. Many indigenous people have turned to cash crop cultivation, often incorporating cash crops into larger swidden systems, in order to limit land encroachment and improve their livelihoods. But to prove they are indigenous, they must construct an identity that is other than Khmer, and therefore other than commercial farmers.

Non-governmental organizations' efforts to assist people with the convoluted legal process of CLT application can reinforce the performativity of indigenous as traditional. In my interviews with NGO staff in Khang Leit, I found that NGOs tended to exalt certain communities that maintained communal governance practices. This reinforces the construction of some communities as traditional (and therefore "real" indigenous communities, in the parlance of the district official) and others as cash croppers–landless wage workers (and therefore "pretending," less desirable targets for NGO projects). For example, numerous NGO staff told me I should visit one village named Manla. One indigenous NGO officer told me, "Manla is the best village. In Manla there are still some people doing shifting cultivation. You will see how we keep the traditional ways there." This village has featured in several academic and NGO publications on land practices in Khang Leit, including my own articles, and is generally held up as a case of effective governance and little deforestation. Manla certainly does provide lessons for researchers. Local governance decisions among elders to limit the conversion of land from food crops to cashew production during a cashew boom in the mid-2000s and the links between elders and youth in governance processes have successfully mitigated the enclosure of communal forest. But the problematic point here is that of certain communities being held up as "good" or "true" indigenous in a way that reinforces the idea that communities that do not fit this model are "bad" or "pretend." These discourses matter because they reproduce inequalities, as NGOs look to support communities that fit their idea of what rural livelihoods should look like. In Manla, five different NGOs were running livelihood projects, including two new projects that started during my fieldwork, while I saw very few NGOs running programs in nearby villages.

In Khang Cheung, NGOs also construct some communities as "good" peasants, particularly those who live primarily from rice-based livelihoods with supplementary collection of NTFPs. People who earn livelihoods from logging or charcoal production are fundamentally at odds with this subjectivity. One NGO conservation officer, for example, told me that his organization gave up working in Srai Saat commune because "people there are too selfish; they don't care about the forest." Ironically, levels of poverty and food insecurity in Srai Saat are much more severe than in nearby communities that attract a higher level of NGO activity. NGOs may not be fully conscious of their own contribution to inequality when they seek to partner with communities that conform to the model of the good peasant or the traditional indigenous, but this practice excludes communities (and farmers) that do not conform, which can further promote inequality between and within communities.

Researchers also reproduce this practice when we work through NGOs to access communities. One foreign researcher frustrated with NGOs pointing him toward model indigenous communities like Manla described this practice to me as "research tourism." The danger for researchers is that if we access research sites through NGOs and are directed toward NGO model villages while we ignore others, we contribute to the idea that we should only support traditional indigenous communities and good peasant farmers instead of seeking to understand how indigenous and Khmer peasant farmers struggle to practice diverse ways of being in changing environments (Frewer 2017; Li 2000).

The Evolution of Struggles for Community Forests and Communal Land Title

Community Forests in Khang Cheung

The fluid livelihood systems among Khmer farmers have been recognized (albeit in a limited way) with the recognition of community forests around the country. NGOs like Ming Tam's Green Cambodia have championed community forests as their central strategy for protecting forestland in the Pheapimex concession area. When community-based natural resource management became a popular paradigm in the mid-1990s, NGOs supported a cluster of CF projects in degraded forest areas in Khang Cheung. The province became a key site for CFs in Cambodia, and two land rights NGOs led the expansion of CF claims over all the districts in Khang Cheung in the mid-2000s. Designated areas of forest are allocated to particular communities, with forest management run by a local CF committee and supported by the government's Forestry Administration. The CF committee creates its own rules for community forest use. In Khang Cheung, community members could gather wild food and firewood from the CF, but logging and charcoal production was prohibited. The tendency of community forestry to focus on degraded forest areas, rather than high-value forests, has drawn criticism from researchers who argue that CFs do not help communities protect the forest that is of most value to their food security and livelihoods (Biddulph 2010). The general insecurity of forest tenure and the difficulties with making a living in rural areas also make forest management extraordinarily difficult, as communities with few resources are constantly battling timber poachers from both outside and within the community.

Ming Tam is passionate about the potential for community-based forest management to protect rural people's way of life, and she believes that CF advocacy is what maintained energy within the community network after the concession company retreated in 2004. The state's swift repression of the community network's 2004 protests (and in particular the bomb thrown at protesters) made villagers and Green Cambodia's funders fearful of state retaliation, and the CF provided a concrete way for local people to save some forest without promoting potentially violent resistance strategies that would raise the ire of the government and external funders. International donors continue to support CF efforts through funding for meetings, forest patrols, and equipment. For donors, CFs promise to engage local people in decision making, save some forest, and strengthen relationships between local farmers and authorities. As one community forestry NGO program head told me, "Even if we have to do this in the less valuable forest, it still saves something; it is the only way to save something." But over time, Ming Tam said, she has developed misgivings about CFs: "At first, the government was against it; we were protesting for the forest and demarcating the borders and doing the forest patrols, and it wasn't about the government. It came from us. And then the government made a formal process for recognizing the community forest. So we can have official permission to catch people who cut the forest, and the government helps us. But now everything depends on the government. So now we are stuck. Because if they don't want it to go anywhere, then they just make sure nothing gets signed and we can't do anything."

As Ming Tam notes, the government essentially co-opted the CF process. The community is now stuck as they must gain government approval to deal with poachers. Multiple state agencies must approve comanagement. These applications are often stalled for years, diverted to areas of degraded forest, or worse, diverted to areas close to villages where people already have private claims to the land. The CF committees in Phnom Mie and Srai Saat communes applied for formal recognition of more than 4,000 hectares of community forest claims in 2008, but after local authorities and one of three required ministries signed the application, the claims were stalled for several years at the central government level. The CFs in Srai Saat broke up as people lost hope in the process. But the CF committees in Phnom Mie continued their efforts: in 2012 they downsized their claim to just under 2,000 hectares and meet monthly to discuss protection measures and the status of legal claims and to draw up schedules for forest patrols inside CF areas. The CF has in this way become the main mobilizing tool for the community network in Phnom Mie. To many people in the commune, the network and the CF campaign are synonymous.

Communal Land Title in Khang Leit

In Khang Leit, indigenous rights NGOs proliferated in the mid-2000s as indigenous struggles gained traction internationally and land grabs in indigenous communities caught international attention. NGOs encouraged indigenous communities to focus their struggles on achieving CLT, and by 2012, more than thirty NGOs worked with over 160 communities in Khang Leit to prepare CLT applications (Ironside, Patterson, and Thomas 2017). CLT recognizes broader land use practices than private land title; it encompasses cultivated agriculture land, fallow land, spirit forest, and burial grounds. NGO officers in Khang Leit assured me that CLT offers more protection than individual property title, because forest is protected and individuals cannot privately sell land within a CLT area: "The CLT stops people from selling land. With private title, once they get the title they will all just sell the land. That's what we see here. But CLT is better because they can't sell the land. The government wants to encourage people to borrow money, you see. And when they start borrowing money and using the private title as collateral, and then they can't pay it back, that's when they lose their land, so it's another form of land grabbing. So CLT is better." This is reminiscent of Hall, Hirsch, and Li's (2011) contention that communal land titling has a paternalistic element, as development agencies selectively advocate for full land rights in some (nonindigenous) communities while protecting indigenous people by limiting the full bundle of rights over property. Other NGO staff told me that CLT is strategic because it provides people with a legal basis to make claims, which indigenous groups can use to protest, even if they are unlikely to win legal battles in court due to corruption and discrimination.

Despite the promise of communal title, it is mired in similar problems to CF claims. By 2016, only eleven communities of 166 who had begun the CLT process had been awarded a provisional title (CCHR 2016). This entire legal process has essentially been sidelined by bureaucratic delay and obfuscation. Similar to the ways people in Khang Cheung spoke about the uncertainty of law (see chapter 5), one indigenous activist noted wryly: "The law is good for indigenous people, but the government thinks only of politics, not of the security of indigenous people. So even if we have the best laws, it doesn't mean much." The legal structure is also convoluted. If the Ministry of Rural Development approves applicant communities' registration as an indigenous group (a problematic process in itself), the communities must then attain legal status from the Ministry of Interior and receive approval from the Ministry of Agriculture, a drawn-out process that is routinely delayed and ignored by officials.

Mounting evidence also shows that communities who have received CLT are still losing land. In 2014, GIZ investigated all seven communities that had received CLT after reports from GIZ's own staff reported land loss within these communities. An internal GIZ memo from Khang Leit field staff confirmed that three of the seven communities with CLT were losing land due to ongoing company encroachment and land sales from people within the community. One NGO officer suggested to me that CLT was not working because the process was driven by NGOs that worked "at base" and could not engage with more powerful actors: "Only having communal title is not enough to have land security. Because land security is not only land but it is about the rights of indigenous people to claim and raise their challenges to concerned stakeholders. Most NGOs here operate only within the communities. This position is not enabling them to solve land conflicts when the conflict is with high officials or powerful people as the conflicts are out of their reach. Also, they worry about their personal security." This NGO officer assured me he still supported CLT. Like others in Khang Leit and Khang Cheung, he felt that advocacy for state recognition of communal land provided a focus to mobilization efforts throughout the mid-2000s in the face of state repression, land expropriation, and out-migration. But the NGO officer's point is that legal land title only provides tenure security when it is enforced, and NGOs have limited power to press communities' claims in the face of the powerful state elite and companies, who can draw on both legal and informal, violent means to control land.

In this context, the Order 01 land reform certainly did not destroy fully functioning CLT or CF areas, nor did the land survey avoid areas that were in the process of gaining state recognition for communal claims. In the following section, I examine the ways private land claims undermined communal claims during Order 01, creating new tensions within rural areas.

Communal Land Claims during Order 01
Community Forests under Order 01

Before the arrival of the student volunteers during Order 01, a Ministry of Environment official came to Phnom Mie and spoke with community network representatives and local authorities. According to Srey Sophorn, the ministry official assured everyone that "the community forestland that is granted or in the process of being granted will be preserved; it won't be titled out." However, in the wake of Order 01, community network members on forest patrol found bulldozers and cleared patches of forest. Srey Sophorn told me, "There are no trees on some of those areas. Now no one knows where the community forest is, because some of it was titled to powerful people and the forest in those places is gone. Now there are just patches, but this is not forest."

I mapped out the extent of the Phnom Mie CF that was titled out to individuals during Order 01 by overlaying the CF map created before the land reform with the coordinates of land titles recorded in the cadastral registry after Order 01 (see figure 13).

The original CF claim was more than 4,000 hectares (the outer boundary line). This did not receive approval from state officials, so it was downsized to a claim of 1,886 hectares in 2012 (the inner black boundary line filled with black shaded dots). The white parcels are private land plots that were titled out during

FIGURE 13. Community forest area including land plots that were titled out to individuals during Order 01.

(Source: Alice Beban.)

the land reform and recorded in the cadastral registry. These private plots are concentrated in the south part of the CF, but they are also scattered throughout the CF. They total around 400 hectares, or 25 percent of the CF area. I do not know who owns these plots of land, as I could not access records of plot names for this area. None of the community network members knew who had taken the CF land either (that they admitted to me). In the wake of the land reform, no one was clear what would happen to the remaining CF land. This uncertainty created tensions among the group, and rumors flew that local authorities and some members of the community network had taken the land. When I asked Srey Sophorn how the community network would proceed now with the CF claim, she drew an outline of the CF on a piece of scrap paper and angrily jabbed her pen into the paper—dot dot dot dot dot—to represent the private plots that lay within the CF area. She said bitterly:

> We can't get that land back, the land that has been titled out. Now we are trying to have that land taken out of the CF and have the rest of the area recognized. But we don't know what will happen with the land that is left. The villagers want the community forest, but the authorities want the land divided into social land concessions for individual families. Now we sit here waiting for them to decide, while all the land is being cleared! You see, it is much easier to clear the forest if there are private plots all around, and we don't know which parts have been claimed. I don't know what will happen!

Srey Sophorn's palpable anger at her inability to know what was happening and the authorities' control over the situation is reminiscent of indigenous activists' anger at the official delays in the CLT process. Meanwhile, as Srey Sophorn says, "all the land is being cleared." I later talked with a village chief in Phnom Mie, who told me it was futile to continue with the CF. He said that any untitled land in the CF area should be designated as a social land concession for poor families in the future because it is no longer usable as a forest. A commune clerk in Phnom Mie also felt the CF claim should be abandoned but said the land should be titled as commune land and then used for schools, Buddhist temples, or public buildings. My discussions with donor agency and Ministry of Land officials in Phnom Penh confirmed there were no guidelines for how the remaining land within the CF claim should be treated.

The community network in Khang Cheung eventually submitted a new application for the CF with the support of Ming Tam and Green Cambodia. This application claimed around 1,300 hectares of noncontiguous land left in the original CF area. But by the end of my fieldwork in mid-2015, this claim still had not progressed, as Srey Sophorn complained: "With the CF, the Forestry

Administration said that we have to get the people's signatures again and submit another application. But we did it all before; we got all the documentation and submitted it all. It was a lot of work. So now we are doing it again. But we don't hear anything back from them. They are just trying to waste time, to make us go back and forth forever with paperwork until we get tired and we stop trying." Srey Sophorn saw the long bureaucratic delays as a deliberate state strategy to waste time—that is, to maintain uncertainty over the status of the community's claim until people lose hope and give up.

The most noticeable social shift when the CF broke up during Order 01 was that the community network fractured as well. In fact, several people contrasted the loss of communal land under Order 01 with the way the concession company grabbed land in the past, arguing that Order 01 turned villagers against each other as authorities titled out communal areas and offered people money or land titles to claim forestland:

> FEMALE FARMER: In the past they got people from outside to get land. Now they give land to people in the village. So now that's why we have been broken. We used to have protests with two hundred people from the village, all together. Now we protest each other.
>
> MALE FARMER: Now we are not afraid of the Chinese company. We are afraid of Khmer and Khmer.

People's fear and distrust of each other were clear during interviews and community meetings. The state elite also actively worked to produce distrust among members of the community network. Local authorities and company management reportedly visited people at their homes in Kbal Srai, threatening or bribing them to stay quiet about the problems with the CF. These actions intensified rumors and accusations as everyone suspected someone—whether local official, NGO staff, or community leader—might in fact be working for the company or authorities. Green Cambodia's Ming Tam said these intrigues were common. In fact, field staff from a neighboring land rights NGO, PPL, and staff from Green Cambodia had stopped talking with each other two years previously when PPL accused Green Cambodia of poaching the best community organizers in PPL's target communities. Ming Tam shook her head as she described this kind of petty competition between the NGOs: "You know, when I started this job, I thought there were just two groups I had to fear: people with power and money, and the company. Then I realized when I worked for a while that there are three: also NGOs. And now, I also have to worry about my own organization; the people with money try to buy us off."

Ming Tam recognizes that as NGOs seek to maintain their funding streams and their relations with state authorities, they end up competing with each other and dividing communities into NGO territories rather than encouraging broader cooperation. When state officials control the terms of the relationship, the NGOs' approach risks facilitating people's land dispossession rather than their land protection.

Communal Land Title under Order 01

While the parceling out of community forest claims in Khang Cheung led to tensions within communities, in Khang Leit the leopard skin reform fundamentally changed the landscape of resistance to land grabbing and the ways that people use and relate to land. In this section I detail the ways in which NGOs and villagers responded when CLT land was mapped out during the land reform.

When Hun Sen first announced Order 01, the prime minister said that CLT land would also be surveyed and provided with communal title. According to a memo signed by the minister of land on 4 July 2012, "For indigenous minority groups registered as communities by the Ministry of Interior . . . the land identification process shall be done in the same working spirit as the one prevailing in the [Ministry of Land Management's] cadastral department instructions on the implementation of the Royal Government of Cambodia's Order 01. . . . [T]he land shall be registered as collective ownership of the community according to the request of its traditional authorities." This document included instructions on how to issue communal titles, even for indigenous groups in the process of registering with the Ministry of Interior.

However, a second document, also signed by the minister of land and dated 26 July, superseded these orders: "In order to implement the Royal Government of Cambodia's Order 01 . . . the determination of boundaries of all parcels being the collective ownership of indigenous communities . . . requires a long time, as well as extensive budget spending. . . . Therefore, registration of collective ownership shall be postponed to be implemented later." In lieu of instructions for issuing communal titles, the second document included a copy of a contract for "indigenous individuals who do not want to be part of an indigenous community and want to live as a private person." The contract, which must be thumbprinted, also stated that any individual who opted for a private title was ineligible to receive the benefits of a communal title.

This shift in state guidelines meant that when the student survey teams arrived in Khang Leit, they ignored CLT claims and encouraged people to accept private titles, undermining CLT claims. A study that surveyed seventy-six indigenous communities in Khang Leit found that more than a third of the communities had active CLT claims that were parceled out into private land plots during Order 01 (Oldenburg and Neef 2014). In chapter 4, I detailed the processes that student volunteer surveyors used to encourage and coerce indigenous people into accepting private land title. Here, I examine further how this process increased tensions within villages between those who opted for private title and those who did not and what the process meant for land advocacy efforts after Order 01.

All eleven NGO staff I interviewed from different NGOs in Khang Leit saw Order 01 as a process that facilitated rapid, negative change in indigenous communities. One NGO staffer said that "communities are broken now. It's really a doomsday. . . . I know it seems over the top but it has shifted everything." Another said bitterly that "Order 01 meant the companies won; it was a political game to get land for the companies and undermine the communal land of indigenous people." These NGO staff recognized that communal land loss had begun much earlier than the land reform, but the land reform was what one indigenous field officer termed "the final nail in the coffin for communal land": "Up to about 2005, there was a lot of shifting cultivation. Between 2005 and 2009, that's when most stopped. People sold land, the companies took land, and people began planting cashew. And then when the students measured the land, this stopped the rest of it. The processes of CLT broke up the community strength. And they only titled the individual family's growing area. So now many people sold up and are moving out."

The other NGO staff I interviewed in Khang Leit agreed with this field officer that Order 01 intensified ongoing processes of livelihood change away from shifting cultivation and left people with little land. Some NGO officers said they worked in areas where 40 percent of people or more had sold their land since they received the Order 01 land title. The NGO staff grew bitter and upset as they talked, commonly pointing to the overwhelming power of the state and companies and the relative powerlessness of the NGOs and indigenous communities. These interviews left me with a sense that the NGOs committed to achieving state recognition of CLT as their main mobilizing platform now had little idea how to support indigenous communities in the wake of Order 01.

Indigenous people in my two Khang Leit study communities were more divided than NGO staff in their opinions of the land reform. Some people told me vehemently that the individual titles brought new tensions into their village. One woman said that people in her village who had opted to receive individual title were staying away from people who had opted to wait for the CLT because "they are embarrassed, the ones who got the land titles. They know we should wait all together for the communal title but now they have broken up the community." Some people who received land titles during Order 01 told me they had waited so long for the CLT to be recognized and the government did nothing, so the individual title was "better than nothing." Others felt that individual title allowed them more freedom to sell the land if they chose or if their children wished to sell land later. Yet others noted that Order 01 did impact their culture, but this was part of a larger process of social change. One man in his thirties shrugged as he told me, "The culture has changed. Now people here think of going to buy motorbikes and things. We still have some music, some traditional culture, but not like before. But we all have to change. It is just that Order 01 makes us change faster."

My experience in Sai Tong commune illustrates the tensions that these NGO staff and villagers are pointing to. During interviews in Panak town (the provincial capital of Khang Leit), I heard that people in one village in Sai Tong were organizing to exchange the individual titles they received under Order 01 for a communal land title. The possibility of gathering up community members' individual titles and exchanging them for a communal title had gained momentum after independent media published claims that indigenous people were coerced into accepting private title during the land reform. In response, Hun Sen publicly committed to a process that allowed indigenous people to convert privately held land to communal land. If successful, Sai Tong would be the first community in the country to take this step. I set out to conduct interviews in this village. But my attempts to conduct research there were thwarted by a high-ranking police officer and village chiefs who intimidated my research team and warned villagers not to talk with us. I was finally able to talk with a group of six community activists from Sai Tong when they came to Panak town to meet with a legal rights NGO. When I asked this group what they thought of Order 01, they noted that the land loss had intensified inequality in their commune:

> WOMAN: Order 01 has taken away our choice. If our field (*chamkar*) has a problem with the company, they have to measure it. If not, we lose it. So now we have to do individual land.
>
> FIRST MAN: Yes, and the main thing, if we look at the results of Order 01, is that people have sold the land. And the company just takes land and we can't do anything against this as individuals. We are too weak!
>
> SECOND MAN: But some do okay. People that have money grow soy or cassava on that land and they can do okay. People that have no money sell.

These community activists express similar sentiments about the individualizing effects of Order 01. Order 01 took away people's choice, as the woman describes; that is, the land reform forced people to conform to private land use systems as the company now (legitimately) cleared untitled land. The first man argues that people must now respond to encroachment as individuals, which he believes is an inherently weak position. The second man recognizes that this process of creating individual subjects accentuates inequalities within communities, as those with money grow cash crops and accumulate more capital, while others sell land in desperation. This man's reflection stresses that indigenous communities are not uniformly affected by the imposition of private property. Just as the land reform deepened class and gender divides in Khang Cheung, social relations within communities in Khang Leit became more strained as class divides grew, undermining the social safety nets that communal land governance provides.

We all sat around a coffee table in the NGO's office, and the meeting focused on how the community activists and NGO staff could work together to persuade people not to sell land until the community secured CLT. The group of community activists was subdued; they said that gathering up people's individual titles to exchange them for a communal title was more difficult than they had anticipated. "Some people have sold the titles already," said one woman, the most outspoken of the group. "About half of the people in my village, they have sold the land to the company already after they got the title in Order 01."

"Yes," nodded a younger man sitting next to her, "we had a meeting all together, with the NGO too. We asked what people wanted, and they said they weren't happy with the amount of land they got and they wanted to swap to a communal title. So that's when we started this activity, to swap. But some of them have sold already. They're still selling the land now. If they didn't sell, the company would put pressure on them to sell."

"The company came to me twice," said a second woman who was sitting next to me on the floor. "And they said that if we don't sell, they will take it anyway. They've already taken the other land, our land. And now they will take this too."

The younger man nodded vigorously and used his finger to trace a long oblong shape on the table. "This is the whole commune; we have about 18,000 hectares of land altogether," he said. He pointed to the top of the oblong and explained that during Order 01, extensive land in the northern part of the commune was titled into individual plots (these are the villages I tried unsuccessfully to access during my survey). But in the central and southern parts of the commune, the majority of land claimants refused to have their land surveyed.

One activist, a man who looked to be in his forties and who continually received texts and calls during the meeting, told me proudly that he had made sure people didn't listen to the students. "I talked a lot with the village elders and the people knew, they understood that the government tricks us into losing our land," he said.

Then the young man swiped his hand from the top of the oblong to the middle. "Now, people in the north who sold their private land are trying to move down to places where there is still communal forestland," he said.

"Yes," said another man. "More than sixty families have already moved down to our part of the commune since the land reform."

Some of the community activists blamed these migrants for new tensions among village elders over whether to allow these outsiders plots in the village communal area. "They want everything!" said one woman. "They already got money for their land, and now they try to get our communal land that we haven't been stupid enough to sell."

The older man next to her shook his head. "It's not about blaming them," he said. "It's the company that tricked them, tricked all of us."

What didn't seem clear to anyone was how a CLT would work if it had to be broken up into small areas in order to excise the land that had already been taken or sold to the company. As the community activists spoke despondently about the possibilities for securing CLT recognition, the NGO officer tried to offer hope to the group. He recalled the ways people mobilized for CLT in the past: "You are brave. And you have resisted in the past. And the community head can talk with the company and the NGOs and has good relationships with the village. You say that you want to change to CLT; you need to organize it yourselves. Call the village meeting; get people organized." The same NGO officer told me afterward that he was in a difficult position, as the community activists implored him to help, but he couldn't help as much as before. "That is one thing that's clear, the government doesn't want the NGOs getting involved in the land titling at all, in the Order 01. So it needs to come from them," he shrugged.

As I was leaving the meeting, one of the women from Sai Tong followed me into the hallway and told me quietly that she had already sold one of the two land titles she received under Order 01. "I needed the money, you see," she said. This woman's quiet comment showed the immense challenge that these communities faced in trying to piece a communal claim together when many of the individual plots were already sold. As with the remaining patches of community forestland in Khang Cheung, it was not clear to anyone exactly how this would be achieved.

Conclusion: How Are Dead People Supposed to Defend Their Rights?

This chapter shows that both private and communal land titles as tools for land rights advocacy in Cambodia are flawed. The land titles available in Cambodian law are legalistic instruments that define certain people as legitimate land claimants and others as illegitimate claimants through narrowly defined practices of land use and tenure. The individual land title under Order 01 denied the ways that farming systems depend on the use of both individual and communal land and the ways that land tenure shifts fluidly through the seasons. The communal land title denies the ways that indigenous communities whose farming systems are no longer confined to shifting cultivation may still depend on both individual rice fields and cropland and communal forest areas. And while advocating for state recognition of communal claims can be a powerful way for people to mobilize collectively, it puts the power to define the process in the hands of state actors whose own interests often run counter to the demands of rural communities. The government has effectively thwarted the process by producing uncertainty using the same methods that I observed in other areas of state practice—obfuscation, bureaucratic delay, and overcomplicated procedures that stymie communities' attempts to gain protection over their land. If all advocacy is geared toward gaining state recognition through land title, what happens to those communities who do not conform to the requirements, whose applications are stuck in process for years, or who still lose land after gaining the title?

The stories in this chapter reveal the way ongoing bureaucratic delay and inaction creates tensions within communities. Order 01 further fractured communal land claims. Some people sought to reassert their communal claims after Order 01, but these efforts faced problems as people had already claimed and sold land within the communal areas. Furthermore, even if the community activists in Sai Tong manage to gather people's private titles to exchange for CLT, and even if the community network in Phnom Mie manages to prepare a new CF application for the remaining forestland, they will face the same state inaction as before. In both Khang Cheung and Khang Leit, community activists spoke bitterly of the way they were continually pushed aside by the state. One man in Khang Cheung said wryly, "Maybe if we wait thirty or forty years we can be successful in this protest . . . like Gandhi. We just have to wait."

Not long before I finished fieldwork, I attended a meeting of indigenous land rights NGOs in Phnom Penh, where people shared similar sentiments. Two communities were in the process of gathering individual land titles to exchange for communal titles with NGO assistance. But as one indigenous activist exclaimed, the government continued to stall: "We just spend time going back and forth on sending complaints to different ministries. They say we can get the communal title but they don't say how; they don't try to help. When we try to get the government involved, they keep sending us to different ministries. So where do we send our complaints? Back and forth, back and forth, no solution. With all this time wasted, the company meanwhile cut down our forest. The whole land sector is a black box, where government actors give no information. How are dead people supposed to defend their rights?" This indigenous activist's eloquent plea sees the "black box" of the land sector as a purposeful state strategy of withholding information and creating delays to produce uncertainty over communal claims.

Despite passionate statements by activists, the NGO sector's overwhelming focus on formalizing claims means that when the title does not transpire—or when the community is awarded title but people still lose land—it is difficult for NGOs and the communities they work with to respond. Discursively, NGO efforts have been so successful that when I attend meetings with highland NGOs, I find it hard to talk about any strategy that does not have to do with going through the steps to securing CLT. Some communities in Khang Leit, and some voices within NGOs and donor organizations, are talking about land tenure security in a much broader sense. But the continued focus on land title limits opportunity for broader conversations, as one NGO officer complained to me: "And now it has become all about title. In the Ministry of Land now, the feeling is that if they have title, then they can make claims. So now if they don't have title, they are seen not to have legitimate claim; they are illegal. But that is a perversion of the law; that completely disregards customary claims that are allowed for in the law. So the conversation has to be about broader rights—not just about possession of a piece of paper."

This NGO officer said he was hopeful that NGO approaches would shift. He showed me the notes from a focus group he had held with six land rights NGOs in order to broaden the conversation about land advocacy. All the NGOs at the focus group had talked about increasing collaboration, and all had recognized the need to follow the agendas of indigenous communities rather than dictate advocacy strategies. Some of these NGOs were already working on alternative forms of advocacy. In 2014, for example, several NGOs in Khang Leit began working together with people from different communes to bring a case to the World Bank against the Vietnamese company HAGL (Bourdier 2019). But the political economy of development funding and the state's repression of dissident organizations limit NGO collaboration.

For the researcher too, the discourse that privileges state recognition of land claims is powerful. I found myself in many conversations in Cambodia where I realized there were certain things I could not say; the critique can only go so far. I recall a German-funded workshop on land titling, a whole day of presentations, one after the other, and most talked about the slow progress of titling, the corruption, the continued problems in areas with untitled land. Then an old German man with white hair and a remarkable handlebar moustache stood up. I believe he was from the European Commission. He said, "In all the conversations I attend about titling, I believe we are missing the elephant in the room—the legal system, the bureaucratic functioning that is not working. So what if we have title? If the judicial system doesn't work, then what meaning does it have?" People didn't reply. The Cambodian speaker gave a pained look to the workshop convener. The meeting went on without comment. At another meeting a month later, I got braver and asked a similar question myself: Given a recent memo showing that indigenous communities with communal land title are still losing land, what other forms of advocacy might be effective? Again, silence. One International Non-Governmental Organization (INGO) official said, "Well, we don't want to talk against land title," and we moved on with the meeting. But that official came to me at the end of the meeting and said, "I understand what you're saying, but many of the NGOs are heavily invested in this. Their funding, their view of the work they have done and can do, it is all so tied to this institution of land title." As this official's comment suggests, the focus on state recognition of communal claims came at the expense of broader advocacy.

The INGO official's comment raises a question at the heart of the current conjuncture for land struggles in Cambodia: If we recognize the problems inherent in strategies that focus on the idea of a singular social contract between citizens and the (unaccountable) state system, what are the prospects for other avenues of struggle? While the INGO official doesn't question the contradictions inherent in the liberal conception of rights itself, my analysis in this chapter of state and NGO notions of indigenous and Khmer land use and governance shows the limitations of privileging the state-capital relationship. This point is powerfully made in McCreary and Milligan's (2014) story of a company seeking to build a pipeline through indigenous Carrier Sekani land in Canada. A recognition of Aboriginal Traditional Knowledge in the project's documents appears to respect indigenous land relations, but "the terms of recognition normalize an ontology in which indigenous difference becomes, above all, a different way of knowing, not a way of being on the land that makes that land something different" (121). The control over the broader landscape of extractive industry in this project remains with the state, while the limited recognition of indigenous land results in the reestablishment of a "terra nullius open again to development but mildly constrained by discrete, localized, patches of Indigeneity" (125).

These "discrete, localized patches" of rural peasant and indigenous landholdings are what was promised in the imaginary of the leopard skin land reform: smallholders coexisting alongside the expanse of "terra nullius open to development." But as I have shown in this chapter, rural Cambodians' understanding of land is not reducible to the notion of land conceived as a bounded object in space surrounded by plantations. The examples of *bonkeur* shifting cultivation, the use of forest- and grazing land, the fluid conceptions of private and common property in wet- and dry-season fields, and the recognition of land's agency through place-based spirits all reveal a complexity that overflows narrow conceptions of land as property. Political recognition of land that promises patches of peasant landholding can thus obscure ongoing projects of accumulation and dispossession of lands while extracting surplus through resource exploitation (Coulthard 2013). What, then, of the prospects for land and property relations that move beyond the primacy of state-capital formations? In the following chapter, I take up this question.

7

AN ONTOLOGY OF LAND BEYOND STATE-CAPITAL FORMATIONS

Mobilizing in the Long Shadow of the Cambodian State

As the dust settled on the Order 01 land reform in 2014, it was clear this policy had not "solved all land disputes" as Prime Minister Hun Sen had confidently predicted a year earlier.[1] Despite a continued nationwide moratorium on new land concessions, reported land disputes rocketed back up after the national election.[2] This upsurge in land disputes is a familiar pattern in Cambodia's election cycle—the state's short-term energy for resolving disputes before elections, together with the ramped-up surveillance and repression of dissent, limits reported land disputes until after the election. In this case, the confusion created during Order 01 also contributed to an increase in disputes in its aftermath. In Khang Cheung, new tensions surfaced after the land reform: alongside the struggle to reassert communal land claims (analyzed in the previous chapter), people found their land plots had been titled in someone else's name, rumors about proposed conservation areas signaled the possibility of losing more land, and a wave of land mortgaging and coerced land sales left some families landless. Then, in late 2014, villagers in Srey Mie commune noticed a black SUV driving slowly through their villages and stopping to place small flags in people's rice fields. This was the first people knew of a massive irrigation dam planned for the area that would cut directly through people's rice fields. I attended an emergency meeting of the community network called to discuss the dam, and the mood was somber. People were deflated; many said they were too *kjil* (lazy/hopeless) to do anything because they did not want to risk a violent reaction from the state or company. Others were defiant. Srey Sophorn said angrily, "The main thing is that the community network has to find ways to stay together so we can fight for our community land and face whatever problems come at us, even if the government threatens us."

Srey Sophorn raises a crucial question for activists in Cambodia, as well as social struggles in other repressive regimes: How do people maintain the strength to continue mobilizing in the face of state and capital violence? In this chapter, I analyze the ways in which people have mobilized over land in the wake of the land reform. In Cambodia, the "long shadow of the repressive state" (Chua 2012, 719) shapes how mobilization develops. The repertoire of resistance that people deploy in the context of fear and uncertainty sheds light on relations of power (Abu-Lughod 1991) and reveals how emotions play central roles in collective mobilization (Jasper 2011).

The chapter is in two parts. In the first part, I analyze people's attempts to "hold onto the traces of the land reform" (Schoenberger 2017) by mobilizing their land titles, survey receipts, and the promises of the reform in their direct appeals to the powerful state elite (rather than through formal legal mechanisms). This mobilization of land rights that is disconnected from the legal system reinforces my central argument that the land reform paradoxically strengthened the prime minister's power through signifying the possibility of his intervention rather than any systematic use of law. This suggests, as Lynette Chua (2012) argues in a discussion about social movements in authoritarian states, that the law "ultimately matters to the movement as a pragmatic concern" (743). Chua's point is that social movements in repressive regimes balance movement survival with advancement when they mount resistance through law (even in the knowledge that the legal system is stacked against them). This tactic ironically "de-centers law" in its self-conscious use of law as a pragmatic strategy rather than as an ideological battlefield (743). In people's use of the land title to appeal directly to Hun Sen, we see a similar de-centering of law and a reification of the existing locus of power that does occasionally produce results for activists.

Beyond a pragmatic tactic, people's use of the land titles also works at a deeper level to subvert fear and produce emotions of hope and bravery in the collective. As one woman in Khang Cheung told me, "At least the title makes us brave enough to protest." The inverse of this potentiality, however, is that those who did not receive a land title become more fearful and insecure. In the second part of the chapter, I look to the broader work of resistance among collectives of rural people that are now fractured between those who received land title and those who did not. When I began fieldwork, I was so preoccupied with the ways fear shapes social relations that much of the work done to resist land grabbing and (as Srey Sophorn says) "find ways to stay together" escaped my notice. The "emotion work" to channel and reshape emotions is a crucial factor in social movement success, albeit an aspect of mobilization that has only recently gained scholarly attention (Ruiz-Junco 2012). In rural Cambodia, emotion work is the labor to subvert fear that takes place in meetings, in casual encounters, through communing together over food, stories, music, and spiritual practices, as well as in overt protest. It is not just the large public demonstrations or meetings with officials that require bravery; community activists work every day to develop what Valeria Procupez (2015) terms "collective patience" to continue their struggles, even as they are faced with the dissembling, delay, and uncertain coercive power of the state and capital. I build on this scholarly attention to emotions in social movements, and connect this with feminist political ecology concerns, by arguing that this emotion work is not just a form of resisting (in the sense of staving off some foreboding future harm to the land); it also draws on, and generates, different relationships between state, society, and land. It is in this articulation of alternative ontologies of land—beyond the primacy of state-capital relations—that these modes of mobilization are significant.

Taking the Title to Hun Sen

Throughout the book, I have shown how the law can be used as a tool of dispossession—powerful people's claims are upheld, while rural smallholders' claims are ignored or mired in delay and obfuscation. But in some cases, rural people who lose land to concessionaires do win land back, and it is this possibility for resolution that is so important to the prime minister's continued legitimacy. To show how the resolution of land disputes depends on people's connections with the state elite, I analyze two cases in which people successfully resolved land disputes with concessionaires and powerful land claimants, and I compare these cases to a land dispute that people in Srai Saat and Srey Mie found themselves embroiled in one year after the land reform.

Case 1: A Community Wins Land Back From an ELC

The first case of success takes place in eastern Cambodia. During Order 01, the volunteers surveyed rural people's land within a South Korean ELC. As Laura Schoenberger (2017) describes in detail, households received land survey receipts, and land titling results were publicly displayed in May 2013. However, the Korean embassy filed formal complaints with the Ministry of Land against the land claimants, arguing that the land was lawfully ELC land and that the company was developing the land in accordance with their ELC contract. In response, provincial officials backtracked on the Order 01 surveys and stated that plans to issue titles could no longer proceed.[3] But land claimants resisted. The community grabbed national headlines when hundreds of villagers marched to Phnom Penh and staged a public protest outside the prime minister's residence. Hun Sen first professed ignorance of the case and placed blame on provincial officials and ministries for "not listening or understanding"[4] and for failing to deliver petitions to his office in Phnom Penh: "I heard that the youth have measured the land, but the titles are not approved. Is it true? Did anyone report to me? For these problems, did all provincial authorities die already?"[5]

Hun Sen went on to threaten the provincial governor with dismissal, warning him that "it's no problem if you don't work to find a solution because we don't lack people who want to be governors."[6] After the prime minister's comments, the Land Ministry resolved the case within two weeks by awarding land titles to 312 families for 1,562 hectares of land that was excised from the ELC during Order 01. Hun Sen's rapid solution for the land claimants, typical of the power of his unwritten rules, was significant for several reasons: it reinforced his power over subnational authorities (including a powerful provincial governor); it showed him standing up against a powerful donor government and large company; and it reproduced his status as the benevolent leader.

Case 2: A Rural Landowner Wins Land Back From A Senior Official

In a second case during my fieldwork in Khang Cheung, a man named Lok Tean managed to win land back after provincial officials claimed his land during Order 01. Lok Tean was not an ordinary rural land claimant. He lived in Phnom Penh with his wife and child, ran a reasonably successful shoe shop, and studied law in the evenings. He had purchased roadside land from relatives in Tmor Muoy village in the mid-2000s, before the rise in land prices. When the volunteer surveyors came to Tmor Muoy during Order 01, Lok Tean's relatives called him and told him to travel to the village to claim his land title. He did so, and when he showed the volunteer surveyors his land documents signed by the Srai Saat commune office, the surveyors measured his land and provided a land survey receipt. However, when Lok Tean attended the land survey display at the village temple a month later, his name was not on the list of land title recipients. Instead, he found another name attached to his land plot. Relatives told him it was the name of a high-up official (*aekadom*) in Khang Cheung, in the Department of Land. Lok Tean's family warned him not to make a fuss because the *aekadom* was too powerful. But Lok Tean felt he had the political connections to take his case forward: "I went to talk to the Department of Land in Khang Cheung. They ignored me. So

I went to the provincial governor, because I know someone who knows him, from Phnom Penh. And he said he would help, but then he didn't do anything. So I contacted an *oknha*, and we went together back to the provincial office, and I said I know the law and I will take [the *aekadom*] to court. And the *oknha* is high up; he has the ear of Hun Sen. And then they found a solution for me straight after I did that." The solution was to divide the land, so that Lok Tean retained half the original land area and the *aekadom* and *oknha* (who intervened on behalf of Lok Tean) claimed the other half of the land. This case is significant as it shows the relatively rare occurrence of a small land claimant standing up to powerful officials. Lok Tean was held up as something of a hero in Tmor Muoy, and his uncle who ran the local noodle shop spoke about the case frequently to me and other customers when I dropped in for a plate of noodles. Lok Tean's uncle particularly reveled in the fact that Lok Tean's political connections went higher than the *aekadom*'s; essentially, Lok Tean was successful because he persisted until he found a patron (the *oknha*) who had enough power for the law to mean something.

Similar to the case in eastern Cambodia, then, Lok Tean's case illustrates how a successful resolution for land claimants depended on pushing through state officials' attempts to obfuscate and delay proceedings. In both cases, the resolution was reached quickly after the cases became politically embarrassing, at a national level for Hun Sen (in the first case) or at the provincial level (when the powerful *oknha* showed he had the potential to take the case to Hun Sen). Neither solution was a result of the systematic use of law or the sustained intervention of NGOs and donor agencies. In fact, rural people and NGO staff I spoke with were adamant that claims could languish forever as they were shuffled from one government office to another, and the only way to create change was to go to Hun Sen. One community activist told me, "The Ministry of Land won't do anything to make big changes unless Hun Sen orders it. And the other problem is with the different ministries; the Ministry of Land hates MAFF, et cetera. So when you raise ELCs with the Ministry of Land, they say that is not our area; you have to go to MAFF. The key is getting to Hun Sen. He is the one who makes all decisions." These two successful cases reinforce what this activist says: Hun Sen is the "one who makes all decisions." The cases acted to further increase dependence on Hun Sen to personally resolve disputes rather than strengthen the state bureaucracy.

The two cases beg the question of what value the land title has in rural Cambodia. Is the title meaningless? I have endeavored to show in this book that the title does have meaning for people in my field sites, but this is not the meaning that donor agencies or neoliberal economists might expect. In Khang Cheung, most people who received a land title during Order 01 valued it—people often kept the document locked away in a box out of the rain, and many people proudly showed me their land title when I asked about it. When asked why the land title was important to them, people commonly said that it meant "This is our land." Some said, "We can use it to get loans." Some just shrugged or asked what I thought. The most common reason people articulated was that "the titles are important for us because Hun Sen gave them to us." The land title in this context has multiple meanings—it signifies personal possession; it abstracts land from place and transforms it into a commodity whose value lies in the potential to take it to the bank; and, foremost, it is a gift from Hun Sen himself. These multiple meanings shape the ways people understand and use the land title in the wake of the land reform.

Case 3: Khang Cheung Community Mobilises Against A New Development Project

I realized the power of the land title as Hun Sen's gift when my study communes became embroiled in a land dispute over a planned development project a year after the land reform. This development, funded by a Chinese concessionary loan, planned to construct a large irrigation canal system and overflow dam through two districts in Khang Cheung over five years. The canal was slated to pass through both Srai Saat and Phnom Mie. When people realized that the project would go directly through their rice fields, rumors started flying that villagers would lose their land. People told me they were not consulted about the project, and they did not trust that their land title would protect them. One villager who had previously lost land to an ELC represents the common feelings people expressed to me: "The irrigation channel will affect three communes but no one dares to protest. We are all worried. Because in the past, they came so fast and we couldn't do anything. Even though I have land title, I am afraid. The authorities won't help us. They got land taken by the company as well. We can't do anything.... We don't dare to protest."

This woman did not dare to protest the irrigation canal even though she had a title for her land. Other people in Srey Mie said they hoped the land title would give them a chance to press their claims with state officials and company management, even if they might not win. "It gives us something," said Ming Tam. "So they can join together, at least they have a chance then." Ming Tam, Srey Sophorn, and other activists held community meetings encouraging people to gather their land titles and lodge a complaint. But the flip side of the potentiality of the land title was that many people who did not receive titles were too afraid to join this group, even if they occupied land in accordance with the Land Law 2001 requirements. One woman from Khang Cheung who did not receive a land title during the land reform told me: "We need to get land title so we can protest. Even if we can't win with the title, at least we have a better right to protest. Now we are too scared." Essentially, then, when this new threat to people's land emerged, insecurity increased among those who did not receive a land title during Order 01, while those who did have land titles were not sure whether (and how) the titles would help them resist the development project.

The community network held an emergency meeting in Khang Cheung town to discuss the irrigation canal. I attended the three-day meeting, and I was struck by how quiet and fearful the community activists were. No one was sure how to respond; it all seemed too overwhelming. And it became obvious during the meeting that the divide between people who had received land titles during Order 01 and those who had not received titles was now manifesting in tensions over who would be most affected by the development project and what the community's course of action should be. Several community representatives from Srey Mie got into a heated discussion:

> FIRST WOMAN: I don't think we should protest. I don't want to be killed or thrown in prison. The authorities won't let us protest. They said we can get compensation if we just sign the paper, so we should do that. And then maybe we can grow rice in the dry season.
> SECOND WOMAN: But we don't know that! We don't know what [the irrigation canal] is for. It's not for us; it's to help the Chinese company. And they'll make us pay for water. . . . We need to protest.
> THIRD WOMAN: (*nodding*) Yes, and we don't know if we will get compensation. Maybe we will only get a little . . . not enough for what the land is worth. And if we don't have land title we won't get as much compensation; that's what I heard.
> MAN: The problem is we're not helping each other. We have to go all together.
> THIRD WOMAN: We have to find out what is happening first. We don't know what is happening. And we have to go to higher levels to protest; we have to go to Hun Sen because the local level doesn't help us.

Two problems lay at the root of this disagreement. First, no one had any idea what the purpose of the development project was, nor how it would affect people's land and livelihoods. People were desperate for more access to water after another season of drought had halved expected rice yields, and the irrigation project promised to bring water to people's fields year-round. But people were suspicious of the project's intentions because the canal ran along the edge of the cassava plantation. As the third woman reasoned, all this might have been a plan to expand the plantation zone. Second, no one had any idea about how the land titles might protect people's land. One man reasoned that the community network should forget about trying to stop the canal project and just focus on getting some monetary compensation, because "the most important thing is that if we have the title, they have to give us compensation." But a woman sitting next to him shot back, "But the title doesn't mean much. . . . Look, they surveyed our land but now they come and put flags on our land to dig it up. So what does the title mean?"

These anxieties revealed people's experiences of place in the leopard skin landscape. Although authorities assured villagers that the irrigation project was completely separate from the concession company, people living within the concession assumed that the "Chinese company" running the cassava plantation had ultimate control over the space and the resources (such as water) that flowed through it. This assumption seemed warranted; Pheapimex concession holders Lao Meng Khin and Choeung Sopheap were on the governing board of the company developing the irrigation scheme. This connection was suspicious, but it couldn't prove whether the people or the company would benefit.

After prolonged discussion at the meeting, the community network decided they needed more information before they protested or agreed to any compensation packages. Over the next month, community network members tried in vain to ask local- and provincial-level authorities about the project, making multiple trips to the Department of Water Management; to commune, district, and provincial offices; and to the Department of Rural Development. But each time, the authorities denied any knowledge of the project. One woman complained to me: "We have been to the local chiefs, to the district, to the province. They don't help us. There has been a reporter, and the NGOs try to help, but no one knows anything. Maybe in the end, Hun Sen will help us. We need to go to Hun Sen. Maybe then we can get all the land back."

Two months after the community network meeting, this woman joined a small delegation from the community that decided to travel to Phnom Penh to protest outside Hun Sen's house. All ten families that joined this protest had received land titles during the land reform. They set out from Khang Cheung on motorbikes and spent three days in Phnom Penh protesting on the pavement outside Hun Sen's residence. They waved their land titles and held up pictures of the prime minister and his wife. I didn't attend the protest, but I spoke with one of the protestors by phone during the protest. A woman in her forties who had helped organize the community network protests in 2004, she told me the community was fed up with waiting: "Some people say we shouldn't protest; they say we should wait for the officials to sort it out. But the [officials] don't tell us anything! If we do nothing, the land will be gone. And we got land titles from the prime minister's land reform, so we come here to say to him to protect our land. Maybe we can't win, but some people win . . . and the Boeung Kak women are helping us."

The protestors were well aware of the group from eastern Cambodia who had secured land by taking their case to Hun Sen. In Phnom Penh, a group of women protestors from Phnom Penh's Boeung Kak Lake neighborhood supported the Khang Cheung protesters, meeting with them to discuss their claims and inviting the protestors to stay at their homes. The Khang Cheung group protested peacefully for two days. But on the second day, armed police officers who had been watching the protestors from the other side of the road confronted the group and threatened to charge them with disturbing the peace if they continued the protest. The families decided to abort their protest and return to Khang Cheung. Men Somning, who took part in the protest, told me that he wanted to stay in Phnom Penh, but the other protesters were scared and had to get home to look after their families: "It's hard because people can only stay a few days; they have to get back home to their children and work. Maybe if we stayed longer. But how long do we stay? We never saw Hun Sen. And the [officials] just ignore us, threaten us. They say we will all go to prison. We will try another way."

The aborted protest reveals the difficulties people faced trying to advocate for their rights: their time and labor were required for social reproductive work at home, and state officials used threats to intimidate them. The group was despondent when they returned to Khang Cheung. Taking their case to Hun Sen had seemed like the only option that might work. But in contrast to the successful protest by the land claimants from eastern Cambodia, the Khang Cheung protesters had failed to gain media attention to their case, and Phnom Penh politicians were focused on other concerns.

Although the protest was not successful at getting the prime minister's attention, it may have influenced the attitudes of subnational officials. Over the next few months, provincial officials visited the commune several times. The officials visited each affected household individually and encouraged people to thumbprint a statement declaring their willingness to exchange their affected land for cash compensation. Community network organizers tried to persuade people to refrain from signing the statement until the community network could coordinate collective resistance to the project. But the authorities spread confusion about the process in an effort to break up community solidarity, as one woman activist described to me: "The authorities are going door-to-door; they tell people to sign the letter to sell their land. When they came to our village, they told us that the people from the lower areas had already agreed. But the truth was that those people were angry too. And when they went to the lower areas, they told people there that we had already agreed. It's a trick. The authorities are trying to ruin the peace in our village, to break up the solidarity of people."

For this activist, these house calls were yet another way state officials produced uncertainty among villagers, deliberately trying to trick them by spreading rumors and lies. Ming Tam said the result of this strategy was the loss of solidarity in the network: "Some people don't think. They take the money, they sell the land,

and then they don't want to talk with others in the group because they are embarrassed about taking the little amount of money. But I want you to look around, and see that this is how the authorities want to break us up. They want us to fall apart, each taking a little money and losing the long-term benefits of the land. It's such a small amount of money to lose our solidarity, our peace in the group."

As more people signed the statements, it became obvious that the project would go ahead. Discussion within the community network turned from protesting the canal construction to getting decent compensation. All negotiations were secretive and made on an individual level, so the community network organizers could not gain an accurate sense of how much money people were offered in order to collectively mobilize for a higher rate. I could not get an accurate sense of what was happening either. The Srey Mie commune chief told me that the company promised a slightly higher rate of compensation for people who held title to their land. However, when I interviewed people around the commune, I found that the rates varied considerably from household to household, whether people held a land title or not. In all cases, the compensation was pitiful, but many people felt it was better to take what they could get than to wait and lose out completely.

By early 2015, most people in Phnom Mie and Srai Saat had signed the paper agreeing not to protest the irrigation project and received some cash compensation. But a small group of people in the community network refused to sign the statement until the company offered a higher rate of compensation. This group waited months, enduring multiple house visits and compensation offers from state officials, as well as intimidation, including anonymous threatening phone calls. Eventually, after several months, the company agreed to pay out a higher rate to this group. The higher rate covered all land—land with title and land without title. The families that had waited were pleased but seemed conflicted. After all, the compensation amounts were uneven across the community. One woman activist in her twenties confided to me that her "auntie and uncle and other relations took the compensation earlier, and now they are still upset because they only got a little and I got more." The state and company's strategy of separating landowners to negotiate compensation appears to have created lasting tensions within families.

By mid-2016, a giant concrete channel had begun to snake its way through Srai Saat and Srey Mie Communes (see figure 14). It is difficult to know what changes it might bring to this area in the future. What this case shows is the limited potential of land title to provide land tenure security for rural people who face dispossession from powerful companies and state actors. Having the land title did encourage people to mobilize collectively and to press for their rights with local officials and central government, but this created a chasm between titled and untitled members of the community network. What had previously been a heterogenous process of claims making—claims made on the basis of various documents

FIGURE 14. Irrigation development project, mid-2016.

(Photo: Courtesy of Courtney Work.)

from authorities, as well as long settlement, generational possession, knowledge of the area and landmarks, stories of grief and migration—now revolved around the land title. But this didn't mean people wielded the title as a legal tool. Rather, people used the law as a pragmatic strategy; it was the material paper with the prime minister's signature on it that gave them hope and meant more than the legal system behind it. The community network members did not expect the land title to protect their rights in a court of law. In fact, they did not even consider taking their case to court. Instead, when their efforts to take their case to local and provincial authorities failed, they took their complaint to Hun Sen himself. This tactic ironically "decenters law" and "repeatedly validates the boundaries of cultural norms" (Chua 2012, 742) by reproducing the appeal to personalized state power. It is through this process of mutual recognition—of making claims and of bestowing access to land—that the political elite's authority is reproduced (Lund 2016).

Beyond State-Society Relations

The story of the new irrigation development project in Khang Cheung highlights the limits of mobilization that privileges state recognition of property rights. The land title provides potential leverage in dealings with the state elite and companies in a context where the dangers of speaking out are very real. But focusing on claims for state recognition places power in the hands of state actors who can obfuscate, delay claims, threaten land claimants, and use these claims for political gain; it also enables the state to define the meaning of land, privileging state and capital formations over more expansive understandings of land. In this second part of the chapter, I look beyond the idea of the leopard skin and the promise of formalized property rights to analyze how rural people engage in mobilization over land in ways that move beyond a focus on state recognition, and I ask what other worlds this work makes possible.

I follow Arturo Escobar's (2017, 238) call for a scholarship that seeks clues for sustaining diverse ontologies (what he terms the "pluriverse," or "a world where many worlds fit") in territorial struggles against extractivism. These struggles, he argues, lay bare "the limits of Western/modern social theory for understanding the range of experiences and knowledges emerging from territorially based worlds" and, in doing so, build a "decolonial view of nature and the environment" that involves "seeing the interrelatedness of ecological, economic, and cultural processes that come to produce what humans call nature" (255). Indigenous writers argue that any attempt to transcend relations of domination with the state requires the "resuscitation of relationships of mutual obligation between land and people" as opposed to deeper engagement with state institutions (Burow, Brock, and Dove 2018; Coulthard 2013). This notion of resuscitation is complex in Cambodia (as in many other contexts), where rural people (both Khmer and indigenous) have deep engagement with market relations and understandings of land shaped by successive waves of state projects of rule that work to make other entangled land relations less visible. But I suggest that diverse ontologies of land are made visible through rural people's collective mobilization. Rural people draw on diverse ontologies to subvert fear and to generate positive affect in land-conflict areas—actions which, in turn, work to renew social relations with land. In the following sections, I recall two stories that illustrate the emotional work of the collective and articulate different relationships between state, society, and land.[7]

Khang Leit

On my final field trip to Khang Leit, I met an organization whose approach illustrates an alternative way of mobilizing that draws on and constructs different social relationships with and through land. This organization, a local NGO called Forest Peoples Programme (FPP), worked with five indigenous communities in Khang Leit. I spent three days staying in one village that the FPP director had worked with for fifteen years. This village was isolated from main roads (I had to wade through a river with my research assistant to reach the village), which made it less attractive to commercial companies than other villages closer to main roads, and people in this village still had access to a large amount of communal forestland, on which they employed a diversity of cropping strategies and livelihoods (including maintaining rotational cultivation alongside cashew plantations).

When I asked people in a group interview why this village was able to hold on to their land when nearby villages had lost most of their land to ELCs and in-migrants, most people talked about the importance of the village elders (*jaa tum*) and traditional chief, who evidently had a lot of power and commanded villagers' respect. People focused on the strong relationships between elders and young people in the village; elders held regular meetings where village youth were able to speak, and young people also respected the elders. The traditional chief boasted to me that "the village chief [appointed by the government] doesn't dare to do anything against me. He knows that the villages support me; I have power here. If there is a question about the village, like about the culture, the religion, the forest trees, where the fields of the different villagers are, then I know all of it."

Beyond the traditional chief and elders, people pointed to the long relationship with the FPP NGO that supported the village. The approach of the villagers and NGO in this area is noteworthy: rather than focusing only on the formal aspects of applying for communal land title, the community first worked on ensuring that all villagers as well as neighboring villages and ELC companies knew where the borders of the communal land was, and they made sure borders were clearly marked. The director of FPP said that they focused on what he called community empowerment as well as legal empowerment: "We believe that two things are most important; one is legal empowerment, and one is community empowerment. We need both. If we only have legal without community empowerment, it won't work, because even if we know our rights we can't fight for our rights. And if we only have community empowerment without legal empowerment, it won't work, because when the company comes the villagers can't back up their resistance."

This NGO director and the traditional chief explained to me that some places with CLT are still losing land because they worry only about the technical rules of securing legal empowerment (i.e., state recognition of their land rights) without community empowerment (i.e., the collective strength to resist land encroachment). In this village, the head of the NGO explained, they did things differently from the process mandated under CLT guidelines: "We don't do the map [for recognition of the communal land area] first. First, we meet with villagers. We mark out our borders and we meet with neighboring communities and get their thumbprints to say they know where our land is. We still work on the CLT application, because without the land title, we will still face trouble if we go to court. But we can't depend on it. If we have relationships with everyone, I think it is easier; that is most important. We have to always work on that."

Then, as one woman explained, "we have a big party." She said that the villagers contacted people from neighboring communities and a manager from the nearby rubber plantation whose son was friendly with some young people in the village. They invited everyone to an evening party at the village meeting hall every few months. They feasted, danced, and took part in collective rituals that celebrated the spiritual power of the land, such as drinking from communal honey wine jars. These ritual practices confirm land's liveliness; spirits authorize human land use and regulate it when it is inappropriate. Then, as one of the elders told me, "At the party, we put up the big maps on the wall to show where our land is. We use the maps we produced with NTFP and the photos of the border markers we've made and the spirit forest and the landmarks. And then we stand up and explain to them all where our land is and how we know it's ours."

The party simultaneously strengthened the knowledge and solidarity of people within the community, confirmed the spirits' relationship with land, and created personal relationships with neighboring villages, authorities, and company personnel. While the party didn't challenge larger structures of oppression, it worked to transform violent affect into hope. And centrally, this strategy worked directly to challenge the state's obfuscation and delays over CLT processes by refusing to wait for state recognition. Certainly, the strategy was not without risk; it was successful precisely because it built on many years of strong relationships within the community and with local-level company management and NGO staff. This strategy is notable because it subverts the state relation to just one among many, and it emerges from a recognition that land is embedded within local socioecological, spiritual relations.

Khang Cheung

I vividly recall the emergency meeting of the community network in Khang Cheung after people first realized the massive scope of the proposed irrigation development project in 2015. Around forty people gathered nervously in the Green Cambodia office in Khang Cheung town. No one knew precisely who was involved with the irrigation project, what the project was for, or what land would be taken. Tensions were high and rumors flew. The meeting grew increasingly quiet as, one by one, people talked about their fear that they would lose their land. Some people cried. Others sat outside smoking, uncertain what it all meant. No one was sure how to respond; it all seemed too overwhelming. People started to bicker with each other. On the second afternoon, two prominent women in the network accused Srey Sophorn of selling out to the authorities.

But as Srey Sophorn angrily stood to defend herself, loud Khmer folk music suddenly blared out from the back of the room. Ming Tam was standing at the back with an old CD player. She stopped the meeting and cajoled people into dancing. Slowly, we all struggled up and joined in a Khmer folk dance in an unruly circle around the room and onto the courtyard outside. I felt awkward at first and confused, but I let myself be dragged into the dance and my jerky hand movements slowly relaxed into the music. After an hour of dancing, people took turns at singing, performing improvised songs about the community; the forest, soils, lake, and mountain in this area; and their love for the people in the network. I was pushed up to the front eventually; I don't recall exactly what I sang, something about people's love for the land, sung badly to the tune of "Stand By Me." The words themselves were of less importance in that moment than the collective affect that was produced. I felt the collaborative performance of the dancing and singing was a conscious effort to resist fear and uncertainty. Our songs introduced a radically different atmosphere to the meeting that released tension I didn't know I had been holding. That evening, people worked in small groups to devise strategies of resistance to the irrigation project. The groups spread out on the floor; laughter and loud conversations punctuated the space. By the end of the third day, the meeting adjourned with concrete strategies for small groups to implement in their own communities, and the community network made plans for a community spirit festival that would call on the land spirits (*nayk taa*) to provide strength and support.

The spirit festival was held a month later. I rode on a wooden cart in a convoy with around one hundred community network members out to a mountain about an hour away from Srai Saat commune. We met around two hundred other community network members from other communes at the mountain. The community network regularly held protest festivals at places where powerful spirits reside; according to network members, some of these mountains were not traditionally spiritually potent places but gained power during the civil conflict because they were sites of mass graves. Holding the spirit festival many hours from a main road on an isolated mountain was certainly not a visible protest strategy. We would not attract the attention of the state or the concession company. Rather, the protest acted to build solidarity among network members from different communes and to harness the power of land spirits for the network. Men Somning explained,

> We did the festival at Phnom Pich to dedicate to the ancestors who died in Pol Pot's time, and to the *nayk taa*. So the *nayk taa* would help us protect the forest. We wanted to do the festival there because the *nayk taa* are very powerful there. In Pol Pot's time, many people died there. When the Chinese company tried to clear the mountain for mining, machines broke and a truck crashed. We're not sure if the *nayk taa* can help us or not, but we have to go and ask, we have to see, so they will know about the problems.

The villagers who attended the spirit festival told me they knew they didn't control the land or the spiritual realm. But they saw their land use practices as something the spirits would support and their struggle as something the spirits would be sympathetic to (as opposed to the "Chinese company," whose destructive land use and labor practices presumably brought on their machinery problems). In this way, harnessing the struggles of past conflict gave hope and strength to the current struggle. I recall the optimism on the bumpy cart ride out to the festival, the dancing and singing, and the excitement of the spirit possession ceremony. The festival could be seen as a way to mitigate fear—not directly confronting the authorities but building up strength, collective bravery, and perhaps divine intervention. It acknowledged that the owners of the land were other than human and that when land is reduced to a natural resource for human exploitation, there will be consequences.

Making Land Something Different

The power of the various acts of mobilization I described in the foregoing sections lies in the unity among the collective—including not just the human elements but the land itself. The recognition of the spiritual elements of land (which took place in both the Khang Cheung festival and songs and the Khang Leit party) calls on a different source of authority. In this place, while the state may have dominion over territory, the local territorial spirit is part of the land and thus has prior claim to authority over it (Work 2011). The spirit is seen by some people to be more powerful than the state in its ability to bring consequences to those who do not treat the land well. Land's spiritual power is not inherently alternative to state power, though; Prime Minister Hun Sen also draws from this discourse of spiritual power. Even as the Cambodian state produces legal subjects through the project of bestowing land rights, Hun Sen produces himself as the *devaraja*, the divine ruler who sits between spirits and people and bestows the gift of land title (Jacobsen and Stuart-Fox 2013). If the true owner of the land is the spirit, and if the king is the bridge to the spirit world, then Hun Sen as the divine ruler has a formidable connection (Beban and Work 2014). But the prime minister's legitimacy is waning. In this sense, as Christian Lund (2016) notes, the process of seeking authority is never finished. When the community network travels to seek help from the spirit of the land, this renews recognition of the spirit's authority, which can challenge the state's dominance over land.

The flip side of people's recognition of the spirit's authority is that the spirit also recognizes—and thus supports—rural people's relationship with land. In the spirit festival, and at the community meeting, a frequent refrain was that villagers "took only what they needed" for themselves and their families; this was contrasted with the companies' bulldozers and trucks, whose thirst for land could never be satiated. The community's relationship to place was affirmed in songs about the specific features of the landscape and the history of settlement. People also emphasized the connection between their land use and food; when the groups from each community unwrapped their cloth-wrapped squares of rice at lunchtime during the spirit festival, a lively conversation sprang up about which family grew the most delicious rice and which community made the best fish paste. The obvious tension between this narrative and the fact that most families also grew cash crops or worked on the plantations to sustain their families (or that some families propitiated the spirits daily through offerings while others seemed skeptical) did not seem to be a contradiction to the people gathered. Their primary point was that their relationship with land was one of securing social reproduction for their family through growing food and earning a small income, in contrast to what they saw as the ever-expanding plantation that did violence to the land. The ritualistic acts of mobilization served as a "collective means of emotional communication" that reproduced the morality of group identity, performing not only who people are but also "what they intend to become in relation to the forces about them" (Barker 2001, 188).

This reaffirming of people's relationship with the land through collective performances of mobilization has effects for individuals, for the group, and for the wider audience of onlookers and opponents (Barker 2001). Within the collective, the party at Khang Leit (like the dance at the meeting and the spirit festival) worked to subvert fear and channel that emotion into bravery and hope. This process of producing "collective self-confidence" must be continuously constructed, as Colin Barker (2001, 201) reminds us: "Unity [i]s always provisional, open to new affective impulses from within and without, and thus ha[s] always to be secured." The party was not just for the benefit of the community members that gathered; it was also explicitly a performance for the benefit of the attendees from nearby villages and the company workers and management. The channeling of emotions worked to produce fear in these other attendees—all partygoers took part in the rituals that confirmed the presence of the spirit, and thus confirmed the spirit's authority to bring consequences to those who did not treat the land well. The subverting of fear into a sense of bravery and joy (and the production of that fear in others) that I witnessed in these acts of mobilization receives less attention in scholarship on emotions in social movements than the channeling of fear, anxiety, and grief into anger (Gould 2009; Jasper 2011). However, in the context of potential state violence, anger is useful only insofar as it motivates people to act collectively, but anger is risky, and often ends up turning itself on the group (such as I witnessed during the emergency meeting when group members began accusing each other of lying).

These acts of mobilizing around the communal, nourishing, and agentic dimensions of land suggest that a different ontology of land is being drawn on by, and generated through, the collective. I term this, following Chung (2017), a feminist ontology of land. This conception of land pushes against the abstraction of land as a commodity and factor of production, instead foregrounding land as life producing—the site and source of social reproduction. It revalues those aspects of land that are not part of the market: those that are oriented toward sustaining the self and community, with the explicit recognition of both women's and men's labor in the work of food production and consumption, as well as parts played by people of different class, gender, ethnicity, and age. A feminist ontology therefore shows that the very idea of a leopard skin landscape is fundamentally flawed. Feminist environmentalists see the roots of the violent transformation of peoples and ecosystems in the dualisms of Western knowledge construction, which posit human identity as outside nature and naturalize domination in both human and nonhuman spheres (Plumwood 2003). The leopard skin abstracts land from its social and ecological relations through the assumption that a zone of capitalist intensification can coexist with zones of indigenous and peasant agriculture (an ontology of land that privileges capital relations and state control and devalues people, nature, and reproduction [Federici 2004]). The leopard skin landscape denies the ecological relations of soil and water that flow through space, the sociopolitical power structures that value agribusiness over peasant farmers, and the peasant and indigenous farming practices that depend on dynamic systems of common and private property. In contrast, a feminist ontology recognizes that neither capital nor the state is the most important actor in this relationship with land, and it seeks to create an ecological culture beyond dualisms that exceeds the temporal-spatial boundedness enshrined in notions of property.

With this understanding of moving beyond dualisms, I expand on Chung's (2017) concept to suggest that a feminist ontology makes room for land relations that do not place humans in a position of control and that recognize land as not only life producing but life itself (Gibson-Graham 2006; de la Cadena 2010). This resonates with indigenous scholarship and with struggles to re-place agency within nature, as well as a growing posthumanist agenda in the social sciences challenging the idea that humans occupy a separate and privileged place among other beings (Coulthard 2013; Haraway 2008; Latour 2013; Todd 2016). Kim TallBear (2017, 187) argues that "indigenous standpoints accord greater animacy to nonhumans, including nonorganisms, such as stones and places, which help form (indigenous) peoples as humans constituted in complex ways." Indigenous peoples are at the forefront of concepts such as *buen vivir* (good life), a Latin American concept now incorporated into the Ecuadorian and Bolivian constitutions that sees well-being as possible only within a community that includes living earth

(Mercado 2015), and New Zealand Māori concepts of the *mauri* (life force) of rivers and mountains that are now considered legal entities with rights of personhood (Calderwood 2016). I employ the concept of feminist ontology rather than indigenous ontology, not to deny the distinctiveness of indigenous worldviews or to appropriate the rich world of indigenous "place-thought" (Watts 2013) but to emphasize the centrality of social reproduction and the diverse practices and understandings of land use in rural Cambodia, where the distinctions between indigenous and nonindigenous identities are contested political constructions (see chapter 6). Land in this understanding is agentic (rather than an inert nature subject to human agency); it is unbounded (rather than bounded property or state territory); it sustains the social reproduction of humans and nonhumans alike (rather than being valued solely for its productive potential); and it is something that humans can never fully control (rather than a resource for our benefit).

Conclusion: Barren Fields

In mid-2016—one year after I completed fieldwork—the Pheapimex contractor harvested thousands of hectares of cassava and abruptly left. The landscape that was once an ocean of cassava bushes has become bare fields (figure 15). When my research assistant Sokun called on Srey Sophorn to ask what was happening, the latter was still in shock:

FIGURE 15. Pheapimex concession plantation area, mid-2016, after the cassava was abruptly harvested and the company left.

(Photo: Courtesy of Courtney Work.)

CHAPTER 7

> The cassava company just left. . . . They took all the cassava, and now they have left the land bare. Now the buffalo are grazing on the land. . . . Maybe they will come back, I don't know. But now they are gone. The laborers didn't get paid, but the district and provincial officials complained and then they got the money back. Now it is so hard. . . . The trees are gone from here, and look, there are no jobs with the companies either. The government says that we will have jobs but then look at this; there is nothing. We are too scared to enter the land, though. Who knows when they will come back, and some of the security guards still drive around.

Srey Sophorn told Sokun that local people were angry because workers had not been paid for their final month of work. Farmers could not access the cleared plantation land to graze their cattle or scavenge for cassava because armed guards still patrolled the perimeter. She continued angrily, "These problems, they are happening everywhere. . . . Nothing is for the people; it is for the rich people, the powerful, not for the normal people."

For Srey Sophorn and others in Khang Cheung, the leopard skin policy has not provided livelihood security. Living within a land concession means living with constant uncertainty, the shock of market expansion swallowing up forestland, the shock of continued drought, and the shock of market crises, such as the cassava price drop that likely caused the company to pull out in 2016. The transformation of forest—which once formed an integral part of people's lives—into secured, barren fields was a stark reminder for Srey Sophorn that "nothing is for the people." My accounts in the first half of this chapter explain Srey Sophorn's anger and reinforce one of my key arguments in the book—land reform has no inherent quality; it takes on meanings in particular sociopolitical contexts.

After talking with Srey Sophorn, Sokun called Puu Tanak's house in Srai Saat. Puu Tanak said angrily that the land in the cassava plantation was now useless, and "I want you to write down that the government should just give it to us farmers." He dictated to Sokun,

> I will farm the concession; they can lease it to us and we'll pay more than the [US$]5 per hectare that those companies are paying. They don't need those companies. . . . Tell that to the government when you write this report! We will look after the land and forests and make sure the people here can make a living and get food. We will plant rice and other crops. But now the companies just ruin the soil and take all our water and trees and then leave. . . . And the rich people are the ones who benefit.

I find Puu Tanak's statement here remarkable; he articulates a vision of rural life that is at odds with the notion of the leopard skin. In his vision, small farmers lease concession land and produce food and agricultural commodities that are more ecologically and socially just than the companies' and provide revenue for the state. This vision implicitly critiques the entire model of global agribusiness production in Cambodia: agribusiness is extractive ("the companies . . . take all our water"), depletes soil nutrients (they "just ruin the soil"), drives deforestation ("we [as opposed to the companies] will look after the . . . forests"), runs on boom-and-bust cycles (they take the "trees and then leave"), intensifies inequality ("the rich people are the ones who benefit"), and makes little to no contribution to formal state coffers ("we'll pay more than the . . . companies are paying"). In contrast to this model of agribusiness, Puu Tanak's vision of small, farmer-led, rural food systems rejects the leopard skin idea of separate, parceled-out space and imagines a holistic system that encompasses the forests, rice fields, crops, and people.

I rarely heard people articulate an explicit vision for their communities as Puu Tanak did here. For most people, it was hard to imagine and put into words a future free from the multiple threats that eroded their hold on the land—agribusiness concessions, threatening state officials, climate change–induced floods and drought, coercive land brokers, loan sharks, erratic global markets, and so on. But the communal practices that work to subvert fear and generate positive affect among communities are another way of building a different understanding of land and social relationships. The meeting, festival, and community party that I described in this chapter worked to knit people together in the face of continued state and corporate attempts to break community solidarity and sow fear and distrust. This emotional work is not something unique to Cambodia; the work of building the collective is a constant effort in all social movements, albeit one that often receives less attention than overt acts of contentious politics (Hennessy 2013). What is notable about the emotional work of rural land activists is that their strategies both generated positive affect among the collective and, in doing so, opened potential for human-nature relations in contrast to the logic of the plantation, and indeed the broader capitalist system.

In making this connection between social mobilization and alternative ontologies, I am aware of a tendency among some nonindigenous scholars to shy away from discussions of indigenous ontologies and ecofeminism because of the risk that these may be perceived as essentializing indigenous or female connections with land (and could be used to make destructive arguments about who counts as truly indigenous or not, as I described in chapter 6. I have those trepidations myself. But as Blaser (2016) argues, this shyness risks reproducing the silencing of these worlds in the academy and thus reifying the human/nature divide and the violence inherent in the understanding of land as a resource to be exploited by humans. In this regard I find Escobar's (2017) discussion of the political work of scholarship on the pluriverse useful. He argues that by making visible multiple ways of being in the world that are always in formation and shot through with power relations, scholars can attend to these worlds not as relativistic spaces but as political challenges to the ontological dualisms in the dominant worldview. There is certainly no essential Khmer connection with land that all rural people share. In both Khmer and indigenous communities, some people brushed aside as backward thinking the practice of propitiating land spirits or agroecological techniques such as using natural fertilizer. Contradictions between people's reluctance to exploit the land and their desire for capitalist development were often visible. But even for those skeptical of the spirit world, the growing prevalence of drought and floods was a reminder that people are not wholly in control: the acts of mobilization described in this chapter were explicitly political in the way they destabilized the privileged position of the state as the supreme arbiter of land (Beban and Work 2014).

Conclusion

As I write this book in the wake of Cambodia's 2018 national elections, I recall the media headlines running up to the election, which revealed widespread concern with Cambodian politics: "Democracy in Cambodia Is Backsliding,"[1] "UNHCR Concerned about Erosion of Democracy in Cambodia,"[2] "Democracy in Cambodia under Threat amid Climate of Fear."[3] Before the 2018 election, the Cambodian People's Party (CPP) ramped up repression of political dissent, imprisoning opposition party members and activists and shutting down independent media outlets and human rights organizations.[4] Well-known political commentator Kem Ley was assassinated, shot twice in broad daylight. As the campaign against civil society and free expression intensified, Cambodia's Supreme Court dissolved the main opposition party, CNRP, and banned 118 senior political party officials from engaging in politics for five years. Alongside this violence, the CPP maintained a politics of gift-giving practices, although these were focused not on farmers but rather on the growing and politically dynamic urban population of garment workers (many of them the sons and daughters of rural farmers), through US$5 handouts for garment workers and raising the minimum wage for factory workers and public servants.[5] But, as in the past, these gifts came with a threat—garment workers were reportedly faced with discipline if they were found not to have voted.[6]

Not surprisingly, the 2018 election was a landslide victory for the CPP. I am deeply concerned about this violence and also about the media's portrayal of Cambodia's political shift as a "backsliding" from some idealized form of a democratic state. It is worth asking: What exactly is this democratic state (from which the country is now backsliding)? My exploration of land and state relations in Cambodia suggests that this idealized democracy has never existed, or rather, that the postconflict Cambodian state has always contained the threat of violent authoritarianism within it. The project of liberal peacebuilding that is focused on instituting capitalist democracy has essentially resulted in economic liberalism without political liberalism—ensuring the freedom of global capital and the state elite while inhibiting the freedom of non-elite Cambodians. The country's economic boom, with massive investment continuing to flow into state coffers from extraction of natural resources including land, sand, and minerals, shows that authoritarian power is quite compatible with extractive resource capitalism. As James Ferguson (2006) notes of contemporary globalized capitalism, it is often not the most stable democracies that attract funding, but precisely those places in which the law can be partially applied, and the state called on to back up global capital in conflicts with local people, that are desirable as sites of investment. This viewpoint recognizes that postconflict is hardly the definitive end of violence; rather, the potential for violence is constitutive of the postconflict state.

The Cambodian government's shift to a more overt authoritarianism is not an isolated case. Throughout the world, governments have come to power with strong nationalist platforms, sweeping away citizen freedoms in pursuit of political objectives (Scoones et al. 2018). Contemporary populist politics shore up exclusionary and even violent political power while offering selective progressive policies—land reform in South Africa, for example, sits alongside deeply conservative practices favoring the elite's claims to land and the threat of state violence (Hall and Kepe 2017). This rise of authoritarianism necessitates the development of innovative strategies by scholars and activists to understand and respond to these shifts. My examination of Hun Sen's politics of fear, violence, and uncertainty suggests that scholars must go beyond analyzing authoritarian leaders as (only) repressive to recognizing the specific ways in which they seek to maintain legitimacy through populist gift giving, discourses of economic development, and production of affects that are violent but may also give rise to moments of political openness.

The dominance of Western discourse and practice is being supplanted by a model that Barma (2016) terms "authoritarian peacebuilding," which focuses on economic growth and infrastructure without pushing for deep reforms (Bliesemann de Guevara and Kostić 2017). This model, according to Barma (2016), defines *peace* as the reassertion of hierarchical state authority over territory, space, and resources and seeks to achieve this outcome not only through military means but also through the control of knowledge production and the channeling of economic resources through patronage networks. Significantly, the discourse of authoritarian peace is not limited to individual states but circulates in sites of international diplomacy in ways that increasingly challenge the global hegemony of the liberal peace. In Cambodia, as in many states in Asia-Pacific that are politically strategic for China, this model is promoted by China as part of bilateral engagement, which has real benefits for people through popular infrastructural projects to increase road and electricity access, but these benefits sit alongside more controversial efforts to improve state surveillance and military capacity and to enable unfettered access to extractivist industries.

China's growing dominance in Cambodia raises the fraught question of what role other donors can and should play in the country. This book shows that democracy does not equate with the object of elections; the installation of elections as the centerpiece of the UN intervention in Cambodia, while ignoring the violent political practices that achieved electoral dominance, has had the perverse effect of reinforcing fear-based governance. My analysis of the donor land-governance program (chapter 1) and NGO efforts to establish communal land title (chapter 6) shows that donors' efforts to bring about change through the establishment of neoliberal rational-legal governance has not worked in Cambodia. The social inequality and ecological harms associated with the imposition of neoliberal economic reforms in Cambodia and elsewhere must shake the faith of even the most ardent believers in neoliberal governance. And even if good governance is perceived as a worthy goal, development efforts in Cambodia place control over the terms of this engagement in the hands of government officials who have an interest in maintaining the status quo. People on the ground are left languishing as their claims are deflected through processes of obfuscation and delay, and this uncertainty tears the social fabric of communities apart and limits imagination for other forms of potential resistance. The international community needs open and deep reflection on what stability at all costs has meant for politics and how this reveals the limits of a liberal democratic agenda.

Throughout the book, I have highlighted the failures of Order 01 to benefit smallholder farmers in ways that economists might expect. But in a narrow sense, the land reform has worked. When I returned to Khang Cheung in February 2019 and once again drove my motorbike along the wide red-dirt road to Tmor Muoy village, I hardly recognized the community. On either side of the road, shrubland has transformed into oceans of mango plantations, high fences, and new structures erected by large agribusiness operations. Many people who were awarded land titles to roadside land told me they sold after land brokers visited their homes and threatened them; many others have since mortgaged their land, fallen into debt, and had their land repossessed. Although land title was not required to access microfinance loans when I conducted fieldwork (see chapter 5), it seems that the possession of a title is now allowing farmers to leverage larger, and multiple, loans. With so many people defaulting on loans, most roadside farmland in the area is now controlled by a few large landowners. Just as neoliberal economics would suggest, those who couldn't compete have exited from agriculture, and larger, presumably more efficient, operators have taken their place. But we really need to question what *efficiency* means here, and the violence that this metric obscures: Is efficiency the large cassava plantation that still lies empty after the Chinese contractor pulled out in 2016? Is efficiency the coercive dealings with land brokers that encouraged people to sell for pitifully low prices, so that families now migrate to urban areas to seek low-paying laboring work or eke out a living on ever-smaller parcels of land? Farmers who received land title during the Order 01 land reform were promised tenure security, wealth, loan access, jobs, and gender empowerment. But this seductive discourse has facilitated the individuation of claims making, the erosion of capacities for social reproduction, and the fracturing of solidarity in rural communities. To quote Puu Tanak: "What do land titles mean when in a few years there will be no land left?" Land reform that is truly intent on achieving socially and ecologically just outcomes must mean a broader restructuring of economic relations so that rural livelihoods are viable.

Beyond Cambodia, this book reframes contemporary debates on property rights. The extension of formal property rights is popularly seen, by both proponents and critics of formalized property relations, to strengthen rural people's relationships with bureaucratic institutions. (For proponents, this relationship with the state increases security and prosperity; for critics, the relationship with the state can be used to extract wealth and controls people.) This discourse assumes that the state is a coherent bureaucracy. But I have shown that in practice social transformation does not occur in the ways the global governing institutions expect. Land titles may strengthen—rather than undermine—the personalized patronage relations with the state elite that Western development agencies hope to subvert, offering the possibility of solving land disputes through individual appeal to the prime minister rather than access to bureaucratic state protection. Technical land titling reform may not guard against land grabs, reduce poverty, or instill bureaucratic market-based rule in postconflict states. On the contrary, land titling may increase social inequalities, facilitate deforestation, and entrench corruption.

Cambodia's project of land reform—and the longer trajectory of donor- and state-supported land management of which it is a part—reproduced gendered, racialized forms of insecurity in rural areas by valuing economic production over ecological and social reproduction, individual over communal relationships with land and state, and patriarchal patronage networks over more horizontal mechanisms of land management. This insight suggests that the World Bank and FAO's focus on creating responsible agricultural investments through tenure formalization is misguided, and it challenges development actors and scholars to dig beneath narratives of "land title as security" and "land title as loss" to show how dynamic constructions of land tenure security differ across gender, age, class, and race and are shaped by collective memory, by the physical landscape, and by relationships with NGOs and state authorities.

This reframing of debates on property rights has implications for literature on property and state formation. The literature on territorialization tends to assume that territorial projects create, or attempt to create, clear rules and boundaries for governing territory and populations. Any deviation from this clarity can thus be deemed a mistake or a lack of capacity. But it is quite possible that there is benefit for the territorializing agent in rules that are half-baked, borders that are undefined, regulations that are overly complex, and policies that are incomplete. The Cambodian state's greatest challenge is that it requires ever-greater resources to satisfy patrons and to maintain the flow of gifts and the promise of development down to local levels, even as this extractive form of development eats away at Cambodian territory and erodes capacities for rural people's social reproduction. The unwritten rules that govern land relations help to provide the state elite with the flexibility to achieve future projects of land control by bringing land back under state control when needed, and at other times parsing land out to capital interests or to rural communities that are politically imperative for the regime's legitimacy. To return to the language of frontier making and territorialization as ongoing cyclical moments, we can understand the production of uncertainty as a form of state-making that creates an ongoing frontier—that is, a space in which rules and established orders are thrown open. The frontier/territorialization movement still occurs, but the throwing open of established rules is not followed with a set of fully realized land relations that stabilize land control; rather, the state's ongoing control over land relies on the flexibility obtained through uncertain, opaque (and thus never quite stabilized) land relations. This terrain of land relations strengthens the position of the politico-business elite, who are seen to have the power to recreate the rules in every encounter.

Recognizing the cyclical process by which the production of uncertainty works to strengthen the elite's control over land, by bringing land under state purview to use (through distribution or capitalization) when politically expedient, shows the contingency of instruments of property law and policy that create seemingly immutable positions of land control. The Order 01 land reform paradoxically worked to regain the state's flexible control over land, even as land was divided into private plots, by claiming the authority to give land away and by reclaiming institutionalized control over large swathes of land that were excised from concessions but not titled out to smallholders. Perhaps the most profound effects of the land reform, as I described in chapters 3–6, were the swathes of former forestland claimed by powerful actors and the land that remained untitled and by implication became legitimately state land—even if it was subject to contestation and customary claims.

Projects of territorialization continue working to regain and retain land under state control. In February 2016, the prime minister announced that after a national review of ELCs (commissioned under Order 01), the government would take back nearly 1 million hectares of public land that had been allocated to concessions. However, there were no maps of that land, nor was there a list of the ELCs being canceled, and official reports from Hun Sen's speeches and ministry and NGO calculations differed sharply over the land size and what it would be used for (Loughlin and Milne 2020). A series of legal reforms in 2016–2017 also brought more land under state control as state public land through the expansion of protected areas and biodiversity conservation corridors (Loughlin and Milne 2020). Protected areas under the Ministry of Environment's control now cover, at least on paper, more than 40 percent of Cambodia's surface area (RGC 2017). The law allows for community development and sustainable-use zones, but it provides limited scope for communities to secure their customary land and resource rights (Loughlin and Milne 2020). Reports from within these protected areas suggest that deforestation continues at a rapid pace.[7] With the CPP, it is difficult to know exactly whose interests are being served, but classically, this extension of state control into protected areas has been used to facilitate highly profitable party-controlled resource extraction from logging and ELC allocation, and there is no reason to expect that this cycle would be any different.

Beyond the substantive focus on land, this book also contributes to feminist scholarship on the emotional dimensions of political rule. Emotions can be used and manipulated for political ends, and a growing literature on the politics of fear post-9/11 shows how nationalist governments stoke fear of the other to provoke racialized appeals to national unity and exceptionalist policies (Pain 2009). There is less attention on how fear shapes social relationships on the ground. But emotions are also a site of struggle that bring people, places, and things together in unpredictable ways. The concept of uncertainty shows the complexity of state-society relations in Cambodia: uncertainty structures not only punishment through the selective application of legal and extralegal means to criminalize people's actions; it also structures reward. People's desire for prosperity and the possibility that the state may be able to provide development encourages people to continue supporting the government. The state's production of fear and uncertainty leads people (including the researcher) to censor themselves, to distrust others, and to view the future with a strange temporality that is at once expectant of possibility and shadowed with foreboding. In the current context of ongoing drought and crop failure in upland Cambodia, this foreboding is also layered with the ontological uncertainty of living with the effects of human-induced climate change, where the possibility of continued existence in a parched landscape is murky (Whitington 2019). I believe that bringing attention to affect as a central component of social and political life within studies of land conflict and state formation enables researchers to center other ways of knowing and to deepen our understandings of state power. This entails working through the complexities of how we know emotions, how we write about them, and how we think through the epistemological and ethical implications of the researchers' own fears and our positions in the production of emotional encounters in the field (Schoenberger and Beban 2018).

Finally, one question haunts scholarship regarding the uncertain potentiality for state-delivered prosperity through gifts of development: How long can the anticipation for development continue to provide some legitimacy to the state? This is particularly acute in the context of rising inequality, where one's disadvantage and others' privilege is so obvious. The difficulty for the Cambodian state is to hold the right amount of tension between potential and repression: Too much feeling of abandonment, and people may resist their subjugation; in this case, the state has to resort to violence through force. Too much gifting, and people may begin to expect the gifts as a regular state provision, a right as citizens that they can hold officials accountable for, which unsettles patrimonial networks. Hun Sen's government is skillful at calibrating violence. The doubling down of fear-based politics since 2017 could be seen as a response to people's growing feeling that the state was not delivering and that the future was increasingly one of foreboding rather than expectation. After the spectacular violence of the opposition party and activists' arrests in 2017, the state's security forces pulled back, and fear was maintained through threats, surveillance, and rumors. Things could change again. When social control depends on maintaining gray areas, there is always potential for these spaces to be filled with different kinds of political projects. However, as Srey Sophorn told me when I visited her recently, "The community network is quiet. Everything is quiet."

But the state does not have absolute power. Governance that relies on fear is always unstable; it requires constant reinforcement of fear and threat, but it can never fully capture affects that are brought forth in encounters. Encounters produce anxiety, fear, and uncertainty, but they can also generate hope and enable new articulations of power (Wilson 2017, 7). The stories in this book show that while encounters with land reform are power laden, the outcomes are never fully predetermined. Some communities used their established relationships with each other and with local authorities to monitor the surveyors (chapter 3); some land claimants were able to negotiate with volunteers by highlighting their poverty (chapter 4). Working in spaces of land violence such as ELCs in rural Cambodia entails the researcher's attention to feelings while participating in and documenting encounters that work to subvert violent affect. This means being attuned to how fear and other affects manifest and how resistance to everyday violence may take forms that are not immediately obvious as resistance.

When I visited Srey Sophorn in 2018, I asked her what she thought about the future. She was silent for a long time. Then she said that she had hope. "The powerful people are scared," she told me. She asked me if I was hopeful. I didn't answer for a moment. "There isn't room for people who have lost hope," she said firmly. And I am hopeful about Cambodia's future. I have met so many inspiring people working for positive change in land-conflict areas across the country and young urbanites forging new political projects that go beyond the models of both patronage relations and Western development. In chapter 7, I analyzed concrete examples of activists' work to subvert fear and generate different affective relations that draw on and construct ontologies of land beyond the primacy of state-capital formations. These stories demonstrate ways of resisting in the midst of fear that the researcher has a responsibility to recognize and take seriously. The stories complicate ideas of human intentionality and move beyond the binaries of human/nature (with its implicit notion of land as a resource for human consumption) and traditional/modern (encrypted with teleological notions of progress) to recognize social reproduction, spirituality, and community as forms of power central to sociopolitical power and possibilities for resistance.

In Cambodia's context of postconflict trauma, these moments that generate positive affect are also sites of reconciliation. Erik Davis (2015) argues that personal reconciliation after the Khmer Rouge occurs explicitly only through the *Pchum Ben* festival of the dead, an annual festival that welcomes back unruly ancestors and brings together families that may normally be separated by rural-urban divides. The ghosts of past trauma and lingering distrust have voice in this space; people talk openly to each other and settle past wrongs. There are other spaces, too, where these ghosts become visible in less explicit ways; Eve Zucker (2013) talks of the role of harvest festivals in recreating forms of community solidarity. I believe that the community network is another space of reconciliation—a space that recreates and develops new traditions for community solidarity. The community network's practices of mobilization articulate a feminist ontology of land that lies in contrast to the logic of the plantation, and indeed the broader capitalist system. This approach seeks to open potential for the collective solidarity and cooperative action that escape structural violence.

Notes

INTRODUCTION

1. Euan Black, "How Cambodia's Record Deforestation Is Driving Crippling Drought," *SEA Globe*, 7 June 2017, 2.
2. Aun Pheap, "Student Volunteers to Be Retired from Gov't Land Title Program," *Cambodia Daily*, 26 December 2014.
3. A commune is a local administrative category in rural Cambodia made up of several villages. Under decentralization policies, commune-level state officials have a significant power over everyday governance (see chapter 3).
4. Multiple terms for *power* exist in the Khmer language. Political power is generally understood through the term *omnaich*, meaning influence over others, while *komlang* signifies more forceful acts of power or energy (Jacobsen and Stuart-Fox 2013).
5. Luke Hunt, "Cambodia's PM Reshuffles Cabinet to Speed Reforms," Voice of America (VOA), 26 March 2016, https://www.voanews.com/east-asia-pacific/cambodias-pm-reshuffles-cabinet-speed-reforms.
6. Bopha Phorn, "Hun Sen Fetes Student Volunteers," *Phnom Penh Post*, 7 January 2013.
7. E. Izadi, "Behold the Ways in Which Male World Leaders Mansplain International Women's Day," *Washington Post*, 8 March 2016. See also Heng Sok Chheng, "Hun Sen Says Change Liberal Women's Law," *Phnom Penh Post*, 5 May 1995, 3.
8. Men make up 80 percent of the national assembly in the most recent election in 2018 (World Bank 2019); 86 percent of district and provincial councilors are men (RGC 2018, 8).

1. DONOR-STATE PARTNERSHIPS IN THE CAMBODIAN LAND SECTOR

1. The World Bank pulled out in 2009 following a land titling scandal at Phnom Penh's Boeung Kak Lake (World Bank 2009), Finland pulled out in 2009 citing concern over the lack of collaboration among donors (Fforde and Seidel 2010), and Canada pulled out in May 2013 citing concern with the slow implementation of communal land titles (Zsombor Peter, "Still No Donor to Take Over Communal Land Titling from Canada," *Cambodia Daily*, 14 March 2013).
2. The law does include a provision for people to gain land title if they can prove they have occupied the land for at least five years prior to the law passing. But, as Springer (2012) argues, in practice this provision excludes many people who cannot prove occupation.
3. See, for example, the 2001 master's thesis of Hun Manet (Hun Sen's eldest son), which discusses the need for use rights and a broader agrarian reform program.
4. For example, Neef, Touch, and Chiengthong (2013) reported that officials promised people SLC land if they vacated their land for ELC development; then the promised SLC never materialized. Essentially, state officials were using the donor SLC program to legitimize land grabbing.
5. Komila Nabiyeva, "In Sweeping Aid Reform, Merged German Agency Becomes Operational," *Devex*, 3 January 2011.
6. BMZ's global food partnership sought food security through public-private partnerships. But the German public, in alliance with peasant movements, decried the partnership, saying that it promoted large agribusiness over small farmers (Dario Sarmadi, "Oxfam:

German Food Project 'Ignores Subsistence Farmers,'" EurActiv.Com, 8 May 2014) and that it paid lip service to ecological concerns (Rokitzki 2016). The program was scaled back in 2015.

7. The BMZ representative's mandate was the much broader "counsellor of the German Embassy," but a GIZ advisor saw the representative's role as "keeping an eye on GIZ."

8. China's aid does require political support at fora such as the Association of Southeast Asian Nations (ASEAN) over the South China Sea issue.

9. Luke Hunt, "A Chinese Takeaway in Cambodia: The Scale of Beijing's Investment Onslaught Is Leaving a Bitter Aftertaste," *Phnom Penh Post*, 31 December 2018.

10. Ben Sokhean, "Government Releases Video Warning against 'Excessive' Rights Use," *Cambodia Daily*, 30 May 2016.

11. Kuch Naren, "Hundreds Order Video of Hun Sen's Land Speech," *Cambodia Daily*, 19 June 2012.

12. Kuch Naren, "Hundreds Order Video."

13. Bopha Phorn, "Hun Sen Fetes Student Volunteers," *Phnom Penh Post*, 7 January 2013.

14. Zsombor Peter, "In Frustration, Germany Ends Land Rights Work," *Cambodia Daily*, 4 February 2016.

15. Zsombor Peter, "In Frustration, Germany Ends Land Rights Work," 3.

16. Tim Vutha, "Germany and Cambodia: 21 Years of Warm Ties," *Business Insights: Essentials*, 31 January 2014.

2. ENCOUNTERING THE LEOPARD SKIN LAND REFORM

1. These settlements formed in the mid-2000s as people in search of agricultural land cleared forest and established new settlements. This is a common process in Cambodia's forest frontier regions, and informal settlements often develop village-like administrative structures under control of military personnel or other local power holders before becoming recognized formally as a village.

2. I could not verify this number with plantation management, but this is approximated from GIS maps of the area and discussions with the Daom Chuur network activists.

3. Tim Johnston, "China and Cambodia: Cassava Diplomacy," *Financial Times*, 14 December 2010.

4. Emily Wight, "Droughts, Flooding, Disease: The Reality of a Cambodia That Has Been Hit by Climate Change," *Phnom Penh Post*, 11 April 2014.

5. Twenty-five percent of survey respondents were married, 7 percent were single, and 18 percent were separated/divorced or widowed. The proportion of women widows was much higher than men (15 percent to 5 percent), which mirrors national statistics.

6. I use Khmer honorifics throughout the text. *Puu* is "Uncle"/familiar older man; *Ming* is "Auntie"/familiar older woman; *Srey* is an honorific for women; *Lok* is an honorific for men.

7. The main indigenous groups in Khang Leit are Jarai, Tampouan, Brou Kreung-Brou, Kavet, and Lum.

8. Rotational cropping systems consisted primarily of food crops (upland rice and mixed vegetables produced in the same field) with a long fallow period (ten to fifteen years) after two to five years' use of the same plot (Gironde and Peeters 2015).

9. Baird (2013a) documents a remarkable 145 different varieties of non-rice crops and 36 varieties of rice growing in the swidden fields of two villages (one Kavet and one Kreung).

3. RECONFIGURING LOCAL AUTHORITY THROUGH LAND REFORM

1. Aun Pheap and George Wright, "South Korean Embassy Defends Rubber Firm, But Villagers Want Its Help," *Cambodia Daily*, 9 July 2014.

4. YOUTH TO THE FRONTIER

1. No official figures are available, and estimates vary widely; this estimate is from a senior Land Ministry official.
2. The UN declares that the "single most important issue facing youth in Cambodia today is employment" (United Nations 2009, 1), with an estimated 300,000 young people entering a tight labor market each year (2).
3. Kevin Ponniah, "Political Eyes on Youth Vote," *Phnom Penh Post*, 9 July 2013, 3.
4. Kuch Naren and Simon Lewis, "Subedi Protest Linked to CPP-Aligned Youth Group," *Cambodia Daily*, 23 May 2013, 2.
5. Zsombor Peter and Kuch Naren, "Hun Sen's Land Titles Receive Rare Praise from Germany," *Cambodia Daily*, 4 April 2013, 3.
6. In a 2013 speech, Hun Sen thanked students from seven student associations that are known to be from pro-CPP networks (Focus on the Global South 2013).
7. Vong Sokheng, "PM Claims Land Scheme Win," *Phnom Penh Post*, 29 January 2013, 2.
8. K. Phearon, "Volunteer Student Sweet Love with Woman in Countryside," 2012.
9. Aun Pheap and Zsombor Peter, "Minorities Decry Loss of Land Under National Titling Scheme," *Cambodia Daily*, 25 April 2013.
10. Aun Pheap and Zsombor Peter, "Minorities Decry Loss of Land," 3.

7. AN ONTOLOGY OF LAND BEYOND STATE-CAPITAL FORMATIONS

1. Kuch Naren and Ben Woods, "Hun Sen Says Land Program Proving a Success," *Cambodian Daily*, 9 August 2012.
2. The human rights group LICADHO says complaints made to its thirteen field offices involved 10,625 families in 2014, compared to 3,475 in 2013 and 5,672 in 2012.
3. Aun Pheap and George Wright, "South Korean Embassy Defends Rubber Firm, But Villagers Want Its Help," *Cambodia Daily*, 9 July 2014.
4. Vong Sokheng and Kevin Ponniah, "The Buck Stops Elsewhere," *Phnom Penh Post*, 14 August 2014.
5. Aun Pheap and Hul Reaksmey, "Officials Trade Blame Over Kratie Land Dispute," *Cambodia Daily*, 14 August 2014.
6. Aun Pheap and Hul Reaksmey, "Officials Trade Blame."
7. I can only gesture toward these ideas within the space of this chapter; see my work with Laura Schoenberger for further treatment.

CONCLUSION

1. Olivia Enos, *Holding the Cambodian Government Accountable to Democracy*, The Heritage Foundation Asia Report, 16 June 2016.
2. Peter Kenny, UNHCR Concerned about Erosion of Democracy in Cambodia, Vatican Radio, 31 October 2015.
3. Sereyvuth Oung and Maly Leng, "Democracy in Cambodia under Threat amid 'Climate of Fear,'" *Radio Free Asia*, 20 March 2017.
4. Oung and Leng, "Democracy in Cambodia under Threat," *Radio Free Asia*.
5. Ben Sokhean and Zsombor Peter, "In Charm Offensive, Hun Sen Promises Workers Raises, Pension," *Cambodia Daily*, 21 August 2017.
6. Tom Allard and Prak Chan Thul, "Crackdown and Cash: Hun Sen's Recipe for Victory in Cambodian Poll," *Reuters World News*, 25 June 2018.
7. Matt Blomberg, "Conservation Group in Cambodia Says Logging in Protected Area Has Increased Amid COVID-19 Pandemic," *Global Citizen*, 4 May 2020.

References

Abrams, Philip. 1988. "Notes on the Difficulty of Studying the State (1977)." *Journal of Historical Sociology* 1(1):58–72.
Abu-Lughod, Lila. 1991. "Writing Against Culture." In *Recapturing Anthropology: Working in the Present*, edited by Richard Fox, 137–162. Santa Fe, NM: School of American Research Press.
ADHOC. 2014. *Report: Land Situation in Cambodia in 2013*. Phnom Penh: ADHOC.
ADI/LIC. 2007. *Land Titling and Poverty Reduction: A Study of Two Sangkat in Prey Nup District, Sihanoukville Municipality*. Phnom Penh: Analyzing Development Issues Project/Land Information Centre.
Agarwal, Bina. 1994. *A Field of One's Own: Gender and Land Rights in South Asia*. Cambridge: Cambridge University Press.
Agarwal, Bina. 2003. "Gender and Land Rights Revisited: Exploring New Prospects via the State, Family and Market." *Journal of Agrarian Change* 3(1–2):184–199.
Agarwal, Bina, and Pradeep Panda. 2007. "Toward Freedom from Domestic Violence: The Neglected Obvious." *Journal of Human Development* 8(3):359–388.
Akram-Lodhi, A. Haroon, Saturnino M. Borras, and Cristóbal Kay. 2007. *Land, Poverty and Livelihoods in an Era of Globalization*. London: Routledge.
Akram-Lodhi, A. Haroon, and Cristóbal Kay. 2009. *Peasants and Globalization: Political Economy, Rural Transformation and the Agrarian Question*. London: Routledge.
Allen, Barbara. 2014. "The Social Construction of Non-Knowledge." *Perspectives: Journal Réseau français des Instituts d'études avancées* 12(9):12–32.
Ansoms, An, and Giuseppe D. Cioffo. 2016. "The Exemplary Citizen on the Exemplary Hill: The Production of Political Subjects in Contemporary Rural Rwanda." *Development and Change* 47(6):1247–1268.
Ashcroft, B., G. Griffiths, and H. Tiffin. 1998. *Key Concepts in Post-Colonial Studies*. London: Routledge.
Baaz, Mikael, and Mona Lilja. 2014. "Understanding Hybrid Democracy in Cambodia: The Nexus Between Liberal Democracy, the State, Civil Society, and a Politics of Presence." *Asian Politics & Policy* 6(1):5–24.
Baird, Ian G. 2013a. "The Ethnoecology of the Kavet Peoples in Northeast Cambodia." In *Cambodia's Contested Forest Domain: The Role of Community Forestry in the New Millennium*, edited by M. Poffenberger, 155–186. Manila: Ateneo de Manila University Press.
———. 2013b. "'Indigenous Peoples and Land': Comparing Communal Land Titling and Its Implications in Cambodia and Laos." *Asia Pacific Viewpoint* 54(3):269–281.
———. 2014. "The Global Land Grab Meta-Narrative, Asian Money Laundering and Elite Capture: Reconsidering the Cambodian Context." *Geopolitics* 19(2):431–453.
Ballard, Brett, and Sovannarith So. 2004. *Cambodia Land Titling Program Baseline Survey Project*. Phnom Penh: LMAP.
Banks, Nicola, David Hulme, and Michael Edwards. 2015. "NGOs, States, and Donors Revisited: Still Too Close for Comfort?" *World Development* 66:707–718.
Banmer, Gabriele, and Michael Smithson. 2008. *Uncertainty and Risk: Multiple Perspectives*. London: Earthscan.

Barker, C. 2001. "Fear, Laughter, and Collective Power: The Making of Solidarity at the Lenin Shipyard in Gdnask, Poland, August 1980." In *Passionate Politics: Emotions and Social Movements*, edited by J. Goodwin, J. Jasper, and F. Pollettta, 51–75. Chicago: University of Chicago Press.

Barma, Naazneen H. 2016. *The Peacebuilding Puzzle*. Cambridge: Cambridge University Press.

Barney, K. 2005. *Customs, Concessionaires, and Conflict: China and Forest Trade in the Asia Pacific Region*. Phnom Penh: DFID.

Beban, Alice, and C. Work. 2014. "The Spirits Are Crying: Dispossessing Land and Possessing Bodies in Rural Cambodia." *Antipode* 46(3):593–615.

Beban, Alice, and Laura Schoenberger. 2019. "Fieldwork Undone: Knowing Cambodia's Land Grab through Affective Encounters." *Acme* 18(1):77–103.

Beban, Alice, Sokbunthoeun So, and Kheang Un. 2017. "From Force to Legitimation: Rethinking Land Grabs in Cambodia." *Development and Change* 48(3):590–612.

Biddulph, Robin. 2010. "Geographies of Evasion." PhD diss., University of Gothenburg, Sweden.

———. 2011. "Tenure Security Interventions in Cambodia: Testing Bebbington's Approach to Development Geography." *Geografiska Annaler: Series B, Human Geography* 93(3):223–236.

———. 2014. "Cambodia's Land Management and Administration Project." UNU-WIDER Working Paper Series 086. Tokyo: United Nations University.

Biddulph, Robin, and Shaun Williams. 2016. "From Chicken Wing Receipts to Students in Military Uniforms: Land Titling and Property in Post-Conflict Cambodia." In *The Handbook of Contemporary Cambodia*, edited by K. Brickell and S. Springer, 169–178. London: Routledge.

Blaser, Mario. 2016. "Is Another Cosmopolitics Possible?" *Cultural Anthropology* 31(4):545–570.

Bliesemann de Guevara, Berit, and Roland Kostić. 2017. "Knowledge Production in/about Conflict and Intervention: Finding 'Facts', Telling 'Truth.'" *Journal of Intervention and Statebuilding* 11(1):1–20.

BMZ. 2012. "Investments in Land and the Phenomenon of Land Grabbing Challenges for Development Policy." *BMZ Strategy Paper 2*. Berlin: BMZ.

Boelens, Rutgerd. 2009. "The Politics of Disciplining Water Rights." *Development and Change* 40:307–331.

Boone, C. 2007. "Property and Constitutional Order: Land Tenure Reform and the Future of the African State." *African Affairs* 106(425):557–586.

Borras, S., C. Kay, and E. Lahiff. 2008. *Market-Led Agrarian Reform: Critical Perspectives on Neoliberal Land Policies and the Rural Poor*. London: Routledge.

Borras, J., and J. Franco. 2011. *Political Dynamics of Land Grabbing in Southeast Asia*. Amsterdam: Transnational Institute.

Bourdier, Frederic. 2018. "Political Livelihoods in the Northeast Borderlands of Cambodia: Legacy of the Past, Territorial Incorporation, and Confrontation." In *Routledge Handbook of Asian Borderlands*, edited by Alexander Horstmann, Martin Saxer, and Allesandro Ripper, 97–108. Oxon, UK: Routledge.

———. 2019. "From Confrontation to Mediation: Cambodian Farmers Expelled by a Vietnamese Company." *Journal of Current Southeast Asian Affairs* 38(1):55–76.

Brickell, Katherine. 2011. "'We Don't Forget the Old Rice Pot When We Get the New One': Discourses on Ideals and Practices of Women in Contemporary Cambodia." *Signs* 36(2):437–452.

Brickell, Katherine, and Simon Springer. 2016. *The Handbook of Contemporary Cambodia*. London: Routledge.

Brigstocke, Julian. 2016. "Exhausted Futures." *GeoHumanities* 2(1):92–101.
Broegaard, Rikke J. 2005. "Land Tenure Insecurity and Inequality in Nicaragua." *Development and Change* 36(5):845–864.
Brown, Wendy. 1992. "Finding the Man in the State." *Feminist Studies* 18(1):7–34.
———. 1995. *States of Injury: Power and Freedom in Late Modernity*. Princeton, NJ: Princeton University Press.
———. 2000. "Suffering Rights as Paradoxes." *Constellations* 7(2):230–241.
Burow, P., S. Brock, and M. Dove. 2018. "Unsettling the Land: Indigeneity, Ontology, and Hybridity in Settler Colonialism." *Environment and Society* 9(1):58–73.
Byrne, Sarah, Andrea J. Nightingale, and Benedikt Korf. 2016. "Making Territory: War, Post-War and the Entangled Scales of Contested Forest Governance in Mid-Western Nepal." *Development and Change* 47(6):1269–1293.
Calderwood, K. 2016. "Why New Zealand is Granting a River the Same Rights as a Citizen." *ABC Radio National*, 9 June.
Carrier, James. 1991. "Gifts, Commodities, and Social Relations: A Maussian View of Exchange." *Sociological Forum* (6):1–22.
CCHR. 2016. *Access to Collective Land Titles for Indigenous Communities in Cambodia*. Phnom Penh: Cambodian Centre for Human Rights.
Chandler, David. 2008. *A History of Cambodia*. Boulder, CO: Westview Press.
Chua, L. 2012. "Pragmatic Resistance, Law, and Social Movements in Authoritarian States: The Case of Gay Collective Action in Singapore." *Law and Society Review* 46(4):713–748.
Chung, Youjin. 2017. "Engendering the New Enclosures: Development, Involuntary Resettlement and the Struggles for Social Reproduction in Coastal Tanzania." *Development and Change* 48(1):98–120.
Cleary, Mark, and Peter Eaton. 1996. *Tradition and Reform: Land Tenure and Rural Development in South-East Asia*. Kuala Lumpur, Malaysia: Oxford University Press.
Cock, Andrew. 2010. "External Actors and the Relative Autonomy of the Ruling Elite in Post-UNTAC Cambodia." *Journal of Southeast Asian Studies* 41(2):241–265.
———. 2016. *Governing Cambodia's Forests: The International Politics of Policy Reform*. Singapore: NIAS Press.
Collins, Erin. 2016. "Repatriation, Refoulement, Repair." *Development and Change* 47(6):1229–1246.
Comaroff, J., and J. Comaroff. 2005. "Reflections on Youth: From the Past to the Post Colony." In *Makers and Breakers: Children and Youth in Postcolonial Africa*, edited by A. Honwana and F. Boeck, 19–30. Oxford: Currey.
Coulthard, G. 2013. "Indigenous Peoples and the 'Politics of Recognition.'" New Socialist, 23 March. https://newsocialist.org/indigenous-peoples-and-the-politics-of-recognition/.
Craig, David, and Pak Kimchoeun. 2011. "Party Financing of Local Investment Projects: Elite and Mass Patronage." In *Cambodia's Economic Transformation*, edited by C. Hughes and K. Un, 219–244. Copenhagen: NIAS Press.
Creak, Simon, and Keith Barney. 2018. "Conceptualising Party-State Governance and Rule in Laos." *Journal of Contemporary Asia* 48(5):693–716.
Das, Veena. 2004. *Anthropology in the Margins of the State*. Oxford: Currey.
Davis, Erik. 2015. *Deathpower: Buddhism's Ritual Imagination in Cambodia*. New York: Colombia University Press.
Davis, K. F., K. Yu, and M. C. Rulli. 2015. "Accelerated Deforestation Driven by Large-Scale Land Acquisitions in Cambodia." *Nature Geoscience* 8(10):1–5.
de Janvry, A. 1981. *The Agrarian Question and Reformism in Latin America*. Baltimore: Johns Hopkins University Press.

REFERENCES

de Janvry, A., and C. Deere. 1979. "A Conceptual Framework for the Analysis of the Peasantry." *American Journal of Agricultural Economics* 61(4):601–611.

de la Cadena, M. 2010. "Indigenous Cosmopolitics in the Andes: Conceptual Reflections Beyond 'Politics.'" *Cultural Anthropology* 25(2):334–370.

de Soto, Hernando. 2000. *The Mystery of Capital: Why Capitalism Triumphs in the West and Fails Everywhere Else*. New York: Basic Books.

Deininger, K., D. Ali, and T. Alemu. 2009. "Impact of Land Certification on Tenure Security, Investment, and Land Markets." Environment for Development Discussion Paper Series, University of Gothenburg, April.

Deininger, K., and G. Feder. 1998. *Land Institutions and Land Markets*. Washington, DC: World Bank.

Deininger, Klaus. 2003. *Land Policies for Growth and Poverty Reduction*. Oxford: Oxford University Press/World Bank.

Derks, Annuska. 2008. *Khmer Women on the Move: Exploring Work and Life in Urban Cambodia*. Honolulu: University of Hawai'i Press.

Deutsch, Robert. 2006. *Beneficiary Assessment of Land Title Recipients under the Land Management and Administration Project*. Phnom Penh: LMAP.

———. 2014. *Survey of Food Security and Land Conflicts in LASSP Areas*. Phnom Penh: LMAP.

Deutsch, Robert, and T. Makady. 2009. *Beneficiary Assessment (BA-II) for the Land Administration Sub-Sector Program (LA-SSP)*. Phnom Penh: LMAP.

DeWalt, Kathleen Musante, and Billie R. DeWalt. 2011. *Participant Observation: A Guide for Fieldworkers*. New York: Rowman & Littlefield.

Diepart, Jean-Christophe, and David Dupuis. 2014. "The Peasants in Turmoil: Khmer Rouge, State Formation and the Control of Land in Northwest Cambodia." *Journal of Peasant Studies* 41(4):445–468.

Drozdzewski, Danielle, and Daniel F. Robinson. 2015. "Care-Work on Fieldwork: Taking Your Own Children into the Field." *Children's Geographies* 13(3):372–378.

Dwyer, Michael B. 2015. "The Formalization Fix? Land Titling, Land Concessions and the Politics of Spatial Transparency in Cambodia." *Journal of Peasant Studies* 42(5):903–928.

Ear, Sophal. 2007. "The Political Economy of Aid, Governance, and Policy-Making: Cambodia in Global, National, and Sectoral Perspectives." PhD diss., University of California, Berkeley.

Edwards, Michael, and David Hulme. 1996. "Too Close for Comfort? The Impact of Official Aid on Nongovernmental Organizations." *World Development* 24(6):961–973.

Edwards, P. 2006. "The Tyranny of Proximity: Power and Mobility in Colonial Cambodia, 1863–1954." *Journal of Southeast Asian Studies* 37(3):421–443.

Eng, Netra. 2013. "The Politics of Decentralization in Cambodia: The District Level." PhD diss., Monash University.

Errington, Shelly. 1990. *Power and Difference: Gender in Island Southeast Asia*. Palo Alto, CA: Stanford University Press.

Escobar, Arturo. 1995. *Encountering Development: The Making and Unmaking of the Third World*. Princeton, NJ: Princeton University Press.

———. 2017. "Sustaining the Pluriverse: The Political Ontology of Territorial Struggles in Latin America." In *The Anthropology of Sustainability*, edited by M. Brightman and J. Lewis, 237–256. New York: Palgrave MacMillan.

Esteves, Ana, Sara Motta, and Laurence Cox. 2009. "Issue Two Editorial: 'Civil Society' versus Social Movements." *Interface* 1(2):1–21.

Evans, P. 1995. *Embedded Autonomy: States and Industrial Transformation*. Princeton, NJ: Princeton University Press.

REFERENCES

FAO. 2019. *Preparing and Accessing Decent Work amongst Rural Youth in Cambodia*. Rome: Food and Agriculture Organization of the United Nations and Humboldt University of Berlin.
Feder, G., and D. Feeny. 1991. "Land Tenure and Property Rights: Theory and Implications for Development Policy." *World Bank Economic Review* 5(1):135–153.
Federici, Silvia. 2004. "Women, Land-Struggles and Globalization: An International Perspective." *Journal of Asian and African Studies* 39:47–64.
Feldman, S., and C. Geisler. 2012. "Land Expropriation and Displacement in Bangladesh." *Journal of Peasant Studies* 39(3–4):971–1013.
Ferguson, James. 1994. *The Anti-Politics Machine: 'Development,' Depolitization, and Bureaucratic Power in Lesotho*. Cambridge: Cambridge University Press.
———. 2006. *Africa in the Neoliberal World Order*. Durham, NC: Duke University Press.
Fforde, A., and K. Seidel. 2010. *Donor Playground Cambodia*. Berlin: Heinrich-Böll-Stiftung.
Focus on the Global South. 2013. *Moving Forward: Study on the Impacts of the Implementation of Order 01BB in Selected Communities in Rural Cambodia*. Phnom Penh: Focus on the Global South.
Foucault, Michel. 2004. *Security, Territory, Population: Lectures at the Collège de France, 1977–78*. London: Macmillan.
Fox, Jefferson, Dennis McMahon, Mark Poffenberger, and John Vogler. 2008. *Land for My Grandchildren: Land Use and Tenure Change in Ratanakiri: 1989–2007*. Phnom Penh: Community Forestry International/East West Center.
Franco, J., J. Borras, A. Alonso-Fradejas, and N. Buxton. 2013. *The Global Land Grab: A Primer*. The Hague: Transnational Institute.
Frewer, Tim. 2017. "The Gender Agenda: NGOs and Capitalist Relations in Highland Cambodia." *Critical Asian Studies* 49(2):163–186.
Frieson, Kate. 2001. *In the Shadows: Women, Power and Politics in Cambodia*. Victoria, BC: Centre for Asia-Pacific Initiatives, University of Victoria.
Frings, V. 1994. "Cambodia after Decollectivization (1989–1992)." *Journal of Contemporary Asia* 24(1):49–65.
Fukuyama, Francis. 2004. *State-Building: Governance and World Order in the 21st Century*. Ithaca, NY: Cornell University Press.
Geisler, C., and F. Makki. 2014. "People, Power, and Land: New Enclosures on a Global Scale." *Rural Sociology* 79(1):28–33.
Gibson-Graham, J. K. 2006. *A Postcapitalist Politics*. Minneapolis: University of Minnesota Press.
Gironde, Christophe, and Amaury Peeters. 2015. "Land Acquisitions in Northeastern Cambodia: Space and Time Matters." Presented at the International Conference on Land Grabbing, Conflict and Agrarian-Environmental Transformations, Chiang Mai University, 5–6 June.
Gironde, Christophe, and Gilda Senties Portilla. 2015. "From Lagging Behind to Losing Ground: Cambodian and Laotian Household Economy and Large-Scale Land Acquisitions." *Revue Internationale de Politique de Développement* 6(1):172–204.
Global Witness. 2013. *Rubber Barons: How Vietnamese Companies and International Financiers Are Driving a Land Grabbing Crisis in Cambodia and Laos*. Phnom Penh: Global Witness.
Gould, Deborah. 2009. *Emotion and ACT UP's Fight against AIDS*. Chicago: University of Chicago Press.
Goshal, B., K. Ku, and D. Hawk. 1995. *Minorities in Cambodia*. London: Minority Rights Group.

REFERENCES

Gottesman, E. 2003. *Cambodia after the Khmer Rouge: Inside the Politics of Nation Building*. New Haven, CT: Yale University Press.

Grimsditch, Mark. 2013. *Women's Tenure Security in Cambodia: An Overview of Key Issues*. Phnom Penh: The NGO Forum on Cambodia.

Grimsditch, M., and N. Henderson. 2009. *Untitled: Tenure Insecurity and Inequality in the Cambodian Land Sector*. Phnom Penh: Bridges Across Borders Southeast Asia.

Grimsditch, Mark, and Laura Schoenberger. 2015. *New Actions and Existing Policies: The Implementation and Impacts of Order 01*. Phnom Penh: The NGO Forum on Cambodia.

Guillou, A. 2006. "The Question of Land in Cambodia: Perceptions, Access and Use Since De-Collectivization." *Moussons* 9–10:299–323.

Gupta, Akhil. 1995. "Blurred Boundaries: The Discourse of Corruption, the Culture of Politics and the Imagined State." *American Ethnologist* 22(2):375–402.

Gyallay-Pap, Peter. 2007. "Reconstructing the Cambodian Polity: Buddhism, Kingship and the Quest for Legitimacy." In *Buddhism, Power and Political Order*, edited by I. Harris, 71–103. London: Routledge.

Hale, Charles. 2002. "Does Multiculturalism Menace? Governance, Cultural Rights and the Politics of Identity in Guatemala." *Journal of Latin American Studies* 34(3):485–524.

Hall, Derek. 2013. *Land*. Cambridge: Polity.

Hall, Derek, Philip Hirsch, and Tania Li. 2011. *Powers of Exclusion: Land Dilemmas in Southeast Asia*. Honolulu: University of Hawai'i Press.

Hall, Ruth, and Thembela Kepe. 2017. "Elite Capture and State Neglect: New Evidence on South Africa's Land Reform." *Review of African Political Economy* 44(151):122–130.

Hamilton, Sarah. 2002. "Neoliberalism, Gender, and Property Rights in Rural Mexico." *Latin American Research Review* 37:119–143.

Haraway, D. 2008. *When Species Meet*. Minneapolis: University of Minnesota Press.

Harris, Ian. 2005. *Cambodian Buddhism: History and Practice*. Honolulu: University of Hawai'i Press.

———. 2007. *Buddhism, Power and Political Order*. London: Routledge.

Harvey, David. 2005. *A Brief History of Neoliberalism*. Oxford: Oxford University Press.

Heder, S. 2011. "Cambodia in 2010: Hun Sen's Further Consolidation." *Asian Survey* 51(1):208–219.

Hennessy, Rosemary. 2013. *Fires on the Border*. Minneapolis: University of Minnesota Press.

High, Holly. 2014. *Fields of Desire*. Singapore: NUS Press.

Hirsch, Phillip. 2011. "Titling against Grabbing? Critiques and Conundrums around Land Formalisation in Southeast Asia." Presented at the International Conference on Global Land Grabbing, Sussex, UK, 6–8 April.

———. 2012. "Reviving Agrarian Studies in South-East Asia: Geography on the Ascendancy." *Geographical Research* 4(50):393–403.

Hoffman, Elizabeth. 2000. *All You Need Is Love: The Peace Corps and the Spirit of the 1960s*. Cambridge, MA: Harvard University Press.

Holston, James. 1991. "The Misrule of Law: Land and Usurpation in Brazil." *Comparative Studies in Society and History* 33(4):695–725.

HRW. 2017. *World Report 2017*. New York: Human Rights Watch.

Hughes, Caroline. 2003. *The Political Economy of Cambodia's Transition, 1991–2001*. London: RoutledgeCurzon.

———. 2006. "The Politics of Gifts: Tradition and Regimentation in Contemporary Cambodia." *Journal of Southeast Asian Studies* 37(373):469–489.

———. 2013. "Friction, Good Governance and the Poor: Cases from Cambodia." *International Peacekeeping* 20(2):144–158.

Hughes, Caroline, and Kheang Un. 2011. *Cambodia's Economic Transformation*. Copenhagen: NIAS Press.

Hun Manet. 2001. *Is Market-Assisted Land Reform an Appropriate Choice for Cambodia at the Present Time?*, MA thesis, New York University.

Hun Sen. 2010. "Address at the 2010 AsiaLink Conversations." Phnom Penh, 3–5 September.

———. 2012a. *Hun Sen Speech to Volunteers at Koh Pich, 19 May*. Accessed 22 January 2016. https://www.youtube.com/watch?v=6SQ_wSljrrs.

———. 2012b. "Presenting Land Titles in P. Sihanouk Pro." *Cambodia New Vision*, 2 December. https://www.cnv.org.kh/wp-content/uploads/2013/02/cnv_178_nov_12.pdf.

———. 2012c. "Presenting Land Titles in Takeo Pro. 30 December 2012." Accessed January 7 2015. https://www.cnv.org.kh/handing-out-of-land-titles-tram-kak-takeo-province.

———. 2012d. "Selected Remarks Made during Speech to Hand Out Land Titles in Andong Meas, Rattanakiri Province, 24 November 2012." Accessed 7 January 2015. https://www.cnv.org.kh/handing-out-of-land-titles-andong-meas-ratanakiri.

Ince, Onur. 2014. "Primitive Accumulation, New Enclosures, and Global Land Grabs: A Theoretical Intervention." *Rural Sociology* 79(1):104–131.

Ironside, Jeremy, Gordon Patterson, and Anne Thomas. 2017. "Swidden Agriculture under Threat: The Case of Ratanakiri Northeast Cambodia." In *Shifting Cultivation Practices Balancing Environmental and Social Sustainability*, edited by M. Cairns, 242–269. Oxfordshire, UK: CABI Publishing.

Jacobs, Susie. 2009a. *Gender and Agrarian Reform*. London: Routledge.

———. 2009b. "Gender and Land Reforms: Comparative Perspectives." *Geography Compass* 3(5):1675–1692.

Jacobsen, Trude. 2012. "Being Broh: The Good, the Bad, and the Successful Man in Cambodia." In *Men and Masculinities in Southeast Asia*, edited by M. Ford and L. Lyons, 86–103. London: Routledge.

Jacobsen, Trude, and Martin Stuart-Fox. 2013. "Power and Political Culture in Cambodia." Asia Research Institute Working Paper Series 200, National University of Singapore.

Jasper, James. 2011. "Emotions and Social Movements: Twenty Years of Theory and Research." *Annual Review of Sociology* 37(1):285–303.

Joseph, Gilbert, and Daniel Nugent. 1994. *Everyday Forms of State Formation*. Durham, NC: Duke University Press.

Karbaum, Markus. 2012. "Cambodia's Façade Democracy and European Assistance." *Journal of Current Southeast Asian Affairs* 30(4):111–143.

Kelly, A., and N. Peluso. 2015. "Frontiers of Commodification: State Lands and Their Formalization." *Society and Natural Resources* 28(5):473–495.

Kelly, Philip F. 2011. "Migration, Agrarian Transition and Rural Change in Southeast Asia." *Critical Asian Studies* 43(4):479–506.

Kelsall, Tim, and Pak Kimchoeun. 2014. *The Political Settlement and the Land Sector in Cambodia*. Phnom Penh: GIZ.

Kenny, Peter. 2015. *UNHCR Concerned about Erosion of Democracy in Cambodia*. Vatican Radio. 31 October.

Kent, Alexandra. 2014. "Conflict Continues: Transitioning into a Battle for Property in Cambodia Today." *Journal of Southeast Asian Studies* 47(1):3–27.

Kiernan, Ben. 2008. *Genocide and Resistance in Southeast Asia: Documentation, Denial & Justice in Cambodia & East Timor*. New Brunswick: Transaction Publishers.

Kosal, Path, and Angeliki Kanavou. 2015. "Converts, not Ideologues? The Khmer Rouge Practice of Thought Reform in Cambodia, 1975–1978." *Journal of Political Ideologies* 20(3):304–332.

Krujit, Dirk, and Kees Konings. 1999. *Societies in Fear: The Legacy of Civil War, Violence and Terror in Latin America*. London: Zed Books.

Larsson, Tomas. 2012. *Land and Loyalty: Security and the Development of Property Rights in Thailand*. Ithaca, NY: Cornell University Press.

Latorre, Sergio. 2015. "The Making of Land Ownership: Land Titling in Rural Colombia—A Reply to Hernando de Soto." *Third World Quarterly* 36(8):1546–1569.

Latour, B. 2013. *An Inquiry into Modes of Existence: An Anthropology of the Moderns*. Cambridge, MA: Harvard University Press.

Le Billon, P. 2002. "Logging in Muddy Waters: The Politics of Forest Exploitation in Cambodia." *Critical Asian Studies* 34(4):563–586.

Ledgerwood, J. 1996. "Politics and Gender: Negotiating Conceptions of the Ideal Woman in Present Day Cambodia." *Asia Pacific Viewpoint* 37(2):139–152.

Ledgerwood, Judy, and John Vijghen. 2002. "Decision Making in Rural Khmer Villages." In *Cambodia Emerges from the Past: Eight Essays*, edited by J. Ledgerwood, 108–126. De Kalb, IL: Northern Illinois University.

Lee, Susan Hagood. 2006. *"Rice plus": Widows and Economic Survival in Rural Cambodia*. New York: Routledge.

Li, Tania. 2000. "Articulating Indigenous Identity in Indonesia: Resource Politics and the Tribal Slot." *Comparative Studies in Society and History* 42(1):149–179.

———. 2007. *The Will to Improve: Governmentality, Development, and the Practice of Politics*. Durham, NC: Duke University Press.

———. 2009. "Exit from Agriculture: A Step Forward or a Step Backward for the Rural Poor?" *Journal of Peasant Studies* 36(3):629–646.

———. 2011. "Centering Labor in the Land Grab Debate." *Journal of Peasant Studies* 38(2):281–305.

———. 2014. *Land's End*. Durham, NC: Duke University Press.

LMAP. 2002. *Project Appraisal Document (January)*. Phnom Penh: World Bank.

Lohr, D. 2011. "The Cambodian Land Market: Development, Aberrations, and Perspectives." *Asien* 120:28–47.

Loughlin, N., and S. Milne. 2020. "After the Grab? Land Control and Regime Survival in Cambodia since 2012." *Journal of Contemporary Asia*. DOI: 10.1080/00472336.2020.1740295.

Lucas, A., and C. Warren. 2013. *Land for the People: The State and Agrarian Conflict in Indonesia*. Athens, OH: Ohio University Press.

Lüke, Monica. 2013. *Human Rights Assessment of the German-Cambodian Land Rights Program (LRP)*. Berlin: German Institute for Human Rights.

Lund, Christian. 2016. "Rule and Rupture: State Formation through the Production of Property and Citizenship." *Development and Change* 47(6):1199–1228.

Macek, Ivana. 2014. *Engaging Violence: Trauma, Memory and Representation*. New York: Routledge.

Maclean, Ken. 2013. *The Government of Mistrust*. Madison: University of Wisconsin Press.

Maffi, M. 2009. "Changes in Gender Roles and Women's Status amongst Indigenous Communities in Cambodia's Northeast." In *Living on the Margins: Minorities and Borderlines in Cambodia and Southeast Asia*, 129–147. Sieam Reap, Cambodia: Center for Khmer Studies.

Mathews, Andrew. 2011. *Instituting Nature: Authority, Expertise, and Power in Mexican Forests*. Cambridge, MA: MIT Press.

Mauss, Marcel. 1954. *The Gift: Forms and Functions of Exchange in Archaic Societies*. London: Cohen and West.

McCreary, T., and R. Milligan. 2014. "Pipelines, Permits, and Protests: Carrier Sekani Encounters with the Enbridge Northern Gateway Project." *Cultural Geographies* 21(1):115–129.

McGoey, Linsey. 2014. *An Introduction to the Sociology of Ignorance: Essays on the Limits of Knowing*. London: Routledge.

McMichael, P. 2011. "The Food Regime in the Land Grab: Articulating 'Global Ecology' and Political Economy." Presented at the International Conference on Global Land Grabbing, Sussex, UK, 6–8 April.

———. 2012. "Food Regime Crisis and Revaluing the Agrarian Question." *Research in Rural Sociology and Development*, 18:99–122.

Marx, K. [1867] 1976. *Capital: A Critique of Political Economy*. Vol. 1. London: Penguin.

Mehrvar, M., C. Kimsor, and M. Sambath. 2008. *Women's Perspectives: A Case Study of Systematic Land Registration in Cambodia*. Cambodia: Heinrich Boll Foundation.

Mercado, J. 2015. "Buen Vivir: A New Era of Great Social Change." *Pachamama Alliance*, 7 June.

Mertha, Andrew. 2014. *Brothers in Arms: Chinese Aid to the Khmer Rouge, 1975–1979*. Ithaca, NY: Cornell University Press.

Milne, Sarah. 2013. "Under the Leopard's Skin: Land Commodification and the Dilemmas of Indigenous Control in Upland Cambodia." *Asia Pacific Viewpoint* 54(3):323–339.

———. 2015. "Cambodia's Unofficial Regime of Extraction: Illicit Logging in the Shadow of Transnational Governance and Investment." *Critical Asian Studies* 47(2):200–228.

Ministry of Information. 2019. *Provisional total for General Population Census 2019*. 7 August. https://www.information.gov.kh/detailnews/326112.

Mitchell, Timothy. 2002. *Rule of Experts: Egypt, Techno-Politics, Modernity*. Berkeley: University of California Press.

MLMUPC. 2014. "Notification." 20 July. Phnom Penh: Ministry of Land Management, Urban Planning and Construction.

Mollett, Sharlene Faria Caroline. 2012. "Messing with Gender in Feminist Political Ecology." *Geoforum* 45:116–125.

Molyaneth, H. 2012. "Poverty and Migrant Selectivity in South-South Cross-Border Migration: Evidence from Cambodia." *Forum of International Development Studies* 41:49–66.

Moore, D. 2005. *Suffering for Territory: Race, Place, and Power in Zimbabwe*. Durham, NC: Duke University Press.

Mosse, David. 2005. *Cultivating Development: An Ethnography of Aid Policy and Practice*. London: Pluto Press.

Müller, F., and G. Zülsdorf. 2013. "Old Policies—New Action: A Surprising Political Initiative to Recognize Human Rights in the Cambodian Land Reform." Presented at the Annual World Bank Conference on Land and Poverty, Washington, DC.

Murtazashvili, Ilia, and Jennifer Murtazashvili. 2017. "Coercive Capacity, Land Reform and Political Order in Afghanistan." *Central Asian Survey* 36(2):212–230.

Musembi, Celestine Nyamu. 2007. "De Soto and Land Relations in Rural Africa: Breathing Life into Dead Theories about Property Rights." *Third World Quarterly* 28(8):1457–1478.

MWA. 2008. *A Fair Share for Women: Cambodia Gender Assessment*. Phnom Penh: Ministry of Women's Affairs.

———. 2015. *Women's Experience of Domestic Violence and Other Forms of Violence*. Phnom Penh: Ministry of Women's Affairs.

Neef, Andreas, Siphat Touch, and Jamaree Chiengthong. 2013. "The Politics and Ethics of Land Concessions in Rural Cambodia." *Journal of Agricultural and Environmental Ethics* 26:1026–1085.

Ní Mhurchú, Aoileann. 2015. "Ambiguous Subjectivity, Irregular Citizenship: From Inside/Outside to Being-Caught In-Between." *International Political Sociology* 9(2):158–175.

NIS. 2013. *Cambodia Socioeconomic Survey 2012*. Phnom Penh: National Institute of Statistics.

Norén-Nilsson, Astrid. 2016. "Good Gifts, Bad Gifts, and Rights: Cambodian Popular Perceptions and the 2013 Elections." *Pacific Affairs* 89(4):795–815.

O'Brien, Kevin J., and Lianjiang Li. 2006. *Rightful Resistance in Rural China*. Cambridge: Cambridge University Press.

Ojendal, J. 2013. "In Search of a Civil Society: Re-Negotiating State-Society Relations in Cambodia." In *Southeast Asia and the Civil Society Gaze: Scoping a Contested Concept in Cambodia and Vietnam*, edited by G. Waibel, J. Ehlert, and H. Feuer, 21–39. London: Routledge.

Ojendal, J., and K. Sedara. 2006. "Korob, Kaud, Klach: In Search of Agency in Rural Cambodia." *Journal of Southeast Asian Studies* 37(3):507–526.

Ojendal, J., and K. Sedara. 2011. *Real Democratization in Cambodia? An Empirical Review of the Potential of a Decentralization Reform*. Visby, Sweden: Swedish International Center for Local Democracy.

O'Laughlin, Bridget. 2007. "A Bigger Piece of a Very Small Pie: Intrahousehold Resource Allocation and Poverty Reduction in Africa." *Development and Change* 38(1):21–47.

Oldenburg, C., and A. Neef. 2014. "Reversing Land Grabs or Aggravating Tenure Insecurity? Competing Perspectives on Economic Land Concessions and Land Titling in Cambodia." *Law and Development Review* 7(1):49–77.

O'Leary, D. 2005. *Pilot Independent Review of Systematic Land Titling Field Systems and Procedures (Transparency and Accountability)*. Phnom Penh: LMAP.

Ong, Aihwa. 2000. "Graduate Sovereignty in Southeast Asia." *Theory, Culture and Society* 17(4):55–75.

Padwe, Jonathan. 2011a. "Cashews, Cash and Capitalism in Northeast Cambodia." In *Cambodia's Economic Transformation*, edited by C. Hughes and K. Un, 123–153. Copenhagen: Nordic Institute of Asian Studies Press.

———. 2011b. "Garden Variety Histories: Postwar Social and Environmental Change in Northeast Cambodia." PhD diss., Yale University.

Pain, Rachel. 2009. "Globalized Fear? Towards an Emotional Geopolitics." *Progress in Human Geography* 33(4):466–486.

Park, Clara Mi Young. 2015. "New 'Webs of Power' and Agrarian Transformations in Cambodia: Where Are the Women?" BRICS Initiative in Critical Agrarian Studies, Working Paper 8. The Hague: Transnational Institute.

Parnell, Terry. 2015. "Story-Telling and Social Change: A Case Study of the Prey Lang Community Network." In *Conservation and Development in Cambodia: Exploring Frontiers of Change in Nature, State and Society*, edited by S. Milne and S. Mahanty, 258–278. New York: Routledge.

Pedersen, Rasmus Hundsbaek. 2015. "A Less Gendered Access to Land? The Impact of Tanzania's New Wave of Land Reform." *Development Policy Review* 33(4):415–432.

Peluso, Nancy Lee, and Christian Lund. 2011. "New Frontiers of Land Control: Introduction." *Journal of Peasant Studies* 38(4):667–689.

Peters, Pauline E. 2010. "Our Daughters Inherit Our Land, But Our Sons Use Their Wives' Fields: Matrilineal-Matrilocal Land Tenure and the New Land Policy in Malawi." *Journal of Eastern African Studies* 4(1):179–199.

Petras, James. 1999. "NGOs: In the Service of Imperialism." *Journal of Contemporary Asia* 29(4):429–441.

REFERENCES

Pitcher, Anne, Mary H. Moran, and Michael Johnston. 2009. "Rethinking Patrimonialism and Neopatrimonialism in Africa." *African Studies Review* 52(01):125–156.
Plumwood, Val. 2003. *Feminsim and the Mastery of Nature*. London: Routledge.
Polanyi, K. [1944]1957. *The Great Transformation*. Boston: Beacon Press.
Pou, Sothirak, Geoff Wade, and Mark Hong. 2012. *Cambodia: Progress and Challenges Since 1991*. Singapore: Institute of Southeast Asian Studies.
Pou, Sovachana, Serey Sok, Courtney Work, Alice Beban, Kevin Nauen, and Theara Khoun. 2016. *Doing Research in Cambodia*. Phnom Penh: Global Development Network.
Procupez, Valeria. 2015. "The Need for Patience." *Current Anthropology* 56(S11):S55–S65.
Rabe, A. 2013. *Directive 01BB in Ratanakiri Province, Cambodia: Issues and Impacts of Private Land Titling in Indigenous Communities*. Phnom Penh: AIPP.
Raffin, Anne. 2005. *Youth Mobilization in Vichy Indochina and Its Legacies, 1940 to 1970*. Lanham, MD: Lexington Books.
———. 2012. "Youth Mobilization and Ideology." *Critical Asian Studies* 44(3):391–418.
Rasmussen, M., and C. Lund. 2018. "Reconfiguring Frontier Spaces: The Territorialization of Resource Control." *World Development* 101:388–399.
Resurreccion, B., and R. Elmhirst. 2008. *Gender and Natural Resource Management: Livelihoods, Mobility and Interventions*. London: Earthscan.
RGC. 2001. *Land Law 2001*. Phnom Penh: Royal Government of Cambodia.
———. 2012. *Council for Land Policy, Instruction No. 20 on the Implementation of the Royal Government's Directive No. 01*. Phnom Penh: Royal Government of Cambodia.
———. 2017. *National Protected Area Strategic Management Plan 2017–2031*. Phnom Penh: Royal Government of Cambodia.
———. 2018. *Sixth periodic report submitted by Cambodia under Article 18 of the Convention on the Elimination of All Forms of Discrimination against Women*. Phnom Penh: Royal Government of Cambodia.
Richmond, Oliver. 2005. *The Transformation of Peace*. London: Palgrave.
Rodriguez, Andres. 2011. "Building the Nation, Serving the Frontier: Mobilizing and Reconstructing China's Borderlands during the War of Resistance (1937–1945)." *Modern Asian Studies* 45(2):345–376.
Rokitzki, Martin. 2016. *The Training Material of the German Food Partnership: Background Analysis*. Berlin: Oxfam Deutschland.
Rosenbaum, H. Jon. 1971. "Project Rondon, a Brazilian Experiment in Economic and Political Development." *American Journal of Economics and Sociology* 30(2):187–202.
Rosset, Peter, Raj Patel, Michael Courville, and Network Land Research Action. 2006. *Promised Land: Competing Visions of Agrarian Reform*. Oakland, CA: Food First Books.
Roy, Ananya. 2016. "Moderators Address on the Panel 'Legibility and the Politics of Non-Knowledge.'" American Association of Geographers Annual Conference, San Diego, 29 April.
Rus, Andrej. 2008. "'Gift vs. Commodity' Debate Revisited." *Anthropological Notebooks* 14(1):81–102.
Ryerson, Christie. 2010. "Peacebuilding and Cambodian State-Civil Society Interaction: An Immanent Critique of the Promotion of NGOs as a Means of Resolving Conflict." PhD diss., York University, Canada.
Sasson-Levy, Orna, and Tamar Rapoport. 2003. "Body, Gender, and Knowledge in Protest Movements." *Gender & Society* 17(3):379–403.
Schedler, Andreas. 2013. *The Politics of Uncertainty: Sustaining and Subverting Electoral Authoritarianism*. Oxford: Oxford University Press.

Scheidel, Arnim. 2016. "Tactics of Land Capture through Claims of Poverty Reduction in Cambodia." *Geoforum* 75:110–114.

Scheidel, A., and C. Work. "Forest Plantations and Climate Change Discourses: New Powers of 'Green' Grabbing in Cambodia." *Land Use Policy* 77:9–18.

Scheyvens, H., R. Scheyvens, and B. Nowak. 2014. "Preparation for the Field: Personal Issues." In *Development Fieldwork: A Practical Guide*, edited by R. Scheyvens, 125–140. London: Sage.

Schneider, H. 2011. "Development at the Expense of the Environment and the Poor: The Conflict for Boeng Kak Lake in Phnom Penh, Cambodia." *Pacific News* 36:4–17.

Schoenberger, L. 2017. "Struggling against excuses: winning back land in Cambodia." *Journal of Peasant Studies* 44(4):870–890.

Schoenberger, L., and A. Beban. 2018. "'They Turn Us into Criminals': Embodiments of Fear in Cambodian Land Grabbing." *Annals of the American Association of Geographers* 101(3):587–608.

Schoenberger, Laura, Derek Hall, and Peter Vandergeest. 2017. "What Happened When the Land Grab Came to Southeast Asia?" *Journal of Peasant Studies* 44(4):697–725.

Scoones, I., M. Edelman, J. Borras, W. Wolford, and B. White. 2018. "Emancipatory Rural Politics: Confronting Authoritarian Populism." *Journal of Peasant Studies* 45(1):1–20.

Scott, James. 1976. *The Moral Economy of the Peasant: Rebellion and Subsistence in Southeast Asia*. New Haven, CT: Yale University Press.

———. 1998. *Seeing Like a State: How Certain Schemes to Improve the Human Condition Have Failed*. New Haven, CT: Yale University Press.

Scott, Joan Wallach. 1988. *Gender and the Politics of History*. New York: Columbia University Press.

Shapiro, Judith. 2001. *Mao's War against Nature: Politics and the Environment in Revolutionary China*. Cambridge: Cambridge University Press.

Shepler, S. 2005. "Globalizing Child Soldiers in Sierra Leone." In *Youthscapes: The Popular, The National, The Global*, edited by S. Maira and E. Soep, 119–136. Philadelphia: University of Pennsylvania Press.

Shulman, Elena. 2012. *Stalinism on the Frontier of Empire: Women and State Formation in the Soviet Far East*. London: Cambridge University Press.

Sikor, Thomas Lund Christian. 2009. "Access and Property: A Question of Power and Authority." *Development and Change* 40(1):1–17.

Singh, Sarinda. 2012. *Natural Potency and Political Power: Forests and State Authority in Contemporary Laos*. Honolulu: University of Hawai'i Press.

Slocomb, Margaret. 2007. *Colons and Coolies: The Development of Cambodia's Rubber Plantations*. Bangkok: White Lotus.

———. 2010. *An Economic History of Cambodia in the Twentieth Century*. Singapore: NUS Press.

Smith, Linda Tuhiwai. 1999. *Decolonizing Methodologies: Research and Indigenous Peoples*. London: Zed Books.

So, S. 2009. "Political Economy of Land Registration in Cambodia." PhD diss., Northern Illinois University.

Springer, S. 2011. "Articulated Neoliberalism: The Specificity of Patronage, Kleptocracy, and Violence in Cambodia's Neoliberalization." *Environment and Planning* 43(11):2554–2578.

———. 2013. "Illegal Evictions? Overwriting Possession and Orality with Law's Violence in Cambodia." *Journal of Agrarian Change* 3(4):520–546.

STAR Kampuchea. 2013. *Shadow Report on Women's Land Rights in Cambodia*. Phnom Penh: STAR Kampuchea.

Stirrat, R. L. 2008. "Mercenaries, Missionaries and Misfits: Representations of Development Personnel." *Critique of Anthropology* 28(4):406–425.

Stoler, A. 2002. *Carnal Knowledge and Imperial power: Race and the Intimate in Colonial Rule*. Berkeley: University of California Press.

Strangio, Sebastian. 2014. *Hun Sen's Cambodia*. New Haven, CT: Yale University Press.

Strathern, Marilyn. 1992. "Qualified Value: The Perspective of Gift Exchange." In *Barter, Exchange and Value: An Anthropological Approach*, edited by C. Humphrey and S. Hugh-Jones, 169–190. Cambridge: Cambridge University Press.

Strauss, J., and D. B. Cruise O'Brian. 2007. *Staging Politics: Power and Performance in Asia and Africa*. London: I.B. Tauris.

Stuart-Fox, Martin. 2008. "The Persistence of Political Culture in Laos and Cambodia." *Journal of Current Southeast Asian Affairs* 27(3):34–58.

Swift, Peter. 2015. "Transnationalization of Resistance to Economic Land Concessions in Cambodia." Presented at the International Conference on Land Grabbing, Conflict and Agrarian-Environmental Transformations, Chiang Mai University, 5–6 June.

Tallbear, K. 2017. "Beyond the Life/Not-life Binary: A Feminist-Indigenous Reading of Cryopreservation, Interspecies Thinking, and the New Materialisms." In *Cryopolitics: Frozen Life in a Melting World*, edited by J. Radin and E. Kowal, 179–201. Cambridge: Cambridge University Press.

Taylor, Lucy. 1997. "Privatising Protest: NGOs and the Professionalisation of Social Movements." Presented at the Annual Meeting of the Latin American Studies Association, Guadalajara, Mexico, 17–19 April.

Thayer, Millie. 2010. *Making Transnational Feminism: Rural Women, NGO Activists, and Northern Donors in Brazil*. New York: Routledge.

Todd, Zoe. 2016. "An Indigenous Feminist's Take on the Ontological Turn: 'Ontology' Is Just Another Word for Colonialism." *Journal of Historical Sociology* 29(1):4–22.

Touch, Siphat, and Andreas Neef. 2015. "Resistance to Land Grabbing and Displacement in Rural Cambodia." Presented at the International Conference on Land Grabbing, Conflict and Agrarian-Environmental Transformations, Chiang Mai University, 5–6 June.

Trzcinski, L., and F. Upham. 2012. "The Integration of Conflicting Donor Approaches: Land Law Reform in Cambodia." *Journal of International Cooperation* 20(1):129–146.

———. 2014. "Creating Law from the Ground Up: Land Law in Post-Conflict Cambodia." *Asian Journal of Law and Society* 1(1):55–77.

Tsing, Anna Lowenhaupt. 2005. *Friction: An Ethnography of Global Connection*. Princeton, NJ: Princeton University Press.

———. 2015. *The Mushroom at the End of the World: On the Possibility of Life in Capitalist Ruins*. Princeton, NJ: Princeton University Press.

Turner, S. 2013. "Red Stamps and Green Tea: Fieldwork Negotiations and Dilemmas in the Sino-Vietnamese Borderlands." *Area* 45(4):396–402.

Ukeje, Charles. 2004. "From Aba to Ugborodo: Gender Identity and Alternative Discourse of Social Protest among Women in the Oil Delta of Nigeria." *Oxford Development Studies* 32(4):605–617.

Üllenberg, A. 2009. *Foreign Direct Investment (FDI) in Land in Cambodia*. Phnom Penh: GTZ.

Un, Kheang. 2005. "Patronage Politics and Hybrid Democracy: Political Change in Cambodia, 1993–2003." *Asian Perspective* 29(2):203–230.

———. 2015. "The Cambodian People Have Spoken: Has the Cambodian People's Party Heard?" *Southeast Asian Affairs* 415:102–116.

Un, Kheang, and Sokbunthoeun So. 2009. "Politics of Natural Resource Use in Cambodia." *Asian Affairs: An American Review* 36(3):123–145.

United Nations. 2009. *Situation Analysis of Youth in Cambodia*. Phnom Penh: UN Cambodia Team.

———. 2015. *World Population Prospects*. New York: United Nations.

Vandergeest, P., and N. Peluso. 1995. "Territorialization and State Power in Thailand." *Theory and Society* 24(3):385–426.

Verdery, Katherine. 2003. *The Vanishing Hectare: Property and Value in Postsocialist Transylvania*. Ithaca, NY: Cornell University Press.

Verver, M. 2019. "Old and New Chinese Business in Cambodia's Capital." *Trends in Southeast Asia* 17. Singapore: ISEAS.

Verver, Michiel, and Heidi Dahles. 2015. "Institutionalisation of Oknha: Cambodian Entrepreneurship at the Interface of Business and Politics." *Journal of Contemporary Asia* 45(1):48–70.

Virak, Ou. 2017. "Moving Beyond the January 7th Narrative." *Future Forum Briefing Note* 6. Phnom Penh: Future Forum.

Warren, Carol B. 2001. "Gender and Fieldwork Relations." In *Contemporary Field Research: Perspectives and Formulations*, edited by R. Emerson. Brooklyn: Waveland Press.

Watts, Vanessa. 2013. "Indigenous Place-Thought and Agency amongst Humans and Non-Humans." *DIES: Decolonization, Indigeneity, Education and Society* 2(1):20–34.

Weaver, John C. 2003. *The Great Land Rush and the Making of the Modern World, 1650–1900*. Montreal: McGill-Queen's University Press.

Weber, M. 1978. *Economy and Society*. Berkeley: University of California Press.

Whitington, Jerome. 2019. *Anthropogenic Rivers: The Production of Uncertainty in Lao Hydropower*. Ithaca, NY: Cornell University Press.

Wilson, Helen F. 2017. "On Geography and Encounter." *Progress in Human Geography* 41(4):451–471.

Wolford, Wendy. 2010. *This Land Is Ours Now: Social Mobilization and the Meanings of Land in Brazil*. Durham, NC: Duke University Press.

———. 2016. "State-Society Dynamics in Contemporary Brazilian Land Reform." *Latin American Perspectives* 43(2):77–95.

Wolford, Wendy, Saturnino M. Borras, Ruth Hall, Ian Scoones, and Ben White. 2013. "Governing Global Land Deals: The Role of the State in the Rush for Land." *Development and Change* 44(2):189–210.

Work, Courtney. 2011. "The Spirits of Cambodia: New Research into Current Practice." PhD diss., Cornell University.

Work, Courtney, and Alice Beban. 2016. "Mapping the Srok: The Mimeses of Land Titling in Cambodia." *SOJOURN: Journal of Social Issues in Southeast Asia* 31(1):37–81.

World Bank. 2009. *Request for Inspection, Management Response and Eligibility Report, No. 3650*. Phnom Penh: World Bank.

———. 2014. *Where Have All The Poor Gone? Cambodia Poverty Assessment 2013*. Washington DC: World Bank.

———. 2019. "Proportion of Seats Held by Women Parliamentarians." *Data Bank*. https://data.worldbank.org/indicator/SG.GEN.PARL.ZS.

World Bank, FAO, IFAD, UN Habitat, and GIZ. 2015. *Report on Deliverable: Data, Tabulations and Descriptive Analysis*. Phnom Penh: World Bank.

Zagema, Bertram. 2011. *Land and Power: The Growing Scandal Surrounding the New Wave of Investments in Land*. Oxford: Oxfam GB.

Zucker, Eve Monique. 2013. *Forest of Struggle: Moralities of Remembrance in Upland Cambodia*. Honolulu: University of Hawai'i Press.

Index

absentee landowners, 10, 150, 151, 152, 154, 155
abusive relationships, 145, 146, 147
affective dimensions, 138, 139, 159–65
  See also fear, confusion and uncertainty; hope; solidarity
agrarian change, 24–25, 37, 108
agribusiness, 7, 8, 10, 209, 213
  smallholder farmers affected by, 106, 144, 172, 206, 209
agribusiness concessions. *See* ELCs; Pheapimex concession ELC
authoritarian peacebuilding, 212–23

cadastral database of land titles. *See* GIZ; cadastral land registry project
Cambodian elections 2018, 211–12, 213, 217
Cambodian National Rescue Party (CNRP), 11, 16, 24, 29, 30, 86 211
  CPP vs., 13–15, 29
Cambodian People's Party (CPP), 12–15, 96, 216
  land titles and, 29–30, 50, 135
  political gift giving by, 13, 18, 20–21, 29, 30, 211
  power of, 12–13, 18–19, 43, 44, 86, 108, 211
  rural people and, 15, 21, 29–30, 70, 85
  youth vote and, 108, 109, 110
Cambodian state, 15, 18, 212, 215
  dissent suppressed by, 84, 106, 189, 211,
  formation of, 24, 27, 36, 107–9, 134
  land as state property in, 7, 8, 34, 38–41, 67, 110, 216
  neopatrimonial nature of, 12–15, 22–24, 84, 103
  peace in, 4–5, 12, 14, 44, 197, 212–13
  postconflict period of, 11–15, 212
  relationship of with China, 14, 44, 63, 213
  repression by, 10, 21–22, 78, 160, 174, 177, 217
cash crops, 58, 93, 108–9, 143, 205
  indigenous farmers and, 75–76, 127, 170, 172, 173, 184, 205
communal land tenure systems, 109, 169–70

communal land title (CLT), 38, 129, 136, 138, 175–77, 189
  community forests and, 174–75
  delays in granting, 176, 181, 186
  donor support and, 38, 175, 213
  guidelines and processes for, 172, 181–82, 201, 202
  private or individual title vs., 9, 129, 131, 178–79, 181, 182, 184–86
  NGO advocacy and support for, 175–76, 180–81, 185, 186–87, 213
  Order 01BB land title reform impact on, 181–84
communal forestland, 67–68, 105, 185, 186, 208, 215
  claiming of, 25, 67, 90, 95, 101–2, 109, 129, 180.
  clearing and/or redistribution of, 28, 37, 61, 64, 65, 70, 82, 152
  ELC and large-scale use of, 65, 69, 72–73, 77, 160
  Order 01BB land title reform impact on, 93–95, 101–2, 113, 150, 160, 208
  traditional use of, 23, 29, 109, 129, 150, 160, 171
community empowerment vs. legal empowerment, 201–2
community forests (CF), 174–75, 176, 177, 179–80
  delays in recognition of, 178, 179–80, 186
  NGO advocacy for, 174, 175
  Order 01BB land title reform impact on, 180
community activist networks, 44, 64, 98–100, 116, 150, 186
  emotions and communication in actions by, 190–91, 200, 202, 203, 205
  forest patrols by, 81–83, 175, 177
  NGO support for, 67–68, 166, 168, 179
  Order 01BB land title reform and, 151–52, 160, 183–85, 191
  Prime Minister appealed to by, 190–91, 192–93, 195, 196–97, 199
  solidarity generated by, 203–4, 218

237

238 INDEX

community activist networks (*continued*)
  strategies and repertoire of resistance in, 66, 168, 190, 19–98, 203, 213, 218
  women as leaders of, 99–102 (*see also* Srey Sophorn)

deforestation, 6, 30,44, 107, 214, 216
  ELCs and, 64, 156, 209
  Order 01 and, 151–52, 156, 160
democracy, 52, 211–12, 213
Department of Land, 38, 100, 113, 114, 210–11
displacement of rural people, 4, 6, 7, 48, 79
  displaced in place, 164–65
donor–state partnerships, 32–33, 41–42, 52
  German government development agencies in (*see* GIZ)
  human rights and, 14, 41–44, 46, 55
  land title program supported by, 22, 27, 32–33, 36, 37–38, 51
  NGOs and, 167–68, 175
  technical outputs as focus of, 30, 33, 46–47, 56
  uncertainty produced by, 19, 30, 33, 52, 56

economic land concessions (ELCs), 5–7, 11, 42, 60–61, 76
  community resistance to, 44, 61, 98, 160, 191–94
  land enclosed and access blocked by, 64, 66, 149–53, 160–61, 176
  fear and uncertainty produced by, 160–64
  government and donor support for, 5, 7, 19, 38
  rural worker employment by, 7, 143, 151, 153, 156–59, 205
  smallholder farmers and, 1, 8, 61, 136, 137–38
  workers complaints about, 157–59
  See also Pheapimex concession ELC
emotional dimensions of political rule, 216–17
emotions and lived experience, 8, 18, 217
  collective mobilization of, 190, 205
  emotion work, 190–91, 200–201, 209
  foreboding, 164, 191, 216–17
  See also fear; uncertainty; hope and bravery; solidarity
extractive industries and resource capitalism, 188, 209, 212, 213

fear, 4, 10, 28, 76, 78–79, 143, 159–60
  of drought and floods, 74, 78, 144, 160, 171, 209, 210
  of the government or state, 10, 11, 16–17, 54, 56, 73, 78, 79, 144
  of land being taken, 8, 63–66, 136, 138, 143, 160–62, 163, 164–65
  perpetuated by officials, 66, 79, 83–84, 95, 97–98, 101–3
  sedimented in the landscape, 65, 165
  social relations shaped by, 17–20, 190–91
feminist ontology of land, 31, 206–7, 218
feminist political ecology, 4, 106, 191
Forest Peoples Program (FPP), 200–202
Forestry Administration (FA), 105, 174, 179–80
forests. *See* community forests; communal forestland

gender-based domestic violence, 145–47
gender norms, 22–24, 29, 58–59, 37, 145, 147, 148–49
  in community leadership, 99
  in land titling and tenure, 67, 69, 122–23
  in settlement of marital disputes, 145–49
  Order 01BB land title reform impact on, 23, 135, 153–56
  among student volunteer surveyors, 106, 123–25
gifts, 10, 15, 20–21, 28–29, 113–14, 202–21
  land titles as, 10, 13, 18, 20–21, 28–30
  obligation attached to, 20
GIZ, 32–34, 37, 45, 53–55
  BMZ and, 42–43, 46–47, 49–51
  cadastral land registry project, 32, 34, 38, 40–41, 47, 55, 181
  investigations and reports by, 40, 41, 46–49, 176
  Ministry of Lands and, 30, 32–34, 36, 46
  See also Land Rights Program (LRP)
Green Cambodia (NGO), 63–64, 170, 174, 179–80, 202
  funding of, 166, 168
  Ming Tam and campaigns by, 63–64, 98–99, 166–67, 174–75, 180–81

hand tractors, 68, 72, 150, 151–52
health services, 18, 40, 62, 76, 77, 78, 141
hope and bravery, 164–65, 190, 205
human rights, 4, 12, 14, 36
  donor agencies and, 42–44, 46, 50, 55
Hun Sen. *See* Prime Minister Hun Sen

in–between–ness, 105, 134–35
indigenous farming systems, 29, 37, 170–71, 206
  cash crops and, 75–76, 127, 170, 172, 173, 184, 205
  vs Khmer land use, 170–74

INDEX

indigenous rights, 4, 38, 55, 175, 176, 177, 186
indigenous ethnic groups, 10, 29, 75–76, 78–79, 106, 108–9, 119–20
   land surveys and, 120–22
   land titles and, 4, 23, 38, 127–28, 129, 131, 188–89
   non–timber forest products (NTFPs), 67, 75, 151, 153, 154, 160, 173, 202
   Siranii's experience, 76–78
   social hierarchies and, 106, 127–31
inheritance norms and practices, 23, 67, 76
intersectional oppression, 105–6
insecurity, 17, 26, 140–41, 153, 195, 214
   food insecurity, 69, 78, 151–52, 173
   tenure insecurity, 131, 138–39, 159–60, 162, 164–65, 174, 214–15
investors, 53, 58, 59, 69, 92, 102, 142
   in ELCs and logging, 4, 7, 42
   urban investors, 69, 92, 142–43
irrigation dam project, 189–90, 195–99, 202
   compensation offered by, 195–96, 197, 198
   fear and uncertainty with, 190, 195–96
   protests against, 195–97

joint land titles, 23–24 48, 49, 122, 125–26, 149
   women's empowerment and, 4, 48–49, 145
judicial system, 11, 17, 89, 106, 187

Khmer communities, 48, 170, 171
Khmer farming systems, 170–72, 174
Khmer Rouge regime, 5, 14, 15–17, 37, 65, 75
khsae networks, 13, 19, 86, 87, 93, 122
kjil (lazy, hopeless), 90, 97, 189

land brokers, 102, 159, 163, 209, 213, 214
   Lok Tiim's experience, 93–94
   Lok Toeurn's experience, 91–93, 94
land claims, 9, 39, 46, 92, 95, 101, 186
   government officials in, 35–36, 92, 93
   local officials in, 87–89, 98
   obfuscation, secrecy, delay and confusion with, 17–19, 26, 169, 176, 202
   possession vs ownership in, 5, 25, 37–38, 67, 161
   See also communal land title (CLT); community forests; delays in recognition of claims
land commodification, 7, 8, 27, 31, 128, 130, 141
land conflict and disputes, 15, 37, 53, 83, 88, 189, 218
   local officials in, 84, 85, 88–89, 95–98

land dispossession, 1, 10, 65–66, 139, 181, 188, 191, 198
land encroachment, 35, 66, 169, 172, 176, 183, 201
land grabbing, 5–7, 42, 52, 64, 66, 87
   legitimation of 46, 53, 56, 117
   by officials, 20, 80, 90–95, 95–98, 101, 135
   Order 01BB land title reform impact on, 46–47
   resistance to 181, 190–91
Land Law, 5, 23, 24, 37–38, 50–5, 95, 194
Land Management and Administration Project (LMAP), 37–40, 41, 44
   problems with, 40–41, 42, 47
landless persons or households, 25, 38, 59, 69, 143, 153
   social land concessions (SLCs) and, 38, 90, 179
land title reform, 7–8, 30–32, 50, 58, 79
   land reform vs, 10, 25–28, 103, 214–15
   See also Order 01BB land title reform
Land Rights Program (LRP), 30, 32–33, 41–42
   gender empowerment and, 48–49
   GIZ and, 36, 42–43, 45, 51, 52–54, 55–56
   statistics for, 46–48
land sales, 60, 91, 138, 142, 143, 176, 189
   forcing of/coercion in, 40, 67, 138, 142, 143, 163–64, 189
   land tenure security (*see* tenure security)
land title distribution ceremonies, 2, 3, 21,28, 31, 98, 111
land title registration databases, 40–41
   problems with, 33, 40, 47, 87
   See also GIZ; cadastral registry project
land titles, 15, 20–30, 31, 56
   as potential collateral for loans, 2, 25, 110, 122, 129, 131, 139,189
   gifting of by state or government, 20–21, 61, 70, 105, 134
   individual vs communal title, 76, 77–78, 121, 127–29, 131
   people waiting to receive, 71, 77, 95
   problems with, 31, 33–36, 48, 96, 102, 132
   as providing protection, 106, 109, 110, 128, 131
   tenure security and, 30, 34–35, 53
   vote buying and, 29–30
   See also communal land titles (CLT); joint titles
land title program. *See* Order 01BB land title reform
leopard skin land reform. *See* Order 01BB land title reform goals and results

leopard skin landscape, 31, 67, 116, 172, 196, 209
 imagined patterning of, 8, 188, 206
 living conditions within, 31, 136–37, 144, 152–53, 164–65, 196, 208
local authorities/officials, 83–84, 97, 104–5, 107, 112
 distribution of land and money by, 84, 89–90
 land grabbing by, 80, 87, 90–96, 100, 101, 102–3
 student volunteers compared with, 113–15
 village chiefs as, 81–84, 85, 87, 93–94, 101, 128, 129–30

mango as a cash crop, 60, 71, 91, 93, 144, 151–52, 154
mango plantations, 143, 152, 155, 213
Men Somning, 65, 98–99, 197, 203
 forest patrol experiences of, 80–83
microfinance institutions (MFIs) and loans, 140–41, 213
Ming Tam, 194, 202–3
 community forests and, 167, 174–75, 179
 community network and, 166–67, 179
 NGO politics and, 180–81
 women recruited by, 98–99
 See also Green Cambodia
Ministry of Agriculture, Forestry and Fisheries (MAFF), 15, 19, 42, 63, 153, 176, 193
Ministry of Land (MLMUPC), 32–33, 55–56, 104, 110, 117, 133
 donor agencies vs, 37, 38, 42
 GIZ vs, 30, 32–34, 36
 land title/tenure disputes and, 34–36

neoliberal capitalism in Cambodia, 4, 6, 20, 24, 28, 106, 213
 applied to land titles, 134, 143, 193, 214
 property reform and, 33, 38, 106
non–governmental organizations (NGOs), 33–34, 42, 53, 73, 84, 97
 exclusion of from Order 01BB land title reform, 44–46
 funding of, 167–68, 180, 187, 188
 Ministry of Land vs, 37, 38, 40, 49–50
 model villages defined by, 173–74
 reports by, 47, 171, 173–74
 See also GIZ; FPP; Green Cambodia
non–timber forest products (NTFPs), 67, 75, 151, 153, 154, 160, 173, 202

obfuscation, secrecy and delay, 17–19, 26, 169, 176, 202, 213
oknha (wealthy donor), 14–15

omnaich (political power, influence), 13, 16, 22
Order 01BB land title reform, 8–10, 23, 28–29, 44–45, 149, 189, 214–17
 changing policies, rules and guidelines of, 9, 19, 45, 106, 115–19, 216
 elite capture of, 9, 84, 92–93, 101, 102, 103
 ELC land and, 8, 35–36, 39
 fear, confusion and uncertainty produced by, 9, 19–22, 63, 78–79, 115, 135, 189
 impact of on communal land use, 149, 164, 166–70, 176–77, 182, 183–85
 indigenous people impacted by, 181–84, 185–86
 local authorities' actions in, 79, 89–90, 93–94, 97, 103, 113, 180, 192
 land titles as political gifts in, 10, 13, 18, 20–21, 28–30, 50, 162
 Prime Minister's management of, 7, 9, 21, 45, 112, 117, 192
Order 01BB land title reform goals and results, 30–32, 78–79, 103, 106, 190, 213–16
 access to loans and credit, 8, 139–41, 213–14
 ELC and plantation employment, 8, 153, 156–59, 164–65
 gender empowerment, 23, 48–49, 122, 137–38, 145–49, 153–56, 214
 increased legitimacy and political loyalty, 21, 55–56, 131–34
 land grabbing and disputes, 35–36, 46, 90–95, 181, 189
 poverty reduction, 18, 26, 29, 137, 145, 149, 164–65
 tenure security, 8, 137, 138–39, 149–53, 165, 198

Pagoda Boys, 109–10, 133
participant narratives
 Siranii (indigenous woman), 76–78
 Sokha (student volunteer), 104–5, 111, 133
 Sokun (research assistant), 1, 59, 61, 104, 200, 208
 Sophea (student volunteer), 109
 Theara (student volunteer), 118, 129, 133
 See also Men Somning; Srey Sophorn; Ming Tam; Puu Tanak
patronage networks, 13, 15, 17, 20, 27, 120, 212, 214
 donor/development agencies in, 14, 19
 in land grabs by officials, 84, 85, 89, 90, 92
 politics and *khsae* in, 10, 86–87, 93, 112, 122–23

Pheapimex concession ELC, 36, 59, 92, 174
  cassava plantation of, 63–64, 73, 136, 157, 195–96, 207–8, 214
  compensation paid by, 136
  in land rights conflicts, 61, 63–65, 98
  as "The Chinese company," 63–66, 70–71, 72–73
  protests against, 101, 167
  work conditions in, 157–59
Phnom Penh, 58–59, 62, 69, 74, 110
political loyalty, 3, 13, 16, 28
  official/authorities and, 85, 87, 96
  student volunteers and, 134
politics of state recognition, 167–69, 177, 182, 186, 187–88, 199–202
postsocialist nostalgia, 16
poverty, 49, 73–74, 78, 117, 126, 143, 173
  indebtedness and, 140–41
  in rural areas, 57, 59, 73–74, 78
poverty reduction. *See* Order 01BB land title reform goals and results
Prime Minister Hun Sen, 3–4, 13–14, 17, 52, 53, 105, 193
  land title reform policy and, 1, 4–5, 7–8, 21, 29, 55–56, 134
  land titles as gifts from, 9, 13, 18, 21, 29, 50, 194
  legitimacy of power held by, 14, 15, 21, 30, 38, 191, 204, 212
  land disputes personally resolved by, 89–90, 192, 193, 195–97
  unwritten rules and oral proclamations by, 4, 17, 35, 45, 116–17, 192, 215
  student volunteer land surveyors and, 21, 31, 84, 103–8, 111–12, 129, 134
  See also community activist networks
primitive accumulation, 6–7
production of subjectivities, 22–24, 27–30, 31, 135
production of uncertainty. *See* uncertainty
Puu Tanak's narrative, 69–72, 73–74, 78, 92, 144, 151
  vision of a holistic system, 208–9, 214

remittances, 62, 69, 72, 152, 155
rice production, 39, 56, 67
  bonkeur (shifting cultivation of), 171–72, 186, 188
  climate change impact on, 66–67, 209
  harvest period, 68–69, 73
  kbal dae (headroom) needed for, 151, 156
  paddy rice, 29, 61–62, 124, 144, 152, 154, 155

  private fields for, 29, 67, 70–73, 161, 172
  rural people and, 60, 62, 63, 66–69, 73, 75
  roadside land used for farming, 60, 69, 192, 213–14
rural livelihoods, 35, 66–67, 78–79, 152, 173, 214 (*see also* participant narratives, Siranii; Puu Tanak; Srey Sophorn)
rural people, 28, 59, 61–63, 70
  community networks and, 98–102, 190–91, 200, 204–5, 209
  local officials and, 80–84, 91–92, 95–98

schooling, 61, 62, 71, 77
shifting cultivation, 127–28, 131, 170–72, 182, 186
  cash crops and, 75–76, 108, 170
  individual titles threatening, 129
  surveying of land used for, 121, 124, 128
  rice production in, 171–72
smallholder farmers,
  ELCs and, 1, 8, 61, 136, 137–38
  land title reform impact on, 4, 8, 18, 40, 159, 191, 215 106, 213
  leopard skin landscape and, 8, 137, 156, 159–60, 188
small-scale logging, 69, 74, 152, 153, 154, 156, 171–72
social hierarchies, 104, 105, 106,119–22
  in Order 01 survey process, 121–31
Social Land Concessions (SLCs), 38, 90, 94
social reproduction, 6–7, 21–22, 158, 205–7, 214, 215, 218
  Order 01BB land title reform impact on, 149–53
solidarity
  built by communities, 99, 202, 203–4, 218
  loss, discouragement and breaking of, 162, 168, 169, 197–98, 209, 214
spirit festival, 203–5
spiritual power of land, 67 131, 170, 202, 204–5
  land spirits (*nayk taa*), 7, 70, 156, 158, 203, 210
spirituality and political legitimacy, 2, 15, 204
Srey Sophorn, 68, 86–87, 99, 102, 208, 217
  community activism and, 73, 100–101, 177, 179–80, 190–91, 194
  life experience of, 72–74, 78
state violence 4, 5, 16, 18,190, 212, 217
  production of fear and uncertainty. *See* fear; uncertainty
  threats and surveillance, 10, 17, 28, 70, 189, 213, 217
  repression, 21–22, 174, 177, 187, 189–90, 211, 217

242 INDEX

student volunteer land surveyors, 1, 8, 21, 111–13, 116–18
   encounters in field by, 105, 106–7, 119–22, 125–26, 129–31, 134, 163, 192
   gendered distribution of labor in, 121, 122–27, 129–31
   land of indigenous ethnic groups and, 127–28, 129–30
   likelihood of land being surveyed by, 119–22
   post–survey period and, 131–35
   recruitment of, 108–11, 115, 132
   strategies of persuasion used by, 128–31
   training received by, 110, 115–16, 134
   See also participant narratives, Sokha, Sophea, Theara
Systematic Land Registration (SLR), 38, 40, 41, 49, 50

tenure security, 7, 33–36, 43, 47, 159–60, 176–77, 215
   land titles and, 34–36, 43, 53, 137–39, 149, 187, 198
   as Order 01BB land title reform goal, 8, 9, 137, 138–39, 149–53, 165, 198
tenure insecurity, 131, 138–39, 155, 159–60, 162, 164–65, 174
   communal land title and, 176–77
territorialization, 24, 27, 215–16
thumbprint as a signature, 125, 141, 145–47
   on land titles, agreements and transactions, 36, 95, 96, 128, 181, 197, 201
timber poachers, 174, 175
transparency, 51, 55–57, 100

uncertainty, 10, 58, 78, 160, 162–65, 202, 203
   in land titles, 20–21
   state's production of, 18–20, 28–31, 55–56, 89, 169, 215, 216–17

women's empowerment, 48, 137–38, 145–49
World Bank, The, 36, 37, 38, 42, 49, 52, 214

youth mobilization, 107–8
youth soldiers, 123, 126–27